LIFE IN PUBLIC SCHOOLS

LIFE IN PUBLIC SCHOOLS

GEOFFREY WALFORD

METHUEN

First published in 1986 by
Methuen & Co. Ltd
11 New Fetter Lane, London EC4P 4EE

© 1986 Geoffrey Walford

Typeset by Scarborough Typesetting Services
and printed in Great Britain by
Richard Clay (The Chaucer Press) Ltd
Bungay, Suffolk

British Library Cataloguing in Publication Data
Walford, Geoffrey
Life in public schools.
1. Public schools, Endowed (Great Britain)
I. Title
373.2'22'0941   LA635

ISBN 0-416-37170-1
ISBN 0-416-37180-9 Pbk

Contents

List of tables

Acknowledgements

Empirically based research is far from being a solitary activity. It is only possible because of the help and support given by colleagues, officials and those who are the subjects of the research.

I am most grateful to the headmasters, staff and pupils of the two research schools for their warm and generous welcome and their patient help. The teachers and their spouses were not only prepared to answer any questions, but also offered me food and drink. They not only tolerated my presence and observations within the school, but also invited me to social occasions outside. I owe them a great debt.

At the University of Aston I would like to thank Professor R. C. Whitfield and Henry Miller for their support during the project. For help with the preparation of the manuscript thanks also go to Roz Hawker and Mark Robson. Tim Devlin, then Director of ISIS, was most helpful in providing national information on independent schools.

I also acknowledge with thanks the publishers of some of my previous articles who have allowed me to use sections of those articles in this book. Chapter four includes some material from 'The changing professionalism of public school teachers' in Geoffrey Walford (ed.) *British Public Schools: Policy and Practice* (Lewes, Falmer Press, 1984). Chapter six includes some material from 'Girls in boys' public schools: A prelude to further research', *British Journal of Sociology of Education* (1983), 4, 39–54.

Chapter eight includes some material from 'The construction of a curriculum area: science in society', *British Journal of Sociology of Education* (1985), 6, 155–72.

Early versions of chapters five and seven were presented at the Teachers' Careers and Life Histories Conference, St Hilda's College, Oxford, September 1983 and at the Centre for the Study of Women and Education, University of Bristol, March 1983, respectively.

1

Public schools and independent schools

'Very well then, let's roast him', cried Flashman, and catches hold of Tom by the collar: one or two boys hesitate, but the rest join in. East seizes Tom's arm and tries to pull him away, but is knocked back by one of the boys, and Tom is dragged along struggling. His shoulders are pushed against the mantelpiece, and he is held by main force before the fire, Flashman drawing his trousers tight by way of extra torture. Poor East, in more pain even than Tom, suddenly thinks of Diggs, and darts off to find him, 'Will you sell now for ten shillings?' says one boy who is relenting.

Tom only answers by groans and struggles. 'I say, Flashy, he has had enough', says the same boy, dropping the arm he holds.

'No, no, another turn'll do it,' answers Flashman.

But poor Tom is done already, turns deadly pale, and his head falls forward on his breast. . . .

(Hughes, 1857)

Of the many vivid scenes recounted by Thomas Hughes in *Tom Brown's Schooldays* it is perhaps this image of Tom being painfully and sadistically roasted in front of an open fire that is most memorable. Flashman has forced every boy in the house to enter a sweepstake for the Derby. Tom draws the favourite and refuses to sell his ticket back to the fifth year bullies. Flashman attempts to persuade Tom of the wisdom of accepting his five shilling offer for the ticket by encouraging and helping in Tom's roasting. A prime example of bullying by older boys on younger boys and the acceptance of such behaviour. Young boys having to fight as best they could against an unjust system where there was little or no control by adults. Thomas Hughes, of course, was writing in the 1850s, and of Rugby School in the time of Thomas Arnold some twenty years earlier. It was a world of stage coaches and sedan chairs as much as Dame's Houses, praepostors and fags. Yet such images of what life is like in public schools still have a powerful influence on the ways in which we see public schools today.

In many ways this is understandable, for the vast majority of people in Britain have no direct contact with public schools. They are seen as strange places that are 'not for us', but where 'they' send their children – a physical manifestation of perpetuated inequalities of class and the impossibility of breaking the wall between the two groups. Lacking direct contact, the majority have to rely on what little information there is readily available to form their impressions. Over the last few years there have been a number of attempts to bring the popular image of public schools more in line with reality. The BBC, for example, allowed the public to view the goings on of Radley College, and Westminster School has also allowed television reporters to peer through its doors. Yet those attempts have not always been successful. The gowned boys at Radley singing in unison and later talking of 'wet bobs' and 'dry bobs' left an assortment of images, but few which could be readily incorporated into most people's everyday worlds. John Rae's (1981) attempt to promote the public school as a dynamic institution responding to the changes of the times and pushing forward with new ideas, was somewhat dampened by writings of his wife some two years later which reinforced old stereotypes with tales of bad teaching, pettiness, seduction of boys by masters and rape of younger boys by older boys (Rae, 1983).

There has developed a complicated myth of what life is like in public schools, based upon the tales of Tom Brown at Rugby, Mr Chips at Brookfield and Billy Bunter at Greyfriars, supplemented by snippets of school life in the biographies and autobiographies of eminent people. As Isabel Quigly (1982) has ably shown, in the late nineteenth and early twentieth centuries there developed a whole genre of English fiction concerned with the world of the public school. Hughes (1857), Farrar (1858) and Kipling (1899), who used the school story as a vehicle to propagate their own ideas of morality and worth, were followed by the somewhat more realistic early writings of P. G. Wodehouse (1909) and Alec Waugh (1917), and even later by the humorous fantasies of Frank Richards' Billy Bunter and Anthony Buckeridge's Jennings. These last novels were supplemented by the weekly instalments of similar stories in boys' comics such as *Gem* and *Magnet*. The image that these later stories presented was romantic and ideal – a safe and secure world where boys could simply enjoy their lives only partially hindered by the restrictions of authority. George Orwell was to describe their mental world as:

> The year is 1910 – or 1940, but it is all the same. You are at Greyfriars, a rosy cheeked boy of fourteen in posh tailor-made clothes, sitting down to tea in your study on the Remove passage after an exciting game of football which was won by an odd goal in the last half-minute. There is a cosy fire in the study, and outside the wind is whistling. The ivy clusters thickly round the old grey stones. . . . Lord Mauleverer has just got another fiver and we are all sitting down to a tremendous tea of sausages, sardines, crumpets, potted meat, jam and doughnuts. After tea we shall sit round the study fire having a good laugh at Billy Bunter and discussing the team for next week's match against Rookwood. Everything is safe, solid and unquestionable. Everything will be the same for ever and ever.
>
> (Orwell, 1940)

Yet the stories were only one side of the developing myth of what life was like in public schools. The biographies and autobiographies, which provided the other main source of information, often presented the barbaric and unpleasant side of these same institutions. In the recently republished collection edited by Graham Greene (1984), for example, he – along with W. H. Auden, H. E. Bates, Anthony Powell, Steven Spender and L. P. Hartley – presents a rather less glamorous portrait of his own school days. Robert Graves, in a similar way, describes his taunting by another boy in *Goodbye to All That*:

> He went out of his way to hurt me, not only by physical acts of spite like throwing ink over my school books, hiding my

games-clothes, attacking me suddenly from behind corners, pouring water over my bed at night, but by continually forcing his bawdy humour on my prudishness, and inviting everybody to laugh at my disgust. He also built up a humorous legend of my hypocrisy and concealed depravity. I came near to a nervous breakdown.

(Graves, 1929)

Such reminiscences brought out rather different reactions from the bulk of the readership who had no direct contact with the public schools. Here, instead of public schools being presented as places of ease, privilege and enjoyment, they were portrayed as brutal, uncultured and to be avoided if at all possible. The combination of the two strands resulted in a complicated myth which was confused and allowed an ambivalent attitude towards public schools to be adopted. Whether such a life was desirable or undesirable was dependent on which aspects of the myth were given the most support.

What is most strange about this myth is that it has lingered so long. Both Billy Bunter and Jennings are still widely available in paperback editions, as is *Tom Brown's Schooldays* and *Goodbye Mr Chips*. There have been recent additions to the genre, too, in the form of R. F. Delderfield's *To Serve Them All My Days* (1972) which became a very popular television serial both in Britain and the United States. The autobiographical fragments also still flow forth. As Tapper and Salter (1984) suggest, 'Thanks to the reminiscences of numerous old boys we are now only too well acquainted with the daily routine of public schools, especially those boarding schools apparently lost forever in the world of past decades'. However, as the later chapters of this book will show, the important word here is 'apparently', for the myth has only tangential contact with the modern reality. This book may be seen as an exploration of the extent of the contact that there is between myth and reality.

Independent schools

In comparison with many other industrialized countries, private education in Britain accounts for only a relatively small proportion of children. In 1983, for example, there were about 515,000 pupils in some 2400 private schools in England and Wales, representing about 6 per cent of the total school population. The percentage of pupils in public schools is even smaller than this, for the public schools form only a part of the private sector.

There is considerable confusion as to which of the many and diverse private schools should be included in the category of public schools. Some of the confusion has clearly been caused by the schools themselves which are now more reluctant to use the term openly of themselves, with all its associations of privilege and élitism, and prefer to advertise themselves as part of a much wider and open independent sector, which can offer a variety of provision for parents according to individual requirements. Critics, on the other hand, are more likely to wish to emphasize that this variety of provision is also available according to parents' ability to pay, and prefer terms such as 'fee-paying' or 'commercial' (Halsey, 1981) which stress the market basis of these schools. Whichever term we choose to describe the wider sector, it is clear that diversity is a major characteristic.

The range of different types of school is enormous. At one end of the spectrum are special schools for handicapped children or children with special learning difficulties. These may only cater for twenty or thirty children and, in fact, many of the pupils may be paid for by local education authorities. Preparatory schools, usually catering for the 7–13 age range, vary from the well equipped and expensive feeder schools for the prestigious public schools, to the downright cheap and shady. Private schools for secondary pupils have a similar range, and at the lower end offer anything but privilege for the girls and boys who are unfortunate enough to be confined to them by their parents. Theirs is a very different experience from that of their peers at prestigious independent day schools such as Manchester Grammar School or St Paul's School, or at public boarding schools such as Eton, Winchester and Harrow.

The various independent schools have grouped themselves into a number of associations, which are primarily based upon differences in age, gender and academic ability of pupils. These associations include the Girls' Schools Association and the Incorporated

Association of Preparatory Schools. In 1972 the Independent Schools Information Service was established to act as an information centre for seven of these separate associations, and the 1350 odd schools in membership can broadly be regarded as the more reputable of the independent schools. Even this is not completely correct, however, for there are several schools such as Summerhill founded by A. S. Neill (1962) which have very high reputations within specific areas, but which have no inclination towards membership of any of the leading associations. In particular, the progressive and libertarian ethos of schools like Summerhill or Dartington Hall (Young, 1983; Punch, 1977) puts them in opposition to those schools in membership of the most important and widely recognized of these associations – the Headmasters' Conference. Most writers now accept that a headmaster's election to the Headmasters' Conference entitles his school to be accorded the status and prestige of a public school.

The term 'public school' has no legal definition. It is a contested accolade, and even its origin is disputed. Some argue that it is derived from the fact that many of the ancient schools established in the fourteenth, fifteenth and sixteenth centuries were originally founded by Merchant Guilds or wealthy individuals to provide free education for the poor. The will of Sir William Luxton, for example, who died in 1556, contained generous gifts to the poor (including prisoners at Ludgate and Newgate), and provision to 'erect and found a free Grammar School at Oundle in the County of Northampton'. It was to have almshouses for 'seven honest men dwellers in Oundle aforsaid to be bedemen for me', attached to the school (Walker, 1956). Sir John Port's will of 1557 was somewhat similar, providing for a 'Grammar School at Etwalle or Reptone' where 'poor scholars' from the neighbourhood were to have their expenses paid from the endowment (Thomas, 1957). Winchester's statute also provided for the 'poor and needy' scholar, but it is unlikely that this meant anything more than 'not exceedingly rich', for the maximum amount of income laid down by William of Wykeham in 1382 which a scholar could receive and still qualify was far more than a high-standing cleric could earn (Leach, 1899). It is much more likely that the 'public school' label derives from a second clause in

Wykeham's statutes which allows for ten fee paying pupils as well as those scholars on the foundation. 'We allow, however, sons of noble and powerful persons, special friends of the said college, to the number of ten, to be instructed and informed in grammar within the said college, without charge to the college.' Whether the original founders intended it or not, most of these ancient schools fairly quickly became the preserve of boys from wealthy families. Girls, it is worth noting, were hardly ever considered. They were automatically excluded from Winchester as its main purpose was to educate future priests, but the foundations in general rarely referred to the sex of the scholars. Finally, some writers argue that public schools are only so called because these schools were open to boys from all over the country and not just boys living in the immediate locality.

Honey (1977) shows that in 1861 the Clarendon Commission, which investigated the horrendous state into which some of the endowed schools had by then fallen, acted as a marker defining nine schools as 'Great or Public Schools'. These were Charterhouse, Eton, Harrow, Merchant Taylors', Rugby, St Paul's, Shrewsbury, Westminster and Winchester. Merchant Taylors' and St Paul's were day schools so automatically had a somewhat different status, so the seven stand as the best list that was available at the time. Honey argues that the use of the term spread as other schools were recognized as equals by schools from within the seven. Marlborough, Cheltenham and Wellington, for example, which were also examined by the Clarendon Commission as examples of recently founded schools, were fairly rapidly taken into the fold. Regular sports fixtures, especially in cricket, were to play a key part in this acceptance of status.

The Clarendon Commission was to have an even greater effect, however, for the catalogue of excesses and misuse of funds found in various endowed schools by the commissioners was so great that many of the schools feared government action which would remove their foundation income. In 1869 Edward Thring, headmaster of Uppingham School, sent letters to the heads of thirty-seven schools which he considered to be leading boys' grammar schools, suggesting that they should meet annually to discuss ways of dealing with this threat to their existence. The first year only twelve headmasters attended, including none of the Clarendon seven, but the following year thirty-four headmasters, including all of the seven, turned up. The Conference has gradually grown from that time and now consists of headmasters from just over 200 schools. Schools are thus generally thought to be of public school status through the election of their headmasters to the Headmasters' Conference. Eligibility depends upon the degree of freedom that the headmaster has in directing the educational policy of the school and the academic standards in the school, particularly as reflected by the size of the sixth form and the number of boys going on to universities (Burnet, 1982). Election is not automatic for a new headmaster taking over a school whose headmaster had been a member, for the opportunity is taken to reassess the standing of the school. A small committee of headmasters spends two or three days at the school of a headmaster who wishes to become a member for the first time, examining the curriculum and facilities of the school. In this way membership is determined by mutual recognition of schools by schools already in membership. The total number of schools represented thus varies from year to year as some headmasters retire and others are elected. In 1984 there were 221 schools in membership with 142,500 pupils. This last figure represents about 3.4 per cent of the appropriate age range in Great Britain.

To use membership of the Headmasters' Conference as the defining characteristic of public school is, perhaps, the easiest way out of the difficulty of limiting attention to the major independent schools. It is the solution adopted by Kalton, for example, in his statistical study *The Public Schools* (1966), and, as data is fairly readily available for this group, it is the solution that I adopt here for much of the quantitative argument. But it is a great compromise, for the diversity of schools with headmasters in membership of the Headmasters' Conference is considerable. They range in size from about 260 at Mount St Mary's to nearly 1300 at Eton. Some have histories that date back to the fifteenth century or earlier, some were founded in the mid-nineteenth century in order to educate the sons of the rising middle class who found their wealth in the rapid industrialization of the period, and others were only founded in the 1920s just before the depression took its toll. A major difference between the schools within the group is in the proportion of pupils who board, for it is the minority of schools within the group where all or even most of the pupils are boarders. Most of the old direct grant schools that chose to become independent as the grant was phased out from 1976, for example, have no boarding provision at all, and even two of the original Clarendon nine were, and still are, only for day pupils.

There is also great diversity in religious affiliation which can have a great effect on the ethos of the school. Nearly all of the 102 schools in the HMC where all or most of the pupils board have a direct connection with one of the Christian denominations. Ten of the schools are Roman Catholic, Ampleforth and Downside, for example, still being run by Benedictine monks. Eight have links with the Methodist Church, two are Quaker and about sixty-six are linked to the Church of England. Historically, a number of the latter schools were established in order to transmit a specific tradition within the Anglican Church. Thus Dean Close emphasized the evangelical tradition, while the Woodard schools, such as Lancing and Worksop, held to the Anglo-Catholic persuasion.

Most of the past sociological studies have tried to restrict their focus to the boarding schools within the group. Dancy (1963) looks at 110 schools which are all or partly boarding, Wakeford (1969) selects 82 large independent boarding schools in England and Wales, Bamford (1967) suggests 106 schools are central, and Weinberg (1967) uses twelve different criteria to define 84 schools. All of these studies thus included all of the well known boarding schools, but they also included many that are not so well known. Somehow, although Ashville College, Giggleswick School, Reed's School and Wycliffe College are all HMC schools with a majority of boarders, for various different reasons they are not prime examples of what most people think of as public schools. Their headmasters' membership of the HMC may entitle them to use the term of themselves, but the weight of history reserves it for a much smaller group – Winchester, Westminster and Wellington; Malvern and Marlborough; Sherborne and Shrewsbury; Radley,

Repton and Rugby – in short, schools 'something like Rugby'. In this account I thus make use of a group of twenty-nine schools which include practically all of the schools that are 'something like Rugby'. My smaller group is formed of two self-selected groups within the HMC one of which, by coincidence, bears the name of the Rugby Group and the other the Eton Group.

J. R. de S. Honey (1977) argues that mutual recognition of broadly similar status is the key element in any grouping of public schools. The Rugby Group of schools consists of seventeen of the major boarding schools in the HMC. It was formed in the 1960s on a fairly *ad hoc* basis through the meeting together of the headmasters of thirteen of the particular schools involved at one of the HMC annual residential meetings. It has now grown to seventeen schools. The Eton Group started a little later and now has twelve schools but, unlike the Rugby Group, includes within it some schools where most of the pupils are not boarders. Both of the groups are informal and have the same basic reason for their existence – they act as a way by which headmasters and senior masters at these schools can meet with their opposite numbers in similar schools to discuss matters of common interest. In the Eton Group the headmasters meet twice a year and masters with other specific responsibilities meet once a year. In the Rugby Group there are seventeen different groups – headmasters, heads of English, heads of mathematics and so on – which usually meet for an extended day at each of the schools in rotation. Each school thus hosts one of the meetings each year.

Table 1.1 shows the schools in membership of these two groups. I do not intend this list to be in any way a definitive list of public schools, for the composition of both groups is heavily influenced by geography and coincidence as much as anything else. Indeed one of the masters I interviewed described his group as 'a bizarre group of schools'. However, the two groups together include all but one (Merchant Taylors' is omitted) of the twelve schools recognized by the Clarendon Commission as 'great or public schools' and, in broad terms, they include most of the schools that are 'like Rugby'. The ethnographic part of this study is based upon research conducted in two of these schools.

Table 1.1   Schools in the Eton and Rugby Groups

Eton Group	Rugby Group
Bryanston School	Bradfield College
Dulwich College	Charterhouse
Eton College	Cheltenham College
Highgate School	Clifton College
King's College, Wimbledon	Harrow School
King's School, Canterbury	Malvern College
Marlborough College	Monkton Combe School
St Paul's School	Oundle School
Sherborne School	Radley College
Tonbridge School	Repton School
University College School	Rugby School
Westminster School	St Edward's School
	Shrewsbury School
	Stowe School
	Uppingham School
	Wellington College
	Winchester College

Public schools and reproduction

It was shown earlier that the number of children in HMC schools accounts for only about 3 per cent of the age range in Britain. While this is tiny, the numbers of children in the Rugby Group and Eton Group schools are even smaller – altogether there were 19,600 pupils in these schools in 1983, roughly $\frac{1}{2}$ per cent of the age population. Why then should we be concerned or even interested in such a small minority?

Clearly, as Ronald Fletcher (1984) argues, 'These proportions seem relatively small, but, given the recruitment from them to higher education and the higher professions, it is *just* their smallness which gives them their high degree of significance'. Public schools have traditionally had very close links with the universities, especially Oxford and Cambridge, and, either through them or directly, with high status professions. Parents have attempted to ensure that their positions of power and prestige within the class structure could be passed on to their sons through payment and attendance at a public school.

The extent to which a public school background has been linked with various privileged and powerful occupational positions in society has been a subject of interest to many. The work of David Boyd (1973), though now dated, is perhaps still the most useful. Boyd argued that any élite group is characterized by:

1 high occupational status;
2 minority form;
3 high status;
4 a distinctive style of life;
5 group consciousness and cohesion;
6 exclusiveness but openness;
7 functional capacity and responsibility;
8 moral responsibility;
9 power, of varying degree.

He then identified eight élite groups in which public school men have traditionally been pre-eminent: the civil service, the foreign service, the judiciary, each of the armed services, the Church of England and the clearing banks. For each of these groups a core of the highest ranking members was defined and the educational background of the members of that core was determined by entries in *Who's Who* of the appropriate year. The methodology was thus uncomplicated, and this very simplicity makes the findings more stark in their impact.

By way of example, Table 1.2 shows the relationship that Boyd found between the top members of five of the occupational groups and attendance at a Headmasters' Conference school up to 1970/71. The prominence of men with HMC school background is seen to be quite out of proportion with the numbers of pupils that these schools educated and, perhaps more importantly, it is only in the cases of the élite in the Church of England and the civil service that there is any evidence for an overall decrease in the proportion over the years studied. In both cases this trend has continued, and the proportion of permanent secretaries in the civil service who attended a Clarendon school declined from one in three in 1950 to one in eight in 1980 (Stanworth, 1984).

Within the armed forces, the army élite is dominated by ex-public school boys with 86 per cent of the officers of the rank of

Table 1.2   Percentage of members of each élite attending public school (HMC)

	1939	*1950*	*1960*	*1970/71*
Civil Service (under secretary and above)	84.5	58.7	65.0	61.7
Ambassadors (heads of embassies and legations)	73.5	72.6	82.6	82.5
Judiciary (high court judges and above)	80.0	84.9	82.5	80.2
Church of England (assistant bishops and above)	70.8	74.5	69.2	67.4
Clearing banks (directors)	68.2	76.3	73.3	79.9

Source: Boyd, 1973

major general and above in 1970 having attended an HMC school. Sandhurst appears to be widening its recruitment base at the moment, but it is still clear that the most prestigious regiments recruit practically wholly from these schools (K. M. MacDonald, 1980). The élites within the navy and air force are less solidly recruited from this group of schools (Stanworth, 1984) but even there in 1971 two-thirds of air force officers of the rank of air vice-marshal and above had attended an HMC school.

The same dominance can be seen in the political sphere. A count of Members of Parliament in the House of Commons for 1982 (from Dod, 1982) shows that at least 42 per cent were educated in an HMC school, 20 per cent of these being from one school – Eton. The school may be different, but one is reminded of the address that Stanley Baldwin made to the Harrow Association in 1926:

When the call came to me to form a government, one of my first thoughts was that it should be a government of which Harrow should not be ashamed. I remember how in previous governments there had been four or, perhaps five Harrovians, and I

determined to have six. To make a Cabinet is like making a jig-
saw puzzle fit, and I managed to make my six fit by keeping the
post of Chancellor of the Exchequer for myself. I am very
proud that it has fallen to my lot to be the next Prime Minister
after Palmerston to come from Harrow.

(Baldwin, 1926)

Margaret Thatcher has not seen the same need to support
Harrow, being from Kesteven and Grantham Girls' School herself, but has still chosen to fill her cabinet with ex-public school
boys. The cabinet of September 1984 contained twenty-two
people, seventeen of whom (or 77 per cent) were educated in
HMC schools. There were four from Eton, three from Winchester, and representatives from Rugby, Stowe, Cheltenham,
Clifton and Shrewsbury. Altogether fifteen were from the Eton
and Rugby Group schools. The Education Secretary, Sir Keith
Joseph, was at Harrow.

It is additionally worth noting the obvious point that these public
schools are largely concerned with the reproduction of a male élite,
or, at least, have been so in the past. Most positions of power and
prestige in our society are still held by males, but such has been the
concern over the role of the public schools in class reproduction
that it has almost gone unnoticed that they have been as, if not
more, concerned with the reproduction of gender relations.
Traditionally, private schools have been single sex schools, and
the private sector has been divided into two very unequal parts in
terms of educational provision. For boys, schooling was designed
to fit them for their eventual positions in various élite groups, but
girls were schooled, with a few notable exceptions, to find their
major rewards in a 'good' marriage and motherhood.

Girls' private schools have not traditionally had the same links
with higher education and the professions that the boys' schools
have had, which has meant that the Girls' Schools Association
(GSA) has never carried as much weight as the Headmasters'
Conference. While some commentators do write of 'girls' public
schools' the use of the extended term itself emphasizes the higher
prestige that the (boys') public schools have. As we shall see in
chapter six, this is one of the areas where there are currently

major changes occurring. In the last few years many HMC schools have responded to pressures and become co-educational either throughout or at sixth form level only. The opening of opportunities to women that has occurred could have acted to weaken the importance of the HMC schools, but, in practice, it would seem that these HMC schools have overcome the threat by providing places for girls as well as boys.

Cultural production, cultural reproduction and social reproduction

The link that has been indicated between high status occupation positions and attendance at public school is part of a much wider theme that has dominated and structured sociology of education in Britain since the war – the relationship between education and the social reproduction of our class society. Changing theoretical fashions have meant that the theme has been dressed in a variety of clothes in those forty years, but the concern to document and attempt to explain the continuities between generations in terms of educational and occupational success has been the backbone on which the sociology of education has developed.

This is not the place to rechart that development in detail. Briefly, however, the birth pangs can be seen as a reaction to the realities of educational provision following the 1944 Education Act. The provision of 'secondary education for all' was intended to lead to greater equality of educational opportunity and, in consequence, greater future equality of occupational success. The early political arithmetic studies, however, rapidly showed that the introduction of the tripartite system had not led to complete equality of opportunity (Floud, Halsey and Martin, 1956). The political arithmeticians, working in a largely social democratic consensus period and with close personal links with members of the then Labour government (Kogan, 1971), carefully documented the class inequalities that they found within the educational system and then used this data as ammunition to fight for a more egalitarian society.

Equality of opportunity was the slogan that was used up until the early 1970s to justify a whole range of educational developments.

The drive towards comprehensive education, the expansion of the higher educational system, the promotion of Educational Priority Areas, to name just some of the major changes, were all promoted in the name of equality of opportunity. The essence of what was meant was that every individual should be given the same opportunity for educational and occupational success 'in the sense that they are all to be treated alike until relevant grounds are established for treating them differently' (Benn and Peters, 1959). These relevant criteria were assumed, by practically everyone, to be ability rather than class, wealth or income, and that judgements on relative ability should be delayed until as late as possible in the child's life. Equality of opportunity was seen as a desirable goal, both for reasons of fairness and in terms of society's need to ensure that highly skilled positions were occupied by the most able and that national 'wastage of ability' was reduced to a minimum.

By the early 1970s, however, the democratic consensus was beginning to collapse, the years of affluence were over, and there was growing evidence that the post-war educational reforms had done little to modify our divided, class-based society. As Halsey, Heath and Ridge (1980) have indicated, rather than the 1944 Education Act marking a decisive turning point in terms of the class basis of educational success, there were only modest differences in the class pattern of educational achievement before and after the war.

The works of Althusser (1971) and later Bowles and Gintis (1976) were crucial in allowing sociologists of education to rethink the role that education played in social reproduction, for these authors suggested that, rather than schools being benign institutions which worked towards individual fulfilment and social equality, schools actually acted to help ensure that our class society was rigidly reproduced. For Althusser the educational system was the major ideological state apparatus which worked on behalf of the dominant class, providing both labour power with the necessary skills for production and also the equally important graded ideologies which legitimated the existing social division of labour and unequal society. Social reproduction thus becomes a mechanical inevitability. For Bowles and

Gintis (1976) the process is equally unproblematic. Any thought of autonomy in the educational sphere is overcome by the structural principle of 'correspondence'.

These early 'reproduction' theories were very influential, but it was generally recognized that both theories were too tight – too deterministic. They left little room for autonomy of action on the part of the individual people involved. As Willis summarizes:

> The notion of 'correspondence' omits the possibility of resistance. By doing so, it ignores the constitution of working-class identities separate from their ideal expression in the bourgeois imagination. In other words, it takes no account of the working class's independent effect on the final construction of the resulting social relationship. 'Correspondence' omits consciousness and culture as constitutive moments of social process and treats human action, apparently, as the consequences of quite inhuman and separate 'structures'.
>
> (Willis, 1981: 53)

The late 1970s thus saw several attempts to document occasions where there was *lack* of fit between the educational system and the requirements of a capitalist economy. Basil Bernstein (1977), for example, developed his concepts of classification and framing which were originally only applicable to schooling and applied them to the industrial system. He showed that there were occasions where, rather than being a correspondence between school and work, there were distinct disjunctions. He argued that for less academic pupils the schools presented an educational code with weak classification and framing, yet these pupils were most likely to enter occupations where strong classification and framing were required.

While pointing the way forward, Bernstein's skeleton lacks flesh, which is exactly what various authors working within what might be generally called a 'cultural' perspective have attempted to provide. In this very loose and divergent group we might place the work of Bourdieu, Willis, those at the Centre for Contemporary Cultural Studies at the University of Birmingham, and also, although with differences in emphasis, that of Corrigan, Turner and Jenkins.

For Pierre Bourdieu (Bourdieu and Passeron, 1977; Bourdieu, 1977) the idea of culture introduced is the culture of the dominant class, which is perceived as having some autonomy from the brute facts of the economy. Bourdieu gives room for human agency in the development and creation of culture, in the generation of new knowledge and new cultural forms. But while human agency is accorded to the dominant class, the dominated class has high culture thrust upon it. Those who control the economic, social and political resources are seen as exerting their power to impose meaning on others, primarily through the institution of the school. It is their culture that is embodied within the schools.

> Just as our dominant economic institutions are slanted to favour those who already possess economic capital, so our educational institutions are structured to favour those who already possess 'cultural capital' defined according to the criteria of the dominant hegemony.
>
> (Harker, 1984)

The dominant culture is proclaimed as objective and legitimate, and the differential access that various classes have to cultural capital quickly ensures that a hierarchical society is reproduced. Bourdieu does not concern himself with any cultural form other than that of the dominant class – he limits any creativity and independence to that group. In the end, although the idea of culture is crucial, Bourdieu presents a fairly static picture which falls easily back into determinism.

Paul Willis' concerns with culture are much more dynamic than those of Bourdieu. His book, *Learning to Labour* (1977), is perhaps one of the best known and most important single studies of the last decade that deals with the problem of education and class reproduction. In it Willis is concerned to document and understand the ways in which groups of young people actively construct their own culture within the restrictions, potentials and possibilities of their own particular historical, geographical and class positions. The fieldwork on which the book is based was conducted between 1972 and 1975 in a small number of schools in the Midlands, but although reference is made to several different young male groups, the thrust of the ethnography and analysis is on one group of twelve young, disaffected, non-academic, working-class males, 'the lads', who he followed through their last two years at school (which coincided with the first year of the raising of the school leaving age to sixteen) into their first six months of working life.

Since the time of the research, of course, the economic and social climate in Britain has changed dramatically. The particular cultural form that Willis describes in detail is now largely only of historical interest. Its importance to present day research lies more in the theoretical framework presented in the book and subsequently modified and elaborated elsewhere (Willis, 1981, 1983). Willis makes clear that his fundamental concern is with the active and creative task of cultural production. He uses the term 'reproduction' to describe the 'biological and generational reproduction of gendered persons in the family' (1981: 49) while 'social reproduction' is the 'replacement of that *relationship* between the classes (i.e. *not* the classes themselves) which is necessary for the continuance of the capitalist mode of production'. These two are very different things and to elide the two 'takes no account of the whole continuum of history, struggle and contestation, and . . . the field of a creative collective self-making in the subordinate class, some of whose processes I designate in my category ''cultural production''' (Willis, 1981: 44). Willis' project is to investigate lived cultures in their particular historical contexts. Cultural production is concerned with the form of living collective, creative and active cultural forms that occur within the determinate and contradictory situations presented to groups within capitalist and patriarchal society. This theoretical framework, then, frees us from the determinism of earlier reproductive theories. It proposes an active and creative response to their particular circumstances, which is never specifiable in detail in advance. This creativity and invention is, of course, partially constrained by the structuring power of history, social location and inherited ideological and cultural discourses, but it emphasizes that social agents are *not* passive bearers and transmitters of structure and ideology. 'Cultural reproduction is the process of the collective, creative use of discourses, meanings, materials, practices and group processes to explore, understand and creatively occupy particular positions, relations and sets of material possibilities' (Willis, 1983: 114). The final category 'cultural reproduction' designates how, from here, through complex ideological and cultural processes, we may perceive certain essential features to be continuous with, and tend to reproduce, limiting forms (racism, sexism, manualism, the private, authority) which predate them but which are now so subjectively inhabited as to provide a sufficient basis for actual decisions and attitudes which allow the maintenance of capitalist production (Willis, 1981: 4).

The ethnographic part of *Learning to Labour* is a rich description of the major elements of the cultural form produced by these particular youths, with all its sexism, racism and hedonism. The lads' culture is strongly anti-school and anti-academic – smoking, drinking, sex and other 'instant' pleasures are regarded as far more important than 'pen-pushing'. It is an intensely 'masculine' culture with hard manual labour being seen as a solid cultural achievement. Being able to 'handle yourself' is vital, and the relationship to authority is that of 'them' and 'us'. 'The lads' regard themselves as being more adult than the conformist 'ear 'oles', more worldly experienced and simply more stylish in terms of what they wear, what they do and what they listen to. As Willis indicates, the particular form that this alternative anti-school culture takes is, in part, determined by current fashions in the wider symbolic system of youth culture.

> Though much of this style, and the music associated with it, might be accurately described as arising from purely commercial drives and representing no authentic aspirations of its adherent, it should be recognized that the way in which it is taken up and used by the young can have an authenticity and directness of personal expression missing from its original commercial generation.
>
> (Willis, 1977: 17)

Being 'one of the lads' is seen as a cultural accomplishment which has to be actively worked at and, more importantly, what being 'one of the lads' entails is itself a cultural accomplishment of the group. The key to Willis' work, however, is that, while the lads' culture is seen as being actively created, it is such that there are distinct continuities between this culture within this anti-academic group of pupils and the culture of the workplaces that these boys are likely to enter. In a sense, then, their culture prepares them for the culture of the workplace far more efficiently than any pro-school culture would do.

Any short summary of *Learning to Labour* fails to do justice to the richness of the ethnography or the subtlety of the argument. Moreover, its fundamental achievement of freeing us from the over-deterministic early reproduction theories should not be underestimated. However, there are several problems which need to be discussed for, in many ways, it is unfortunate that Willis' theoretical framework should have first been applied to this particular group of disaffected males. There has been an unfortunate tendency amongst commentators on the work to assume that the particular cultural form that these twelve lads produced is in some ways representative of all anti-school cultural forms. (At its worst some commentators seem to have taken this particular cultural form as being representative of all 'traditional' working-class cultural forms. See, for example, Binns and Mars 1984; Weiss, 1983.) A more careful reading of the book makes it clear that this is not intended, and Willis states explicitly that other ethnic and gender variations are not examined. At the level of the working class as a whole, an important point of the argument is that the variety of cultural forms that are produced leads to differing perceptions of work and of the 'kind of person' who does that work, and thus to self-defeating divisions within the working class. However, Willis does write of '*the* male white working-class counter-school culture' and states that a good proportion of working-class boys in the study school took up this oppositional culture.

Very little evidence is given for this and, even if we accept that it was true then, for that particular school, there is very little reason for expecting it to be more widely applicable. Work carried out a few years later by Raby and Walford (1981a; 1981b) in a very similar working-class, but mixed sex, West Midlands school, indicated that only a tiny minority of these working-class boys wished to assert their masculinity through entering hard manual labour occupations. On the contrary, the majority cultural form constructed by the boys in this school affirmed a dislike for hard manual labour and a desire to 'skive' and have a softer, easier and cleaner job if possible. It would seem that the continuities of cultural form experienced by Willis' twelve lads betweeen the school and the workplace may not have been so widely applicable as is commonly thought. Any particular cultural form produced is dependent on the particular historical and social circumstances – the rapid changes that occurred in the economy after 1975 may alone account for the different findings a few years later. It is evident that a few years later still, with the massive youth unemployment of the 1980s, the lads would have experienced a sharp discontinuity between their anti-school culture and the culture of the dole. Indeed, in some more recent work, Willis himself states that young working-class people now want the power of 'skills' in the marketplace of jobs (1984: 224). In the end, Willis fails to answer in any significant way his basic question of how working-class kids in general get working-class jobs. These particular lads appear to be a special case, rather than a major part of the general pattern.

In many ways it might have been more fruitful to have studied in greater depth the variety of cultures produced by the 'ear 'oles', for their produced culture may, in fact, have been more creative and active than that of the lads. Willis repeatedly claims that the lads' culture is a 'creative and self-made form of oppositional and cultural style', yet he gives very little evidence for this actually being true. It is only by assuming that the school acts as the central site for cultural production, rather than the home or other activities outside school, that Willis is able to sustain the illusion that the lads' culture is actually creative and self-made. In practice, the major elements of the lads' culture would appear to be very similar to those of their working-class fathers, although the book gives too few details of the family lives of most of the boys to enable a check to be made. It would seem likely, however, that at least the sexist, racist and manualist aspects of the lads' culture is passed down the generations from father to son in the home or outside the school environment. There is little necessity to posit any great 'creativity' on the part of the lads. The 'ear 'oles', on the other hand, also being from working-class families, may in fact be being much more creative and active in their produced cultural form. Here the home background may well be still oppositional to school, but the 'ear 'oles' somehow manage to construct a culture that transcends this.

The most important aspect of the concept of cultural production is that it grants a degree of autonomy and creativity to what appear to be essentially similar groups of actors within the same structural constraint. It opens up to analysis the potential variety of cultural forms that can be produced. Unfortunately, there has been a tendency in the past to close down this potential and restrict the potential diversity of cultural forms at the very moment when the possibility has been sighted. Willis' bi-polar division of white working-class males in his school into 'the lads' and 'the ear 'oles' is far too neat and tidy.

While he does allow for some boys to be on the fringes of the lads' group, the essence of the thesis is that there is a decisive break in cultural form between the responses of these two groups within the working class. The data are presented in such a way that continuities between the groups are neglected. More recently, Richard Jenkins (1983), in his study of youth in a Belfast housing estate, drew three broad divisions into 'lads', 'citizens' and 'ordinary kids'. Here, however, the groups are not seen as static and firmly differentiated from each other, but are seen as 'ideal types' and the individuals involved in each cultural form, or life style, are seen as changing over time and even for various activities.

As will be seen later, such fluidity of involvement is characteristic of the varieties of cultural form found within public schools. The idea that public schools act merely as vehicles through which the 'high culture' of the dominant class is passed unproblematically and unaltered to its young, is quickly seen to be far from reality. For cultural production occurs in public schools just as much as in working-class secondary moderns or comprehensives. Those 'warm, gendered, concrete bodies' (Willis, 1983) that eventually inhabit particular social positions, create for themselves a culture that may incorporate many elements of the dominant culture, but which also includes many other elements from the diversity of cultural forms that surround them.

A note on method

The overall aim of the study on which this book is based was to investigate, describe and analyse the various cultural forms to be found in British public schools – to find out how life is lived by the numerous groups of people involved in public schools. Its aim was thus wide and somewhat open-ended, for my interest was not only with the pupils but also with the teaching staff and various other adults whose lives are structured by the never ending pressures of the school. Inevitably such breadth of interest was traded for depth of understanding of any one of the particular groups involved. It was not possible to gather the sort of extremely detailed ethnographic data collected by Willis (1977) or Jenkins (1983) in their studies. Nevertheless, it is hoped that the data collected and reported here do have the rather different strength of being more generalizable than either of those studies, and it is to that point that I now turn.

Case studies of individual schools based on a range of ethnographic techniques have now become a recognized and uncontentious part of the sociology of education. The methods developed by anthropologists to study exotic foreign cultures have been applied to a wide range of individual schools, the researchers seeking to understand and describe the inner workings of these microsocieties. This continuity is perhaps best seen in the path-setting studies of schools conducted by Hargreaves (1967), Lacey (1966, 1970) and Lambart (1976). As Lacey (1982) describes, these three were initiated from an anthropology department at Manchester which contained both sociologists and anthropologists and, after reading for an MA, Lacey claims that 'I was ready by the department's own reckoning to begin fieldwork and this could just as easily have been among the Eskimos as among the inhabitants of Hightown' (Lacey, 1976). Luckily for sociology of education, the attractions of life in the north of England were greater than those of the far north, and Lacey's study of a grammar school was to provide a pattern and benchmark for future studies.

In the not too distant past we have thus seen studies of infant schools (King, 1978), middle schools (Meyenn, 1980); and a whole group on various aspects of comprehensive schooling (Woods, 1979; Turner, 1983; Burgess, 1983; Ball, 1981). In the United States there has been a similar flood of reported studies, including two of the more notable on junior high schools by Metz (1978) and Everhart (1983). Somewhat similar studies, but concerned more with the life of youth outside the school structure, include the work of Corrigan (1979), Hebdige (1979), Jenkins (1983) and, of course, Willis (1977). However, although case studies of individual groups and schools are now common, and such work now forms one of the backbones of the discipline of sociology of education, there are still nagging doubts about problems of representativeness and generalizability. How common is it, for example, for headmasters to organize morning assemblies as if they are the Master of Ceremonies in a vaudeville show as Woods described in *The Divided School* (1979)? Are the precautions taken by another headmaster against 'trouble' at the end of term, described by Burgess (1983), an extreme case of paranoia or an example of recognizably similar activity in most comprehensive schools? Perhaps more importantly, did the process of differentiation and polarization, and the consequent development of two radically different sub-cultures, occur just at Hightown Grammar, or did it occur elsewhere as well (Lacey, 1970)? And how common was it that institutional support for mixed ability classrooms was based more on social control aspects, as described by Ball (1981), than on more acceptable educational reasons?

The problem is by no means new. If we do research whereby a reasonably sized representative sample is drawn from a wider population, then (assuming that the research has been competently conducted) we can fairly generalize any findings to that wider population. We can never be sure that what we have found in our sample also applies to the rest of the population, but we can calculate what the probability is of any error. On the other hand, any findings from a detailed ethnographic case study cannot be legitimately generalized to any wider population. If we study one boys' comprehensive school in detail, for example, we have no way of knowing to what extent the activities found in that school are typical of other boys' comprehensive schools without also investigating them. A sample of one is quite simply not a sample at all.

One way of countering this problem is to argue that large, randomly selected samples are not always necessary. Hammersley and Atkinson (1983) argue that the selection of critical cases for intensive ethnographic study may be more fruitful. Glaser and Strauss (1967) are more concerned with the use of ethnography for theory building, so suggest that sampling should be strategically developed as the research moves from stage to stage. They argue that cases should be selected in such a way that as many categories and properties of categories as possible are produced.

In practice, however, the location of case studies in the sociology of education has rarely been based on such criteria. Schools have been chosen because of geographical convenience, prior contacts, willingness of schools to allow access and serendipity. The location of the university department at which the research was based has practically always been a deciding factor with regard to geography. This is inevitable and, given that we can't make valid generalization from one case study anyway, not necessarily any disadvantage. But the problem is that generalizations have been made and will continue to be made. In spite of any caveats that authors may place in their reports, readers, whether they be sociologists or otherwise, have tended to generalize to a wider population of what they consider to be similar cases. Perhaps the worst example of this is the misuse of Willis' work already described where his carefully selected handful of lads in the Midlands have been taken by so many authors to be representative of the whole of British working-class white youth. Readers draw upon their own stock of 'commonsense' knowledge to link the descriptions of what occurs in one context to many other cases that seem to be 'similar'.

There is, of course, no simple answer to the problem of lack of generalizability. In one sense there is a simple trade-off or compromise that has to be made by every researcher between the insight that can be gained through case study and the breadth and generalizability that can be achieved through more extensive work with a representative sample. For a number of reasons, however, the compromise that has to be made in the case of the study of public schools is not as stark as those which have to be made in the study of the various forms of state maintained schools. There are several possible strategies open to the researcher of public schools. The first is simply to study in detail the world of some particular named school, on the assumption that that individual school is important enough alone to make this worthwhile. Thus, for example, in the United States, Peter Prescott studied Choate, one of the major independent schools of New England (1970) and Ellis and Moore (1974) have described life as a cadet at Westpoint. The lines between sociology, journalism, history and anecdote are difficult to draw, but while the books on Eton fill many shelves, there are no studies of named schools in Britain that would be widely regarded as sociological.

At the other end of the spectrum of possibilities is the use of a representative sample. Weinberg (1967) used a questionnaire to headmasters as the major source of his new information and was able to obtain a sample of 'nearly two thirds' of his defined population of eighty-four boarding schools. Lambert's team visited one in three of the HMC schools for a period of about two weeks, and in four schools they 'studied them minutely during a period of continuous observation and survey lasting in each at least half a term or more' (Lambert, 1975). Lambert's team were thus able to achieve depth and breadth.

Wakeford's study was methodologically between the two extremes. He used the boarding school at which he had been a pupil as the main research site, spending three periods of four to eight weeks in participant observation as a temporary assistant master. He was given access to personal documents, essays and confidential reports and carried out informal interviews with staff and pupils. His concern with possible unrepresentativeness of his main school led him to also visit six other public boarding schools for periods of two or three days. He states 'these visits enabled me to appreciate their common systemic features, and emphasised for me that these features might be not the result of deliberate design, but rather the effect of their status as public boarding schools' (Wakeford, 1969).

The research reported here is mainly based upon periods of intensive study in two separate major public boarding schools from within the Eton and Rugby groups. Both of the schools have about 600 pupils, a teaching staff of roughly 50 and had fees of around £4500 per year in 1982. One of the schools had girls in the sixth form only, the other was for boys only. I spent a four week period in one school in 1981 and a whole term in the second in 1982.

The study of two schools, of course, does not in itself help very greatly with the problem of generalizability, but the key factor here is that the population from which the sample of two was drawn was small – only twenty-nine schools. I have argued that the schools which form the Rugby and Eton groups include practically all the major public boarding schools, and that the presence of a school in one of these groups is an indication of a degree of recognition of similarity of status. The schools within the groups are still varied, but not as varied as within the HMC as a whole and certainly not as varied as within the whole of the independent sector.

A further advantage with regard to generalizability is that, while in most research the bulk of the population is completely unresearched and very little detailed information is easily available, in the case of the Rugby and Eton group schools an immense amount of information is available about the whole population. All of the schools produce a prospectus and various other advertising literature. Practically all of them also have at least one full length history and there are numerous histories of the public schools, schoolboy reminiscences and biographies which give information. Much of this is dated and of little relevance, but it is still possible to make some estimate of the degree to which the two schools studied differed from the others on a multitude of dimensions. Generally, it was the similarities that were striking rather than the differences, and, indeed, this was my intention in approaching these two schools originally. In other words, I did not study Eton, for to do so (if I had been given the chance) would have been to have studied a school where the differences of experience between living at that school and any one of the others would probably have been great.

Apart from the availability of documentary material on the whole population, I was able to gather oral material too, for the interchange of staff between these schools is fairly high, and I was able to interview staff who had taught at other schools in the group. Many knew several of the schools in their group well. The existence of the Rugby Group and Eton Group also meant that staff automatically had a greater knowledge of other schools in the group. They visited other schools regularly and the senior staff all knew personally their opposite numbers in most of the schools in the group. I was able to be present at two of these meetings myself. All of this information could be used to judge in which areas these two case study schools seemed to be similar to the others and in which different.

In my account I avoid those areas of the life of the two schools which appeared to be idiosyncratic. In no case did this mean that a vital area had to be omitted. In the account I have used material from both of the schools usually without identification, for I hope that by doing so I can conceal the identities of the two specific schools involved. A few details have also had to be changed to retain anonymity.

The two schools chosen were not my first choice. Five refused before the headmaster of the first was prepared to grant me entry. The second school, which was my next choice, readily gave me access after checking with the first headmaster. The fact that I had previously taught for two terms at another of the schools in the group, and had spent my teaching practice term in yet another, clearly helped considerably in negotiations over access at all stages.

In both schools my major role was that of an open researcher. Staff and pupils knew that I was at the school for the specific purpose of writing a book about public schools. In the first school, because of shortage of time, I did no teaching, but in the second I taught two sets of lower form boys – six periods a week for the first half of the term and three thereafter. During that time I lived in accommodation provided by the schools on the school site. In both schools my research method was eclectic, and I tried to gather information about the world of the schools in as many different ways, and from as many different sources, as possible.

I talked with boys, girls, masters, wives, secretaries, other staff and headmasters. I became involved with the various aspects of school and community life including sports, visits, drinking at the local pubs, dinner parties and other activities. I observed lessons, chapel, meals, sports and meetings of masters, parents and prefects. I conducted eighty taped semi-structured interviews with academic staff who were part of a stratified, pseudo-random sample. I only had one outright refusal to be interviewed, but two more 'never had time' on several askings. I also gave a questionnaire to about 200 of the lower form boys in one of the schools, which included questions on background, activities in school, friendship groups, attitudes to school, and aspirations for the future. In general, I lived with the masters, but broke rules with the boys.

2

Everyday life in public schools

'Triste lupus stabulis,' began the luckless youngster, and stammered through some eight or ten lines.

'There, that will do,' said the Doctor; 'now construe.'

On common occasions, the boy could have construed the passage well enough probably, but now his head was gone.

'Triste lupus, the sorrowful wolf,' he began.

A shudder ran through the whole form, and the Doctor's wrath fairly boiled over; he made three steps up to the construer and gave him a good box on the ear.

(Hughes, 1857)

The scene is instantly recognizable. We are in a school classroom where the pupils are being expected to be able to show mastery of some work previously set. The unlucky boy picked by the master makes a gross error and the master's anger 'boils over'. Hughes assures us that this was the last time that Doctor Arnold hit a boy in class, for displays of physical anger on the part of masters were not to be part of his new scheme. It was certainly as unnecessary then as it is now, for the masters and the schools have far more potent and effective methods of control at their disposal than a box on the ear.

The instant recognizability of 'what is going on' in Tom Brown's Rugby indicates a basic sameness of experience between what Hughes was writing about then and our own experiences and mythologies about schools. Have the changes only been superficial ones, like the removal of physical punishment in class, or have there been deeper changes too?

In a sense, this is one of the underlying themes of the book, and can only be answered gradually as the various aspects of present day public schools are discussed. But, in order to look at the detail, it is first necessary to give an overview. This chapter thus aims to give a general description of the way in which everyday life is structured in present day public schools. It is, in essence, a skeleton and the flesh will be provided in later chapters. It concerns itself mainly with the structural aspects of institutional life in which cultural production occurs. It takes the formal organizational structures of the school and house system and outlines the nature of life for the boys in these institutions.

Teaching and the formal curriculum

A public school is not simply a school with facilities for pupils to board. The fact that pupils live at the school structures and influences the curriculum and the ways in which teaching and learning proceed in the classroom.

At the simplest level this can be seen in the six-day teaching week to be found in these schools, rather than the five of day schools. It is felt that pupils need both routine and to be kept busy for as much of the time as possible, and that Sunday's break in routine is sufficient rest. Six-day teaching also means that the terms can be significantly shorter than in day schools, which allows long vacations and slightly reduces school fees. Most lessons occur in the mornings, when on weekdays there are usually five forty-minute periods, and on Saturdays four. In addition, on three afternoons each week a further two lessons are held in the afternoon. The timing of these afternoon lessons depends on the season. During summer they occur directly after lunch, and the pupils are then involved in sports or other activities for the rest of the afternoon. In winter, however, the lack of light in the early evening means that football or rugby is played directly after lunch and pupils return, somewhat exhausted, to lessons at about 4.30 until 6.00 p.m.

Each major public school differs slightly in the scope and nature of the formal curriculum offered, but the radical difference between these schools and comprehensives is, of course, that the curriculum for all pupils is directed towards O and A level GCE examinations. The Charterhouse prospectus explains simply that:

> As the majority of our pupils are proceeding to the University emphasis must be laid not only on intensive academic teaching but on the development of their own intellectual initiative. They must learn to cope successfully with the public examinations which are essential steps in future careers. The aim of the curriculum is, while remaining flexible and varied, to prepare each pupil for these examinations at what is, for him, the most suitable time.

We must leave open at the moment the question of whether the actuality matches the rhetoric in terms of the development of intellectual initiative and whether the curriculum might be less than ideal for those pupils who do not 'proceed to the university'. What is clear is that the curriculum centres on the demands of GCE examinations.

The pupils start work on a two- or, more commonly, three-year course designed to enable them to achieve two good fistfuls of O levels. The range of subjects studied is usually very wide. At Oundle, for example,

> In the Third form the curriculum is very general and requires no important decision to be made. The subjects which are taken are English, French, Latin, History, Geography, Divinity, Mathematics, Physics, Chemistry, Biology, Art and Music. In fact the only point that needs to be made is that all boys take Latin in the Third Form, even if they have not studied the subject before, because of its relevance to University entry in certain Art subjects.
>
> (Oundle School, Commemoration Book)

At Malvern the now unusual compulsory Latin is dropped and

> He studies Divinity, English, Geography, History, French, Mathematics, Biology, Chemistry and Physics. Most boys study Latin, though Spanish can be taken as an alternative. A boy who is interested in the Classics may also study Greek.

German can be studied in the second year. Periods are also devoted to Art, Music and P.E.

(Malvern College Prospectus)

In most public schools, a small number of the most academically able boys take their O level examinations after just two years at age 15, but the majority of boys take one or two O levels at this stage and the bulk after three years at the school. There may be some slight narrowing of the curriculum in the second and third years in the school as boys begin to choose between subjects in options, but most will still take between eight and ten O level examination subjects. As a general rule, the public schools will have nothing to do with the Certificate of Secondary Education, for to enter a boy for such an examination would be tantamount to admitting that the school had failed.

As the pupils board at the school there is little need to include very much sport, art, music, or design education within the formal curriculum. Boys will be given a taste of these during their time at the school, but will be expected to follow this sort of pursuit in free time or on 'activities' afternoons. Practically all of the actual lesson timetable is fiercely academic.

What, then, are lessons like in public schools? It is clearly impossible to give an accurate generalizable picture of the nature of teaching and learning in all public schools. Differences occur from school to school, subject to subject, master to master and class to class. Further, the actual experience of being in a particular lesson will be interpreted differently by each pupil, by the teacher and by any observer. Some attempt at description must, however, be made based on my own experience of observing and teaching at the schools.

While I was living at the two schools I spent several weeks 'following' boys through their lessons timetable. I chose a boy who was willing to be followed, obtained his timetable, and wrote notes to all of those masters who taught him to say that I wished to attend those lessons. None of the masters refused me entry into their classrooms. They were, of course, aware that I was going to be present in their lessons, and may well have initially prepared their lessons rather more carefully than they would have done otherwise. However, the pressure on time from other lessons and activities means that it is unlikely that any extra preparation could continue for very long. As I usually sent out my letters about a week before I was due to visit, I frequently got comments like, 'I thought you'd forgotten me' or 'I thought you were coming last week', which indicated that lesson preparation was unlikely to be very different from usual. After a few visits I felt that the lessons I was visiting had become, in the words of one of the masters, 'fairly normal'. He said, 'On the first day they were rather quiet, the second day they were rather noisy, on the third day there was still a little bit of play to the gallery, but more or less a normal lesson'. On the fourth visit he said, 'Today was just another lesson. There are loads of lessons just like that.' Checking with the boys, they agreed that by then the novelty of having someone else in the room had worn off and that the lessons were just as tedious as ever. 'Surely', asked one 14-year-old, 'you don't want to come to any more of these boring lessons?' Yet if the boys did interpret the lessons as boring, this did not mean that they were either disruptive or inattentive in the lessons. Individual teachers, of course, varied in the degree of control they exerted over, or expected from, their pupils in the classroom, but the overriding impression was one of order and directed work activities. I observed nothing approaching a riot, very little openly disruptive behaviour and few pupils wandering aimlessly around the room. This can perhaps best be illustrated from an account based on fieldnotes of a day's teaching for one 15-year-old who would soon, in fact, be taking two O levels, but who would wait another year before taking the remaining seven.

It was necessary to 'follow' one boy rather than a group as the majority of lessons were set by ability. Only a small group of four or five attended the identical lessons, the remainder were in the same set for some lessons but not for others. The lessons for the day were maths, French and divinity before break, followed by English and German. After lunch, for this was a full day, there was chemistry and geography. It is worth noting that here, as in most secondary schools, pupils moved from room to room and were confronted with differing environment, subject matter, academic and social expectations in each of the lessons. Within each forty-minute lesson the activity that occurs is completely independent of what follows or precedes it. The teacher does at least have the continuity of subject discipline but, for pupils, attention has to be switched rapidly from one topic to another quite unrelated area at each change of lesson. Without notes, by the end of the day I found it difficult to even remember the subjects taught, let alone the content of the lessons.

My original intention had been to use some sort of systematic observation schedule based upon the work of Flanders (1970) in addition to unstructured observation. There are now several schedules which have been developed for specific purposes, for example those of Galton, Simon and Croll (1980), Eggleston, Galton and Jones (1976) and Wragg and Dooley (1984), which have been used for the systematic observation of primary classrooms, science teaching and disruptive behaviour respectively. I had intended to develop the latter schedule in these public school classrooms. Unstructured observation, however, soon made it clear that such structured observation was unlikely to produce very interesting results within the time available for observation, simply because so little of the interaction was pupil initiated, and so much interaction was 'on task'. It was felt that unstructured observation would better reflect the 'feel' of the lessons.

For example, the first maths lesson I observed on the fourth day was held in a special mathematics teaching block. Boys queued in a casual way outside the classroom door and walked in when the teacher arrived and asked them to do so. They quickly found their desks, quietened down and organized their books. The teacher's first words inside the classroom, a mere one minute after the bell, were 'Right, there's quite a lot that needs to be said'. He proceeded for the next twenty minutes to say what was to be said, with no interruption whatever from the class. There were two questions from the boys, and I spotted from the back of the class only one pupil/pupil interaction – and that was to borrow a pencil. The whole twenty minutes was practically totally teacher talk on two set examples.

In the second part of the lesson the boys were set some examples to do. I saw one pupil/pupil interaction and a further two pupil/teacher questions. All teacher talk was 'on task', with no jokes, diversions or discipline problems. One boy was, however, not spotted reading another book quietly at the back of the room rather than doing the set work. The final five minutes of the lesson were spent in a quick-fire question and answer session between the teacher and the whole class, boys being picked to answer specific questions. The lesson ended on the bell.

A brisk walk to a nearby building led on to French. Again boys queued outside the room, some rapidly revising a word list. In spite of the five-minute gap between lessons, the teacher this time was four minutes late. The boys already knew that they were to get a test, so his opening words less than a minute later were 'Okay, just do your best, there's only a few. I'll give you a few sentences first. Okay, number one.' The class was completely silent as the boys coped with translating nine quite complicated English sentences into French. The boys swapped books with a neighbour and marked each other's work. The marks received were a matter of considerable importance to most boys. They gently 'bargained' for marks with the teacher, claiming that one part was 'quite hard' and thus deserved one and a half marks rather than one, another was easy thus was 'really only a half'. Questions were asked about what could be counted, and how many marks should be given for various attempts. In the end the nine sentences were marked out of $16\frac{1}{2}$. The '$\frac{1}{2}$s go up on Mondays' so the boys thus gave marks to the teacher which ranged from 8 to 17. There was a space of about five minutes which was filled with gentle French banter before the bell called the lesson to a halt.

A further walk led to divinity, which again was a test on work the boys should have completed. The master wrote on the board '1. Describe the four visions of Amos and their significance. 2. What happened when Amos went to Bethel?'

Several of the boys complained that he had said it would be 'one word answers', but decided in practice that essays were just as easy. They took slightly longer to settle down this time, but three minutes after the start they were completely quiet. Until the very end of the lesson there was no teacher/pupil interaction and I saw only three pupil/pupil interactions.

After break, English and German demanded a more active response from the boys. In English they were studying *Romeo and*

Juliet and the teacher led them through the text, using an audio recording first, then slowly, line by line, picking out difficulties of language and interpretation. In this lesson there were many teacher initiated questions on the text and also several pupil initiated questions. The boys seemed prepared to reveal their ignorance for they were fairly sure that, unless it was gross, it would be taken seriously. The boys had expurgated versions, the gaps in which the teacher duly filled. 'And what does expurgated mean?. . . And why might your versions be expurgated?' 'Because girls might read it, sir?' Some gentle noise was quietened by 'Right, gentlemen – that will do.'

The German lesson started with a quiet question and answer session on a random ten out of twenty questions previously set. Again here there was quite a lot of interaction between pupils and the teacher and between pupils. At one stage the master made all the boys stand up, and then allowed them to sit again when they got a sentence correct. Although the boys were all about 15 they did not appear to mind this and accepted it as a part of the lesson. Again there were no problems of discipline – a quiet word occasionally was sufficient to maintain order. At the end of the lesson the master set some work to be done outside of timetabled lessons. Several complained, not at the fact of having to do work, but at the amount he was setting.

Somewhat refreshed by lunch, the next lesson was chemistry, where we sat in a small room with a demonstration desk at the front. The first four minutes of the lesson were spent by the teacher in making final adjustments to the equipment on the bench, while the boys talked quietly to each other. They quietened on the first 'Okay, I'm ready.' The lesson then continued through demonstration of the way in which metal elements combine with hydrogen, chlorine, bromine and iodine. Questions were practically all teacher initiated and drew from the boys an account of what they had seen in terms of colours of gases and so on. They were invited to suggest why things had occurred as they had, and what underlying mechanisms might be involved. Again, for the most part, boys listened attentively and made notes on what was happening as the lesson continued. There was very little pupil/pupil interaction. The lesson ended just on time with the master telling the boys to write up the experiment in their notebooks before the next lesson.

Geography started with a short question and answer session which revised the work completed in the last lesson. Two boys asked the teacher questions about the work. In this room the boys were seated at long flat tables and close together. There was still very little 'off task' interaction. I spotted the occasional kick under the table and playing with pens, but as far as I could see all the boys did what was required of them. They first of all copied out a map which the master had put on the overhead projector, which dealt with the geographical aspects of the siting of dams on rivers. For a quarter of an hour the teacher then explored the map through a further question and answer session. 'Where would they site dams?' 'Why?' 'What were the consequences?' and so on. The bell finally rang and a ripple of lively relief was evident.

It is worth spending some time outlining the way in which lessons were structured for this particular boy on this particular day. It cannot be said to have been a representative day that could be generalized but it was certainly not atypical either. The boy in question was of quite high ability so that about half of these lessons were for the highest ability sets. But I was careful to follow some boys who were at the lower end of the ability range too. The surprising thing was how little difference there was between the classroom experiences of the two sets – for all boys in the school follow an O level course, even though some of them will not necessarily pass the examinations in the end.

However, it does need to be indicated that not all lessons were as quiet or well disciplined as those I have just described. In one lesson I watched a pair of boys scare another with a stick insect that had been captured in a tobacco tin. The joke continued throughout the lesson and, by the end, the third boy had moved his desk some six feet from the original position, away from the offending insect. In another lesson I saw a boy quietly reading a science fiction novel all through a maths lesson, and in another a boy sat half the lesson absentmindedly carving his name (or perhaps something else) into the desk. The occasional book was pinched and shirt splattered with ink as in most schools, but here misbehaviour was minimal, and done in such a way that teaching usually proceeded uninterrupted.

There are many possible explanations which can be used to account for the nature of the control exerted by teachers in these classrooms. One obvious explanation is that all of the classes are far smaller than in comprehensive schools. In the lessons described the largest group was 23 for divinity and the smallest was 14 for German. For Headmasters' Conference schools as a whole the staff–pupil ratio in 1984 was 1 : 12.0, which compares with 1 : 16.2 in state secondary schools (ISIS, 1984; DES, 1985). In the public boarding schools the ratio is nearer 1 : 11 or 1 : 12. Strangely enough, although it seems self-evident to most parents and teachers, the research evidence about the relationship between class size and academic success is mixed. The widely influential reports of Coleman (1966) in the United States and Plowden (1967) in Britain, for example, both claimed that class size did not make any difference to academic achievement. However, as Glass *et al.* (1982) make clear, both of these studies were non-experimental and if the experimentally based studies are reviewed where children were randomly assigned to classes of differing sizes, then in 80 per cent of cases children in smaller classes did better. They argue that, additionally, affective areas of attitudes and feelings depend on class size:

> Class size affects the quality of the classroom environment. In a smaller class, there are more opportunities to adapt learning programs to the needs of individuals. Many teachers avail themselves of these opportunities; others would need training to do so. Chances are good that the climate is friendlier and more conducive to learning. Students are more directly and personally involved in learning.
>
> (Glass *et al.*, 1982)

They further claim that larger classes will affect adversely pupil attitudes and interest, teaching practices and teacher morale, and, indeed, most teachers and teacher unions are adamant in their demands for smaller classes. At the lowest level this could be simply that smaller classes are easier to control.

There are other factors, too, which make teaching easier for teachers in public schools. Although the numbers in each class are small, the classrooms themselves are usually not. Most classrooms have single desks or tables which are spread widely throughout the room, thus separating the boys from each other. A raised dais at the front of the room for the master's desk is also not uncommon, ensuring far greater visibility of potential deviants.

But the major explanation for the highly ordered classroom environment most likely resides, not in these physical and architectural elements, but in the facts of boarding itself and pupil motivation to succeed. Timetabled lessons are not separate from the rest of life in a boarding school, but are integrated within the organization of the boarding school as a whole. The various aspects of life overlap and interact with each other. Thus the master who teaches the boys physics or English in the morning, may later be found umpiring cricket and later still, acting as housemaster. Any significant infractions in the classroom have implications not only there, but in each aspect of the boy's life at the school, for they are reported to housemasters who have control over rewards and privileges and ultimately may give corporal punishment. The latter is very little used. Several housemasters made a point of telling me that they had never used any form of corporal punishment. 'There it is,' said one, actually showing me a cane, 'but I've never used it.'

Order, whether it be in the classroom or outside, is rarely maintained by overt force. Within the classroom, relationships between masters and boys were generally fairly formal, but friendly and easygoing. There was little need for masters to continually threaten, as the whole system is organized around the idea that boys *do* work. Boys expected that they would be forced to work – they might well still try to avoid it if possible, but they did not expect to be successful very often. A network of checking and reporting on work and progress ensured that any failings would be temporary and it was quite simply easier to do the work in the first place.

For boys up until O level, and sometimes after, the usual way of monitoring each boy's work is through a complicated regular two, three or four week assessment procedure. In each subject boys are scored for effort and for attainment and often given a position order in their sets. This means that each piece of work that is marked is recorded by the master and becomes part of the 'orders' for that period. Most boys give a fair degree of seriousness to these marks, for they will eventually have to answer for any bad marks to their housemaster or his assistant in a regular personal meeting. These are the semi-formal occasions where praise and blame are apportioned. Within this atmosphere the sort of 'mark grubbing' that I described in the French lesson makes sense. It may only be an odd half mark here or there that an eager boy can bargain, but this may make a considerable difference to his position in his set. One really poor mark and his position can plummet. The more cynical and calculating boys, of course, recognize that there are ways of playing the system so as to maximize praise, or at least acceptance, by their housemaster, yet minimize effort. Working on the assumption that the vacations are long enough for almost anyone to forget what went before, the new term starts with a moderately clean slate. Only the foolhardy would attempt to come top in the first session of the term, for he can only expect to fall from this peak. The wise boy aims for moderate success in the first session, followed by gradual improvement throughout the term. Unfortunately, while such calculations are easy to make in the abstract, the combined product of twenty boys attempting similar strategies is less easy to calculate, and some calculations go badly wrong.

Truancy is another problem that masters at these schools do not have to face. Although very occasionally a boy will fail to supply a good reason for not turning up at a lesson, the close community of the school is highly likely to lead to detection. Boys cannot claim to be ill if they are not, simply because a list of boys who are ill is readily available. Neither can they easily stay in their houses, for the chance of being caught by the matron, housemaster or his wife is high. Having got out of bed and dressed for breakfast, as all boys must, there are few places to hide – it is quite simply easier to turn up at the lessons. If boys do miss lessons, whether it be for illness or so that they can take part in a special activity, it is their responsibility to make up the lost lessons. Teachers thus rarely have to repeat work due to absences, which can be so potentially tedious for those pupils who actually attended.

The academic work of the school is far from being restricted to timetabled lessons. Work is regularly set in all of the academic subjects for completion out of lessons in prep. Prep, or preparation, periods are fixed quiet times in the evening when boys work on their own. Schools, and even houses within schools, vary, but about $1\frac{1}{2}$ hours divided into three blocks seems to be common for the younger boys. This means that during the week there may be some fifteen extra fixed work periods and maybe even some more on Saturdays. The youngest boys are usually supervised during their prep, either by older boys or by masters or housemasters. The older boys work in smaller studies, unsupervised in detail but still unable to make any significant noise. The technological breakthrough of the micro headphone is much appreciated by many of the boys.

While it would be foolish to think that all of the boys sit quietly working for an hour and a half, the expectation on the part of the masters is that the work will be done, and the expectation on the part of the boys is also that, one way or another, it will be done. This helps to explain the nature of teaching activity in timetabled lessons, for the number of 'tests' in the day described was not unusual. In planning a week's work the teacher must take account of preps as well as lessons. An English set might have seven lessons and three preps, while a chemistry group has three lessons and two preps. The difficulty is that the preps must be such that they can be done individually by a boy in his study using only those resources immediately available to him. It is little wonder that there are many 'read for a test' or 'learn for a test' type preps set. It is also little wonder that, once the test has been given in the lesson, papers are exchanged between pupils rather than being individually marked by the teacher. Teacher survival strategies demand that the amount of marked work is reduced to sensible proportions, yet the existence of preps automatically generates large volumes. The teacher who asked boys to write on the 'Visions of Amos' and 'Amos in Bethel' may well have had an easy lesson (one which, incidentally, he used to mark work from another set) but may also have regretted his decision not to ask short answer questions when faced with his twenty-three essays. At only five minutes each, they would have taken nearly two hours to mark.

Teaching and the formal extra-curriculum

Boarding schools differ from day schools in the extent to which 'extra-curricular' activities are formalized. While in day schools extra-curricular activities are, by definition, ultimately optional, these very same activities become part of the formal expectations of the school for boarders. This is especially so with sport where boys are not only expected to take part in the main sport according to season, but must also indulge in some other sporting activities. At Clifton College, for example,

> Facilities for physical activities include a gymnasium, training rooms and a remedial gym; a heated swimming pool; a racquets court; eight fives courts; three squash courts; ten tennis courts (six hard and four grass) and a miniature rifle range. The school owns 86 acres of playing fields and has a boathouse on the River Avon.
>
> (Clifton College Prospectus)

This scale of provision for sport is in no way atypical of the major public boarding schools. The facilities are there not only for spare-time, truly optional activities, but to enable the school to ensure that all boys are occupied for large portions of the day in what are seen as 'constructive' ways.

All boys usually are forced to take part in the major games of the school whether they wish to or not. This is generally rugby or soccer in the winter and cricket or rowing in the summer, and may occupy three or four afternoons each week. During summer those playing cricket may find that it fills five or six hours most days of the week, and for the school team there may be even an occasional two-day event away from the school. The school's expectations do not end there, however, for it is common to set aside a further afternoon to minor games which can include those more individual sports such as golf, squash or swimming, or the team games such as basketball, hockey or water polo. Competitions are organized on both school and house bases for most of these sports. The range is so wide that a good sportsman can find himself competing in something for his house practically every day, and the pressures of small numbers in each house are so great that even boys who are not particularly keen or able still find themselves involved at a competitive level.

Schools are usually also well equipped for cultural and artistic activities which again are not wholly optional and thus form part of the formal extra-curriculum. In music, for example, no boy is actually forced to play an instrument, but encouragement to do so is high. Young boys may find that they have become part of the choir simply by performing well on a voice trial in their first days at the school. Concerts are arranged where outside musicians play to a 'volunteer' audience. Music tuition is, in fact, usually very thorough and taken seriously by school and parents. Private tuition from highly qualified staff is usually one of the 'extras' that parents pay for separately, and most of the major schools run several orchestras or musical groups which make public performances.

Drama also has a tendency to engulf more people than those who initially have the feel for greasepaint. Annual house plays are common, which tend, by the time the play goes on, to involve most of the boys in the house either front- or backstage. Those who are especially keen can, of course, audition for school plays. Everyone goes to Stratford or the local theatre for the O level English play if the professional theatre has checked its schedules properly.

The formal extra-curriculum extends still further into each boy's life. Art and craft are areas where encouragement rather than compulsion is all that is generally applied, but there is usually a whole set of additional societies and activities which boys must take part in. At Cheltenham, for example, there is,

a host of smaller societies, which do or discuss. Boys are required to belong to at least one society as well as being encouraged to pursue an activity. Half holidays, after games, the weekend and Thursday evenings are earmarked for activities and societies, and a boy has therefore every opportunity to discover the art of using his leisure time well.

(Cheltenham College Prospectus)

There follows a list of thirty-seven varieties ranging from chess and cycling, to mah-jongg and mountaineering and to stamps and sub-aqua, a wide enough choice indeed, but each boy has to choose at least one to be interested and active in.

Chapel is perhaps one of the most contentious parts of the formal extra-curriculum. It undoubtedly plays a smaller part in the lives of the schools than formerly. It is now more usual to have chapel services two or three mornings each week rather than six, and these services rarely last longer than five or ten minutes. Most of the schools do, however, retain compulsory chapel on one occasion each Sunday. This is usually compulsory for all boys, except those of firm different faith, no matter how loud a boy shouts that he finds it meaningless. It is generally recognized that to allow some boys not to go would mean a mass exodus, as is shown by the remarkably smaller attendance at any voluntary services.

The other major area of contention in the formal extra-curriculum is that of Combined Cadet Forces (CCF), which is still compulsory for all boys in some of the major schools but which has become voluntary in many. The common pattern is now for the younger boys to spend one afternoon each week on non-military but challenging outdoor activities such as canoeing, orienteering or climbing. They will probably learn map-reading and first aid, too, and may have to try their luck at the Tarzan assault course. At the end of the first or second year boys are able to volunteer to join the CCF usually either in the army, or air force sections. Here the training is more para-military in nature and boys usually have to attend an annual summer camp. Even though boys now usually volunteer for CCF, it does not mean free time for those who don't, for usually CCF is timetabled against Voluntary Service and those who do not wish to serve their country through military means are forced to demonstrate that they will do so through service to the community. The work that these 'volunteers' do in the community varies from school to school, work in those near towns being likely to involve getting shopping for old people or digging their gardens. Some schools have highly developed services which include plumbing, helping handicapped people and reclaiming farm land. While some of the reasons for the boys becoming involved may be less than altruistic, there is little doubt that much useful work is done and that the boys, the recipients and the school's reputation locally all gain from the transaction.

Formal social life

It can be seen that a public school boy's life is a busy one. The formal curriculum is extensive and is supplemented by an equally extensive programme of formal extra-curricular activities. But there is still a further side to the formal expectations and control that the school has over the boys through what might be called the formal social curriculum, whereby activities which are elsewhere unstructured and in the private domain come within the framework of the school's control.

At a boarding school the rule of the clock pervades social as well as academic and extra-curricular activities. Boys have to go to bed and wake at set times; they have to eat, see the matron, queue for money and even bath at set times of the day. To the outsider, bells may seem to ring for more occasions than anyone could possibly sort out, yet the boys recognize each and respond to them. Typically the day begins with a wake-up bell at 7.30 a.m. All boys have to be up and into breakfast by 8.00 a.m. and out again to chapel or assembly by about 8.40 a.m. Lessons usually start at about 9.00 a.m. A break after the first three periods allows the boys time to go back to their houses, make coffee and find their books for the next two. Lunch is usually at about 12.50 a.m. and may be served in the houses or in a separate refectory according to the school. The afternoon activities depend on the day of the week. The formal academic curriculum continues on Monday, Wednesday and Friday, followed by an assortment of formal extra-curricular activities, while on Tuesdays, Thursdays and Saturdays it is sport that usually dominates. At Wellington College:

> Games are played in the afternoon; tea is from 6.00 to 6.35 p.m. and prep begins at 7.00 p.m. In the Lower and Middle School

boys are given three preps each lasting 45 minutes. Middle and Lower School boys are expected to have their lights out by 10.00 p.m., the Lower Sixth by 10.30 p.m., the Sixth Form by 11.00 p.m., and prefects by 11.30 p.m.

(Wellington College Prospectus)

The rule of the bell is a periodic reminder to the boys of the extensive set of rules and regulations under which they live. For, in boarding schools, the restrictions on behaviour, dress, and where a boy is allowed to go, relate not only to a relatively short period in classrooms, but regulate the whole of life during term time. School rules are often finely graded by age, such that as boys grow older they are given greater responsibilities and have fewer restrictions, but the restrictions are always harsher than those demanded by the law of the country, and boarders find themselves encumbered by far more constraints than boys of their own age outside. An obvious example is that while teenagers can legally smoke and buy cigarettes at 16, schools do not allow any pupils to do so. Again, while young adults can drive and own motorcycles and cars at 17, they are not allowed to do so while at school, except under very special circumstances. Rules with alcohol are equally restrictive. Even 18-year-old men are not allowed to possess alcohol, buy it from a shop or go to a public house. They are, however, allowed to buy restricted amounts of beer either from a junior common room or house bar, and usually this privilege is obtained at 17 on certain nights each week. Betting, 'dabbling in the occult' and possessing fireworks are forbidden. At a more personal level, restrictions are placed on length of hair, on chewing and eating in public and on whether a boy may walk with his hands in his pockets. Dress rules are always long and detailed and usually there are three levels of appropriate dress from the formal Sunday chapel wear, through the everyday classroom wear, to informal attire. The 'informal' clothes permissible are not necessarily as informal as many boys might wish, however, for any flamboyant clothing is often automatically debarred. Regulations as to where boys may be at any particular time of day are also pervasive. Older boys are allowed to go further away from the school and more often than younger boys, but not only are pubs and betting shops automatically out of bounds, so are certain shops and coffee bars. Schools near towns will often make the centre of the town out of bounds except under special circumstances. The younger boys will only be able to visit cinemas as part of an organized group, but even the older boys will have heavy restrictions placed upon their visits to cinemas and theatres. One of the research schools only allows boys to go to pop concerts during term if they can persuade a master to go with them – something that did, in fact, occur.

In addition to school rules, each house has house rules which may well differ between houses at the same school. These may relate to how frequently and when television may be viewed, or when the house bar is open and for whom. House rules also cover the duties expected of each boy in the work of the house. Thus younger boys may sweep floors and clean dormitories. Where meals are served on a house basis they may lay tables, serve food and clear away plates and cutlery. In every house some boys will have to clear up the small kitchens used by the boys for coffee and snacks. Someone will also help prepare and clear away any snack meals provided.

Most of this work is done by the younger boys – those in their first two years at the school – and may be called duties, work or fagging. Schools often make a special point of mentioning fagging in their prospectuses:

> 'Fagging,' termed 'officing' at Stowe, is not permitted on a personal basis, but during his first year or so every boy is expected to 'office' by doing communal tasks in his House or in the school.
>
> (Stowe Prospectus)

> The old disciplines of fear and fagging are now gone, though junior boys are still called upon to carry out certain tasks for the good of the community.
>
> (Oundle Commemoration Book)

The prospectus for Monkton Combe School states simply

> personal 'fagging' does not exist.

While schools do, of course, have paid cleaning staff it is clear that

> With the prevailing cost of domestic help, boys are required to play an increasing part in the care and daily cleaning of their own property and of their studies.
>
> (Oundle Commemoration Book)

At Uppingham, too, 'In every House its members are expected to help with some of the domestic chores'.

These domestic chores in the houses and the enforcement of regulations on the houses and school are overseen by boys holding positions of responsibility. These positions are still myriad and finely graded. A 'fag' who empties the waste paper bin may rise to one who washes the coffee cups. The 'top fag' has responsibility for organizing the rota of jobs for other fags. Boys may be in charge of a study or in charge of a dormitory. They may rise to become house monitors or prefects and school prefects or praeposters. They may become head of house or head of school.

With each new position come increased responsibilities and increased privileges. Those in higher positions have authority over subordinates to ensure that the house or school rules are kept. They thus have the ability, and indeed duty, to give punishments to the younger boys. These punishments never now include corporal punishments and are usually trivial in nature. The common way in which prefects can punish younger boys is through the giving of lines and this is usually restricted to only one or two hundred. Alternatively boys may be told to do extra cleaning or perhaps get up early the next morning. The punishments themselves are designed more to reinforce the authority and legitimacy of the prefects than to be retributive, and they represent ways in which the prefects can maintain control without any adults being directly involved. Failure to comply with a punishment of this sort leads to swift escalation in the severity of the punishment, first through prefects, but ultimately through housemasters. Offences against the rules which only justify these paltry punishments may be recorded but need never become the knowledge of the housemaster, for he will only expect to have to deal with persistent offenders or major breaches of discipline.

The system thus recognizes that most boys are going to break rules at some time, and that it would be impossible and indeed undesirable for masters to act as police in these matters. For the house to run smoothly it is necessary for the older boys who actually live in the house to be given legitimate authority over younger boys – if it were not legitimized, and thus limited, by school rules, it would inevitably occur anyway.

It is worth quoting at length the rules of one of the research schools which indicate the delicate nature of this relationship.

> In their Houses, boys in their first year are the special responsibility of the House Sixths, who should help them with interests, advice and encouragement. They are available to their Sixths for House duties, but all members of the House should help to perform these.
>
> First year boys are entitled to the courtesies that all [boys of the school] should enjoy. They may not be sent out of bounds on errands. They should not be entrusted with large sums of money and should not be given financial reward without the knowledge and approval of the Housemaster.

Thus while first year boys may not be sent out of bounds on errands, they may be sent on errands, and they may also be entrusted with small sums of money, and given financial reward with the knowledge of their housemaster. Thus boys may be sent to buy a newspaper as long as the shop is within bounds at the time and they may certainly be sent to buy some food from the school shop when it is open. A boy may be well satisfied with a non-financial reward bought from the same shop as a reward for his labours.

In some schools all fagging of this type is officially banned and the only fagging legitimized is that of chores for and within the house. It would be unrealistic, however, to expect that more individual transactions do not occur. In practice a younger boy may have more to gain from being a fag than the older boy has from having a fag, and it is not always the case that it is the younger of the two who is the one exploited.

3

Home from home – the boys

'And now, Tom, my boy,' said the Squire, 'remember you are going, at your earnest request, to be chucked into this great school, like a young bear, with all your troubles before you – earlier than we should have sent you perhaps. If schools are what they were in my time, you'll see a great many cruel black-guard things done, and hear a deal of foul and bad talk. But never fear. You tell the truth, keep a brave and kind heart, and never listen to or say anything you wouldn't have your mother or sister hear, and you'll never feel ashamed to come home, or we to see you.'

(Hughes, 1857)

Squire Brown's last words to Tom, before finally sending him off on the Tally-ho to Rugby, were the end product of a long medi-tation on how to prepare him for this new world. He found it a none too easy task, for he did not wish to enumerate the sort of temptations Tom might meet, yet wished to ensure that he would be prepared to resist them. In the 1980s many fathers of public school boys would have had even greater difficulty than Squire Brown, for while he at least had some experiences to draw upon, the chances are that parents now have no experience of public school themselves on which to base their advice.

Irene Fox (1984, 1985) has recently reported the results of a survey conducted with 190 sets of boys in traditionally indepen-dent (as opposed to ex-direct grant) schools. She found that about half of the parents of these boys were themselves educated in the state maintained sector, usually in grammar schools. Further, she found that the parents of boarders were remarkably similar to those of day boys, and that 43 per cent of the boarders had parents who jointly had no experience of boarding themselves. Indeed, of the fathers who had boarded, about a third were sending their sons to public school as day boys.

These findings are in general agreement with information obtained from my two research schools. In a sample of about 200 boys in one of these schools, only 45 per cent of the fathers had been boarders and only 52 per cent had been to independent schools. The figures for mothers were even lower, as only 26 per cent of the mothers had boarded as girls. Thus it can be seen that very many of the boys at my research schools and in the sample studied by Fox were 'first generation' public school boys. Their fathers had no comparable experience on which they could draw to pass on advice to their sons. Even where the father had boarded there were fewer cases than might be expected where the father had attended the same school as the boy. Table 3.1 shows that in 1961 some 27 per cent of the pupils in my main research school had fathers who had themselves been educated at the same school. This was still true in 1967, but by 1972, perhaps as a result of the shifts in attitudes of the 1960s, a great change had occurred and only 17 per cent had fathers from the same school. By the time of the research only 14 per cent had a direct link in this way.

Table 3.1 Proportion of pupils with fathers who attended the same school. Statistics for all pupils in one of the research schools

	1961	1967	1972	1977	1982
Fathers went to same school	27%	27%	17%	16%	14%

Source: Annual lists

The task of this chapter is twofold. First it is to look at the experiences of the boys at present in these public schools and to see, in a broad way, whether even these 14 per cent of fathers who had known the schools in their youth might have been able to pass on any worthwhile tips to their sons. In general, the question here is, how does a boy's experience now differ from that of the 1950s or 1960s, and how does it differ from our traditional picture of Tom's experiences in the 1830s at Rugby?

Secondly, the chapter attempts to describe some aspects of the way in which cultural production occurs in these schools. The schools, at the formal level, are structured so as to encourage the transference of a particular version of high culture and the legitimization of acquisition of some part of that culture through examinations and certification, but this does not mean that the boys simply and passively accept this particular culture. Just as working-class boys in secondary modern schools create their own various cultural forms within particular determining conditions so, too, do boys in public schools. In practice their cultural forms may be more actively creative, for they draw upon elements from their own cultural backgrounds (which, as we have seen, are not so homogeneous as might have been expected), from the culture provided and nurtured by the school, and also from various popular youth and working-class cultures. The fluid and variable cultural forms found amongst the boys in public schools may well incorporate creatively elements of working-class and popular cultures that are in clear conflict with the cultural forms of their parents.

The new data used in this chapter are derived from the periods of participant observation at my two major public boarding schools, where I was able to talk with boys and become involved in many of their activities, and also from a questionnaire given to about 200 pupils in one of the schools. The questionnaire used was a shortened version of that used by Lambert *et al.* in their studies of boarding schools (Lambert and Millham, 1968; Lambert, Bullock and Millham, 1970; Lambert, 1975). In their case a three- or four-hour questionnaire was completed by practically all of the sixth form pupils in six boarding schools – a total of 1238 pupils.

In the present case a much reduced version was constructed which could be completed within one lesson period, and it was given to junior rather than senior pupils. The questionnaire was completed by practically all of the first and second year boys at the school (i.e. 13–15-year-olds) in class time, in class groups.

A further difference between Lambert's data collection method and the one used here was that his pupils completed their questionnaires under 'exam conditions', while mine were encouraged to ask me questions if they did not understand what was required or were in doubt about meanings. In practically all cases the pupils worked quietly and eagerly on their own, with just an occasional question to me. Generally the boys welcomed the chance to tell someone what they thought, and treated the process of completing the questions with due respect. The aim was to have the questionnaire completed by all boys in the first two years of the school; however, three boys were ill or away at the appropriate time and thus did not take part. Moreover, not every question was answered by every pupil, but the lowest response rate was 90 per cent. About 2 per cent of the answers had to be discarded as individual pupils had given facetious replies. However, an indication of the care and seriousness with which most of the pupils answered is exemplified by one group, where we started late, who stayed voluntarily some ten minutes into their coffee break to complete the questions.

I cannot claim to have collected ethnographic data from the boys anywhere near as rich as that collected by Willis (1977) or Corrigan (1979) in their studies. However, what is evident is the non-uniformity of responses to their particular determining conditions. I found a complex of cultural forms, some of which were highly supportive of the school and others that were strongly oppositioned, but no clear divisions were evident. On the contrary, cultural forms were seen as fluid both in time and in membership.

Why do parents send their sons to public schools?

Thomas Hughes (1857) allows us to enter into the mind of Squire Brown when he is thinking through his meditation which eventually led to the advice to Tom already quoted:

Shall I tell him to mind his work, and say he's sent to school to make himself a good scholar? Well, but he isn't sent to school for that – at any rate, not for that mainly. I don't care a straw for

Greek particles, or the digamma; no more does his mother. What is he sent to school for? Well, partly because he wants to go. If he'll only turn out a brave, helpful, truth-telling English-man, and a gentleman, and a Christian, that's all I want.

Parents still may not care about Greek particles or the digamma, but they certainly do care about academic success. Irene Fox's survey has shown that, whether boys board or not, there are two major advantages that parents wish to purchase by sending their boys to public school – 'the ability to produce better academic results and to develop the character by instilling discipline' (Fox, 1984). Boarding itself was not a primary consideration for most, and only 10 per cent gave this as a reason for choosing a public school. The boys in my sample were also asked an open-ended question on why they thought their parents (or guardians) had sent them to school there. Overwhelmingly they claimed it was for better academic results. About 70 per cent of the boys replied that their parents wanted them 'to get a good education', 'get educated well', 'get good exam results' or similar comments. Some additionally drew explicit comparisons with the state main-tained sector – 'to keep me from the comprehensives, which would be a waste' or 'because I wasn't doing well at my compre-hensive'. Examination results and academic success were thus seen as the most important factor for parents sending them. That the boys generally agreed with the importance of this emphasis was backed by much of the more ethnographic data and by two further questionnaire replies: 'because they love me and see the need for a good education', and 'good qualifications, I hope'.

Boys were also aware of the second of the reasons described by Fox – to develop the character by instilling discipline – but they tended to place it well below that of academic success. As might be expected, they also phrased it somewhat differently, for example, 'So that, with any luck, I won't turn into some hooligan'. Others replied in terms of 'courtesy and manners' and many wrote of the aim of independence and learning to live and organ-ize oneself without constant parental help.

The boys put forward a wide range of supporting reasons for their attending public school; some indicated that it was a family tradition which went almost unquestioned, while others gave rather less socially acceptable reasons than parents would probably have wished them to admit. One claimed that 'they can't stand the sight of me', and another that 'it gives them more free time', while others suggested that their parents were more interested in the status that a public school education afforded, both to them and to their son, or in the probability that it would lead to a good job later. About 20 per cent of the boys indicated that it was not all a matter of delayed gratification. Some claimed that they were at the school because the sports facilities were good, because their brothers had enjoyed it, or because they themselves thought they would enjoy it. Several were emphatic that it was their choice rather than their parents, some going further and arguing that 'my parents didn't want me to be a boarder – it was my choice' or 'they didn't want me to stay, but I love it, and they agreed'.

That many of the boys actually wished 'to be sent away to school' is worthy of further discussion. The way in which individuals interpret today's reality is, of course, dependent on past experiences. But children have only limited experience to draw upon and tend to accept whatever comes much as it is. Eighty per cent of the sample of boys questioned had come to public school directly from a preparatory school, and only about 10 per cent had come from the maintained sector, usually comprehensive schools. Of the boys from prep schools, most had already experienced boarding. Table 3.2 shows the ages at which the boarders first boarded, and it can be seen that about half had boarded from before they were 11. The most common age for first boarding was, however, 13, indicating that those boys had started boarding on transfer to public school.

At first sight it would seem unlikely that boys of 6 or 7 would find boarding particularly congenial; however, only 4 per cent of

Table 3.2 Age at which boarding boys first boarded

Age	6	7	8	9	10	11	12	13
Percentage	1	15	16	9	8	13	10	28

Source: Questionnaire sample

pupils said that they hated their prep schools most of the time, and even these did not have the usually anticipated reasons for their hatred. One stated:

> I hated it most of the time because the school catered for 8-year-olds and not really 12-year-olds, and they treated you in a babyish way.

Another elegantly stated:

> It was fucking boring, and the masters were about 100 years behind the times. I'm not used to being boxed in a 1 mile square for 2 years, and that's that.

Thirteen per cent said that they had been 'unhappy in the early years but happy enough in the last ones'. Many of these boys had been early boarders. One stated:

> At first I was teased and bullied, however, as I progressed up the school, life became more tolerable, and I began to enjoy life.

Another stated simply:

> At first I didn't like the boarding – I missed home.

Perhaps more startling, however, was the 30 per cent who 'thoroughly enjoyed it' and the further 40 per cent who said that they were 'happy most of the time'. Within this 30 per cent were the full range of boys from those who had first boarded at 6 to those who had been day boys throughout. Included within the group is one who remembered:

> I enjoyed it all the time except Common Entrance Term which was hell.

A further 11 per cent had, quite unexpectedly, enjoyed it in the first years, but had not towards the end. These boys practically all stated that the petty restrictions of the prep school had eventually become tedious. They felt that they had outgrown prep school, and yearned for greater freedom in public school. Their reasons mirrored some of those comments from boys who preferred to classify themselves as having hated it all the time, but several also included comments about teachers who had become tiresome. The overall picture seems very similar to that reported by Lambert:

> However, the progress from the ritualistic casting aside of teddy bears at the end of the first term to the dizzy heights of dormitory captain seems to pose few problems for most boys. They seem happy, highly committed and fulfilled in the gregarious world of pre-adolescence.
>
> (Lambert, 1975: 144)

The same general pattern of responses was found on a question of feelings towards present school life, as table 3.3 shows. Here 74 per cent of the boys either thoroughly enjoyed or had a reasonably pleasant time at the school. Only 6 per cent claimed to be really unhappy. This was very much in accord with my own perceptions during observation at the two schools. Boys appeared, for the most part, to enjoy being at the school. This does not mean, of course, that they enjoyed everything about it. Most lessons were still seen as tedious and being made to work hard is rarely enjoyed by anyone, but the many other advantages of life at the school more than balanced these disadvantages.

The most mentioned advantage, from the boys' point of view, was that being away from home allowed them more independence. Many felt that it allowed them to stand on their own feet

Table 3.3 Responses to the question 'How have you enjoyed your years at this school? On the whole have you . . .'

thoroughly enjoyed being here?	28%
had a reasonably pleasant time here?	46%
enjoyed it at first but not recently?	5%
been happy in the last years but not so in the earlier ones?	10%
had a tolerable time?	6%
been unhappy much of the time?	2%
disliked being here most of the time?	3%
really hated it here most of the time?	1%
	101%

Source: Questionnaire sample

and look after themselves, but it also got them away from what they often saw as the clawing and pervasive demands of their parents. At a simple level some boys wanted to 'get away from the old man' or just 'get away from parents'. The advantage was that 'you don't have to communicate with your parents if you don't want to' and also that 'you can do a lot of things and your parents won't know, e.g. smoking and drinking'. It means that 'parents can't nag at you all the time' and that 'you can do your own thing without parents always watching you'. Perhaps more positively, many of the boys felt that being away from home had improved their relationships with their parents. This group wrote that the holidays had become much more enjoyable than they would otherwise have been, and that there were fewer arguments between the members of the family. In answering a question on the effects of boarding on family relationships, one boy wrote, fairly typically:

> I think it has brought the family closer together. Being away from home most of the year makes the time spent together extremely enjoyable.

Another stated:

> It is one of the nicest things possible to go home after a hard term and to really enjoy your family's company and to do things together happily.

Opinions differed as to who had made the changes. Most related changes in themselves, for example: 'It has made me appreciate home much more' or 'I don't get so fed up with my parents.' Others saw change in others: 'Since going to boarding school my parents are much nicer when I go home.' Others imply changes on both sides:

> It has made us a lot closer, because they do not see me so much in comparison to before. They look forward to it much more, or at least, I hope they do.

This feeling of benefiting from alternating periods of close contact with parents and times away at school is reflected in answers to a question on how they enjoyed living at home during the holidays. Table 3.4 gives the responses. The largest group enjoyed being there during the holidays but did not wish that they could be at home longer. Only 30 per cent enjoyed it very much and wished they could be there far more. At the other extreme, only 2 per cent were actually unhappy at home, but 24 per cent enjoyed it part, but not all, of the time. One of these explained, typically for the group, that 'family arguments depress one after a time, periods over two weeks become a strain'.

Table 3.4 Responses to the question 'How do you find living at home during the holidays?'

I enjoy it very much and wish I could be there far more	30%
I like being there throughout the holidays	44%
It's all right but I'm glad to get back to school when term starts	12%
I like being there for some of the holiday but not all	12%
I find it a bit of a strain for much of the time	1%
I don't like being there much	0%
I'd honestly rather be there as little as possible	1%
	100%

Source: Questionnaire sample

Relationships with family were only a part of the advantages that boys saw in being at the school. Many spoke of 'having friends with you all the time' and some of the better facilities for sport and hobbies. A few wrote of better provision for music too. They wrote of there just being more to do for them at the school and of finding home restricting and boring.

We have seen that a few of the boys did not find being away from home so advantageous. While most wished to maintain a respectable distance between themselves and the watchful eyes of their parents, a small minority did not. Some wrote that they could see no advantages whatever in being away from home. Others grudgingly argued, 'None as far as I can see. Might possibly increase your independence' or 'None, apart from getting you used to being without your parents'. They wanted closer contact with their families and the feelings of security and well-being that being in a supportive family provides. For them, the disadvantages outweighed the advantages, but even for those where the balance was tipped in the opposite direction, these boys were clear about what they were missing by being away from home. About a third indicated that they did not see as much of their parents as they wished. Occasionally they wrote in terms of homesickness but more often it was in terms of not knowing the family as intimately as they wished or their being unavailable to discuss the boy's own experiences and problems. Some had more instrumental attitudes towards home, and wrote of the missed 'luxuries' of home where they had free access to television, their own bedroom, a comfortable bed and plenty of good food. About 10 per cent complained about the quality and quantity of food at the school and about 5 per cent complained about the uncomfortable beds.

About 10 per cent of the younger boys seemed as concerned with the lack of contact with their pets as with their parents. In writing of the disadvantages for them, comments included 'Miss the family and the animals' and 'not having a good relationship with your pets', 'I miss the dog'. At the extreme was one who wrote 'miss the animals – but that's all'. It must be remembered here, as elsewhere, that the boys who answered the questionnaire were aged 13 to 15.

About 20 per cent of the boys wrote about the effects of their being away on their friendships at home. Boys found that they 'lose friends at home' or that they 'don't have any friends at home'. Some explicitly 'find it difficult to become friendly with boys from state schools', and several wrote that they had lost friendships that they had before, because their friends no longer accepted them. Inevitably, going away had disrupted peer groupings in the home town and previous relationships had withered due to lack of contact. This was one of the reasons for boys finding holidays 'dull' and 'boring' after a while. Their friends from school were said to 'live all over the country, so it is hard to see them during the holidays'.

In practice, although friends are still probably widely geographically spread, they are now unlikely to come from 'all over the country'. In the last ten to twenty years public schools have become much less public in the sense of being national rather than local schools. As Salter and Tapper (1981) argue:

> the trend is towards parents selecting a school within a fifty mile radius of their home – a comfortable day's return journey by car.

This type of claim is difficult to verify, but some indication of its veracity can be seen in table 3.5. This shows the proportion of pupils in one of the research schools whose family lived reasonably nearby. The definition of 'nearby' was the arbitrary one of whether or not the home was in the same county as the school, but the figures do show a distinct pattern of increasing geographical concentration. Part of this is due to increases in the numbers of day pupils at the school, who almost by definition have to live locally (but not in this case necessarily within the same county). However, a similar pattern of greater geographical concentration was found for parents of boarders with, by 1982, about a quarter of these being within the county. A definition of proximity in terms of distance from the school shows that Salter and Tapper's (1981) assertion is correct for, again by 1982, about 60 per cent of parents lived within about forty miles from the school, which, as they put it, is a 'comfortable day's return journey by car'.

Table 3.5 Proportion of pupils from 'local' area. Statistics for all pupils in one of the research schools

	1961	1967	1972	1977	1982
Proportion of pupils from 'local' area	7%	7%	17%	26%	33%

Source: Annual lists

Greater proximity of parents to the schools has considerably affected the degree to which these public schools are 'total institutions' (Goffman, 1961), for many of the boys now see much more of their parents during term time than did pupils twenty years ago. Schools have varying rules which regulate the number of times that boys can have direct contact with their parents. Some encourage parents to visit whenever they wish at weekends after Saturday lessons, while others make some restrictions. Some schools now have weekly boarding rather than full boarding, and these boys return to their homes at weekends. This is not a general pattern, however, as it is disruptive for the pupils who remain, and, more commonly, boys are allowed to return home on one or two weekends during term if they wish to do so. Visits by parents to the schools are also more common, the usual pattern being to arrive just after Sunday chapel to take the son, and perhaps a friend, out for Sunday lunch and an outing. The cars would return just before eight and house 'call-over'.

Teaching and learning

We have seen that the majority of boys felt that they were at public school because they and their parents believed that they would be more likely to be academically successful by being there. Parents were seen as buying good teaching and facilities for learning, and boys often made it very clear that they too saw the transaction in these terms. In the questionnaire the boys were asked how satisfied they were with the teaching at the school. Seventy-six per cent said that they were satisfied and 15 per cent said they were not. The remaining 9 per cent, perhaps wisely, said that it was not possible to generalize about the teaching in this way and that, while they felt that the teaching was satisfactory in most cases, there were some areas where it was not. The comments given in addition to the simple replies were, perhaps, of greater importance than the numerical totals, for in many cases boys qualified their responses by giving examples of named departments and individual teachers where they felt that the teaching was simply not good enough. These comments were not, however, the moanings of boys complaining about being forced to work too hard, but usually complaints that they were not being forced to work hard enough.

Several other researchers in schools have noted complaints from the pupils about their teachers' lack of preparation, knowledge or teaching skills. (See, for example, Hargreaves, 1967;

Furlong, 1976; Gannaway, 1976.) Recently Turner (1983), reporting the views of a sample of well-motivated teenagers in a comprehensive school, has highlighted the way these pupils regard
teachers as resources which differ in quality and usefulness. The
pressures on these pupils to obtain a satisfactory number of O
and A level examination passes led to complaints about inade-
quate preparation for lessons on the part of teachers, inability to
explain material well and lack of concern that pupils complete
homework or are fully prepared for the examinations.

This sort of comment was echoed by boys at both of the research
public schools. Boys of all ages gave examples of bad teaching,
cases where they felt the teacher had not done adequate preparation, where he used the textbook too much and was unable or
unwilling to explain in any other way, and where teachers did not
mark work or set enough prep. Being in the schools as an independent researcher, pupils were keen to ensure that I heard their
complaints, simply because they wanted something done to
improve matters. But they were also keen to ensure that I was
aware that their comments applied only to a very limited number
of teachers, and the same named teachers and departments
recurred consistently in conversations with boys and in their
questionnaire replies. For these boys it was simply a matter of
obtaining 'value for money'. They saw a need for academic
achievement in the form of certification and felt that their
parents' considerable financial investment should provide them
with a consistently high standard of teaching.

In answer to a further question, 77 per cent of the boys felt that
most of the teachers were good teachers, only 6 per cent believing
that 'the majority don't do their job properly'. They were not,
however, quite so generous in their assessment of their teachers'
motives for doing the job, as only 26 per cent believed that their
teachers 'really believe in the value of teaching'. More positively,
72 per cent felt that most of their teachers were 'friendly out of
school', and only 5 per cent felt that most were 'not really interested in the boys'.

Although there were overall similarities between the expectations of teachers held by pupils at these two public schools and
those held by pupils at Turner's (1983) comprehensive, there

would also appear to be differences in emphasis. Only very few teachers were singled out for special blame at the public schools, even though the expectations from pupils were probably more demanding. Pupils expected their teachers to be prepared to help them on many occasions out of lesson time as well as in, and they expected prep to be marked thoroughly and quickly. They made it clear that the vast majority of their teachers did, in fact, meet their high standards. The impression given by Turner is that a rather greater proportion of teachers was the subject of complaints in his comprehensive school. A further difference would appear to be in the nature of the complaints made. It was very rare indeed for boys at these two public schools to complain about lack of subject matter knowledge; they acknowledged that virtually all of their teachers were more than sufficiently academically knowledgeable to teach them. The most common complaint was that some teachers did not force them to work hard enough either in class or in prep. These boys thus recognized that essentially it was *they* who had to do the work, rather then the teacher. They saw the teacher's job as being that of ensuring that pupils did, in fact, work hard enough to enable them to pass the examinations at the end. In the comprehensive studied by Turner complaints about lack of teacher knowledge and inability of teachers to control classes appear to be more common. Pupils also seem to be more likely to assume that it is the teacher who must work hardest rather than they themselves. Perhaps the greatest difference, however, was in the age at which the pressure of examinations was felt by pupils. It was a group of 13- to 14-year-olds at public school who wished me to intervene on their behalf to ensure that something was done with a particular teacher who was not giving them enough work. It would seem that such pressures are not so keenly felt by pupils in Turner's comprehensive school, nor at such an early age.

While practically all of the boys believed that their long-term futures were dependent on educational success, and were aware that this would require considerable work on their part, this does not mean that work was always completed on time or that it was given the full attention and effort that it deserved. Again, there are common elements here between the work restriction norms found by Turner (1983) and others in state maintained schools and what occurs in public schools. Turner states that the most important pupil-peer-group-reinforced norm that he found was one which regulated the amount of schoolwork that it was permissible to do. Pupils would make it clear by insults and sometimes sanctions that to work too hard could mean the loss of friendship and the risk of being labelled 'a swot'.

> 'Swots' are regarded as unintelligent. 'Swots' have to make up with hard work what other pupils already have in terms of ability. This enables them to do well at school but in a way that is taken to be illegitimate.
>
> (Turner, 1983: 119)

It is not that doing well is regarded in itself as being undesirable, it is just that having to work hard in order to achieve is taken to imply that the person is 'really dumb'. Such a label is thus to be avoided if at all possible, which results in work restriction norms both in and out of the classroom. If a teacher is weak and allows some boys' misdemeanours to be overlooked, self-respect within the peer group forces most of the other pupils to engage in bad behaviour too. Most pupils who are in any way examination orientated thus demand that a teacher be able to control a class, because only in that situation will he and his friends be able to work without breaking peer group norms and without being labelled 'a swot'. (See also Connell et al., 1982: 102.)

Very similar pressures to restrict work output and not to be seen to be totally accepting of the school's formal values were present in some groups in the research public schools, but to a far lesser extent. Over 80 per cent of the questionnaire replies indicated that to be too friendly towards masters would make a boy unpopular, but only 44 per cent said that 'working too hard' in itself would have the same effect. Items like 'unwillingness to join in things', which was endorsed by 64 per cent of the sample, were seen as being far more likely to make a boy unpopular than working too hard. Indeed, from a separate question, some 61 per cent felt that the majority of boys in the school were reasonably hardworking, and only 23 per cent thought that the majority did 'only a bare minimum of work'. The difference is probably due to the more total nature of boarding school education. In day schools it is possible for a pupil to work hard in the evenings at home without any of his friends knowing. He can 'mess around' and be one of the lads in lesson time but still keep up with the work by working at home. Such audience segregation makes it possible for a pupil to develop an identity in school which is in line with peer group norms and limited work output, yet still enables him to achieve academic success.

Such strategies of 'image management' are not usually available to boys in boarding schools, where practically all of the time is spent in the company of others, and where every activity is cruelly monitored by peers. If work is to be done out of lesson time it has to be done in the house, which, as we shall see later, will most often mean that such activities are watched by closest friends and thus by those who have the most power to impose peer group norms. In such a situation a rigid norm of work restriction becomes impossible; the boys themselves do not want it to develop.

However, many of the boys do not wish to perceive themselves as conformists – they wish to negotiate and maintain a self-image as one of 'the lads'. Fifty-four per cent of the boys in the questionnaire sample thought that most of the boys at the school were 'out for a good time', yet this was not perceived as being incompatible with working hard at academic studies when the occasion demanded. In practice the school often did demand hard work, and had at its disposal a range of sanctions to enable it to ensure that the work was done. The pervasive nature of the school's control enabled these boys to justify working hard in terms of the unavoidability of doing so. The peer group norm of work restriction was thus modified in such a way that work was done 'when it was not possible to reasonably avoid it', and where the sanctions for avoiding it were likely to be more intrusive on preferred activities than compliance. It is important to recognize that being one of 'the lads' demanded at the public level that work was not done because of any intrinsic interest or even primarily because one was interested in gaining qualifications for a future career. It was done because the school forced it to be done. The school's strong control structure enabled these boys to negotiate a way out of the contradiction between two desired aims – peer group approval and academic success.

The house

We saw in the last chapter that the physical social facilities for the boys are usually divided into houses. The house is both a physical building, a grouping of people and an ideology.

It is difficult to overemphasize the importance of the house to the experience of being in a public boarding school. The influence is so great that it is almost as if the boy joins a house rather than the school. In a number of schools this is exactly what happens; it is the housemaster who accepts boys into his house, and thereby into the school. Each separate housemaster maintains his own list of prospective boys and interviews boys and their parents before acceptance. The actual procedure varies from school to school, but in practically all cases the housemasters officially play a major role in selection. The headmaster's role is often restricted to the admission of a limited number of pupils each year on headmaster's nomination. The houses endeavour to promote the idea that selection for each particular house is an honour which has been won in competition with others and that, once accepted, each boy has a prime responsibility to his own house. We will see in chapter eight that in reality the competition may not actually be great, but neither boys nor parents are aware of this at the time.

The houses have been developed to become a vital part in the motivational apparatus of the school. Boys compete with other boys practically always under the banner of their houses, and 'house spirit' and group solidarity is reinforced throughout the boys' life at the school. Sports are one of the main areas where this occurs. Each house will have teams for football or rugby, cricket, hockey, swimming, rowing or whatever the main sports of the school are. In each case there will be several teams to suit the full age and ability range. When it is remembered that houses usually have only about ten or twelve boys in each year, it becomes clear that to provide teams in all these sports means that practically all of the boys have to become involved and play for their house. Sometimes sporting activities are organized such that *every* boy has to take part on a competitive basis for their house. Athletics, for example, is perhaps one of the most individualistic of sports, but to maintain house competitiveness all boys were required in both of the research schools to attempt to attain certain 'standards' in the field sports, the results of which led to failure or success in the house standards competition. Houses also competed within music and art, drama and craft, and, of course, academically. Cups and trophies were given each year to successful houses, which were then usually arranged in the house hall or other main room of the house.

Clearly, different groups of boys attached varying degrees of seriousness to these competitive activities. There were occasions during the long hot summer, while house cricket was being played, when it seemed as if all the housemasters were keenly watching their teams yet hardly a boy could be seen. Burgess (1983) has noted in another context this tendency for competition between houses to become competition between housemasters. Yet it was rare to find any of the boys totally at odds with the basic framework of competition. Just under half of the question-naire respondents thought that being 'full of house spirit' was one of the things that made a boy popular at the school, and it was hard for any boy to detach himself from the pervasive influence of house wins and losses. The presence or absence of silver cups and trophies on the appropriate shelves served as a constant reminder of the general standing of the collective. Few boys, after all, wish to be part of a house which is recognized by other boys as being 'useless', and since it is almost impossible to change houses after admission, self-image and peer group pressure usually work together towards a collective strategy.

On the questionnaire boys were asked whether they had par-ticular friends who they 'went around with'. The overall results were fairly similar for both the third and fourth years with about 19 per cent saying they had no one in particular and, of those who did have particular friends, 62 per cent said their friends were from within the same house only and 38 per cent that they were from various houses or another house. The slight differences were in the direction of increasing house influences in the second year, as friendships between boys who had been at the same prep schools, but were now in different houses, waned and new in-house friendships grew.

The figures show that there is still a surprising in-house pressure on friendships, for, it must be remembered, each year only has about ten or twelve boys in each house which is a very limited number of people from whom to choose close friends. This was partly recognized by two of the boys who, in answer to a further question on what sort of things they liked doing together, replied 'not a lot' and 'we all basically have the same attitude to school. But mainly drawn together by circumstances rather than free will.' There is an element of satisficing indicated here which is probably common throughout.

It is clear, however, that house and house spirit are not as strong as they once were. They are still important, most friendships will still develop from within the houses, and boys will still spend much of their school lives within the house, but it is now possible to develop other loyalties too, and to not always compete. Moreover, it was clear that boys did not always stay in the same tight friendship groups. Individual interests in a variety of activities meant that different boys would be involved, and groups would have overlapping membership.

Dossing and festering

We have seen from chapter two that boys' lives at public schools are busy ones. Schools generally attempt to ensure that each day is full and structured, and that as much time as possible is 'usefully' spent. Thus the rigorously timetabled academic activities of the school are extended into the formal extra-curricular activities and then extended further into the formal social life of the houses, so that eating, going to bed, waking up and even brushing one's teeth become activities which, at least in theory, are conducted at set times of the day. Non-academic time is filled as much as possible by various forms of 'useful' activity. Sports, which often occupy large slices of afternoon time, are there not simply so that boys can learn to play games well, or even enjoy playing, but to ensure that time is 'usefully' spent. The range of extra-curricular clubs and societies and cultural activities is also designed to ensure that boys don't become idle. What might be called the Protestant Work Ethic still has a strong influence for the staff of these schools. Several times I was quoted (usually wrongly) the words of Isaac Watts – 'For Satan finds some mischief still / For idle hands to do' (*Divine Songs for Children*, XX, 'Against Idleness and Mischief') and, while masters quoted it in such a way as to emphasize that they did not believe in Satan, they clearly believed in the truth of the underlying idea. Boys were boys, and were likely to get into trouble in unplanned free time.

The boys were well aware of the pressures on them to 'do something useful' with their time. Housemasters in particular were keen to ensure that boys were actively involved. We have seen that the younger boys at public schools are usually actually forced to take part in some hobby or society on one afternoon a week and are pushed by their housemasters to do much more than this. Boys know that the school expects them to take an interest in some form of cultural activity and that this will help to excuse their other failings. While the younger boys can be persuaded to try out new activities because they might enjoy them, the older boys sometimes become involved for highly questionable reasons. One group of boys I spoke to about a forthcoming Duke of Edinburgh Award overnight trip they were about to undertake saw it as a bore and a waste of time, but they felt it would look good on their forms of application to university. I received similar comments from boys involved in debating and some sports. Some of the relatively unsporting boys felt that they needed to be able to say that they were involved in some sort of sport when they went for university interviews. Voluntary and community service also had a share of boys whose motives were less than altruistic. It was often seen as the least painful alternative and, again, was something that 'looked good' on application forms.

Pressure on boys came not only from the school but also from parents. One boy, for example, told me that his parents had kept nagging him to take full advantage of all the school facilities as they were paying 'a fortune' for them. To please them, yet at the same time to assert his independence, he had made a canoe, which had cost them even more money for materials. The important point is that, while he enjoyed making the canoe and canoeing, this was not the major reason for his building it. He had made it so that staff and parents could see that he was 'doing something useful' with his time. This was far from being an isolated example, and indicates that the extension of the school's control into areas that would usually be leisure activities has the effect for many of the boys of making leisure activities into 'work'. Hobbies and activities were thus done not only, if mainly, for their intrinsic interest but because the school or others required it. Thus, while some of the boys I spoke to in the craft workshop or art room were enthralled by the act of painting or making a clay pot, the reactions were more usually not ones of unalloyed enthusiasm. They were fulfilling expectations of them by masters and parents and in truly free time the art and craft facilities were not heavily used. The library was usually deserted. The one area where a dedicated group of boys would have to be persuaded to leave at the end of the day was computing, and here it was not clear whether the interest was more in computer games or in programming.

We have seen already that, in the questionnaire, boys did not generally mention the good facilities for sport, art, music or craft as advantages of being at the school. Nor was the array of clubs and societies pinpointed. It was as if these structured 'useful' activities had become a part of the formal curriculum for most of the boys – the formal extra-curriculum. They were largely not seen as pure leisure activities, but as an awkward hybrid activity which, while being enjoyable, was not a preferred activity. What then were the preferred leisure activities?

Try as the schools may, boys find spaces in their busy, structured lives to fit in their own leisure activities and, while the occasional boy does rush to the tennis courts or to practise piano, the majority of this time appears to be spent in 'dossing' and 'festering'. In answer to a question on what sort of things boys liked doing with their friends, by far the most common reply involved ideas of 'dossing', 'messing around', 'socializing', 'listening to records' and 'festering'. One boy thoughtfully defined the latter as 'sitting about studies, talking and drinking coffee'. The thread drawing these ideas together is that this is unstructured time not under the control of the school or masters. Time is spent 'doing nothing' or just 'doing nothing in particular' rather than being engaged in a specific leisure activity.

As Paul Corrigan (1979) has argued, it is essential to recognize that, even though the boys themselves refer to these activities as 'doing nothing', it is very much a positive activity. Boys choose to pass their time in a way that is unstructured and definitely would not be regarded as positive or 'useful' by teachers or parents.

Corrigan's work was with a group of boys who were very different from those at public schools. He describes the school experiences and leisure activities of working-class boys from an estate in Sunderland, and explains the way in which 'doing nothing' is a major activity for these boys. They are regularly on the streets, standing around and talking amongst themselves, enjoying that activity as an activity in itself. They have few alternative venues as youth clubs are seen as too highly organized and authoritarian, and commercial entertainment is too expensive for most of the boys except on an occasional basis. Homes are small and usually mean close supervision by parents. The street, on the other hand, offers the boys a place of relative independence and freedom from direct supervision. The street is a place where they can do what they want when they want, with only police and residents occasionally interrupting this freedom. It offers a place for the boys to be themselves and talk together, not necessarily because they have information to communicate, but simply because of the enjoyment of being together. In this way it corresponds closely to the street corner society described by Whyte (1943) in Italian New York.

Corrigan is specifically interested in the ways in which his boys in Sunderland get into trouble, and describes a process through which 'weird ideas' can lead to 'trouble'. He argues that these boys are looking for interesting and exciting things to happen. While 'doing nothing' may be a way of spending time more congenially than staying at home, it is not particularly exciting and, especially on the festival of Saturday night, the boys wish to maximize the chance of something exciting occurring. In this light 'weird ideas' can be seen as one of the most important ways that boys can ensure that something exciting, or at least a little more interesting, does occur. One broken milk bottle leads to all the milk bottles in a road being smashed, or a few well chosen words of insult to other boys passing by can lead to a full-scale fight. As Corrigan notes:

> The sort of interaction that we are referring to here is not the *planned* smashing of things. It is not that the boys go out on a Saturday night looking for milk bottles or other things to smash. Rather they use smashing as something interesting to do.
>
> (1979: 130)

At first sight all this might seem to have little to do with boys in public schools. Public school boys, after all, do not generally walk the streets of an evening or eventually get into trouble with the police as a result of their 'weird ideas'. None the less, they do still enjoy similar periods of 'doing nothing' and many also have 'weird ideas' and carry them out. Moreover, while these activities are less likely to lead to involvement with the police, they may differ from the activities of the boys from Sunderland only in degree.

The main reason that public school boys do not wander the streets is, of course, that they are not allowed to. It is highly probable that many of them would do so if they could, and indeed, some of them do anyway even though the punishments for being out of the house can be severe. But public school boys have less need to be outside than do the kids from Sunderland, for they have within their houses spaces which they largely control. Unlike the estate homes of Sunderland, the studies of public school houses are not closely supervised. Within limits, the studies are spaces in which boys can be themselves, away from the direct supervision of adults. The studies are thus places that can play a similar role in a public school boy's life as the streets can for boys in working-class housing estates. Studies and the various 'study-room cultures' that dominate this aspect of boys' lives are a key aspect in attempting to understand what life is like for boys in public schools. The culture that develops is unlike any other, for their situation is unlike any other – where else can a boy have such independence from adult control and yet be within a control structure dominated by older boys?

It is, of course, practically impossible for any adult to penetrate very far into this study-room culture. However, I was able to spend several evenings in houses talking with boys into the small hours of the morning, and I was also lucky in that my own accommodation at one of the research schools overlooked the studies of a nearby house. This enabled me to observe, fairly unobtrusively, some of the activities of two particular study-room groups. This information was supplemented by conversations with many boys on the importance and nature of this micro world.

The various studies provide physical envelopes within which pupil-produced cultures thrive and proliferate. In houses, where boys are given a more or less free choice as to who they share with, the differences can be substantial. One well-kept, tidy study may house a group of three or four highly academic, conformist boys who decided fairly early that an Oxbridge place was worth working for. The bookshelves are full, work is completed well before time and coffee is a civilized pleasure. The study next door, however, may be a chaotic mess, with cloth hangings from the ceiling, red and blue flashing lights and 30 watts of amplified sound.

Different schools vary as to the size of the space they provide for boys. In practically all cases, younger boys get the worst deal, with either more people sharing the room or the worst part of the study for themselves. Although called studies, and usually being the place where work is done, most of the boys do not seem to see them primarily in this light. Most take great care with the decoration of the rooms to make them good social places as much as good places in which to work. Posters and pictures, soft chairs and carpets are often more prominent features than work tables. Pride of place is frequently given to the sound system, and an important part of choosing who to be in a study with is the quality of the sound that can be jointly produced.

'Doing nothing' or 'festering' consists of groups of boys talking, listening to records and drinking coffee. Primarily it is simply the sharing of conversation just for the sake of doing so. It is very similar to boys on the streets, or, for that matter, to a middle-class dinner party. The purpose of a dinner party is not to feed the guests, but to establish an occasion in which conversations can be shared. It too is 'doing nothing in particular'.

Corrigan's kids, however, get into trouble with the law because their weird ideas are performed on a public stage. The boys in public school can have weird ideas too, but these are performed generally within the enclosed world of the school. The weird idea may be to start flicking water at someone and end up with boys battling it out with the fire hoses, or it may be to throw a pencil out of the window and end up with a mound of papers and books on the ground outside. It may start with one pillow and end with a full-scale dormitory fight, or start by removing someone's sheets and end with the whole bed hanging from the rafters. Not that these are necessarily everyday occurrences, of course, but they are the result of waiting for something interesting to happen and supplying it yourself if it doesn't.

Perhaps unsurprisingly, Saturday night was the main night on which 'trouble' occurred, and this was expected by house-masters. It was on Saturday nights that boys were most likely to return to houses drunk or very late, some sort of disorder might occur in the house, or someone might get into trouble 'down town'. It seems that the special desire that Sunderland kids have to liven up the end of the week is also shared by boys in public schools.

Some of the boys specifically stated in their questionnaire replies that they liked doing 'dangerous, risky things' with their friends. One example given by these 13- to 15-year-old boys was 'pissing on the 1st XI square at midnight', a fairly harmless pursuit, but one with the highly symbolic element of attacking one of the fundamental 'sacred' symbols of the school. It carried the risk of a very serious sanction, but without a great probability of being caught. The nature of 'risky things' to do, or 'weird ideas', varied with age of course. Younger boys could make their world more exciting by simply raiding the kitchen or being out of the house at night. One boy I found taking a totally illegal midnight swim explained that it was much more fun to swim then because of the added excitement of possibly being caught. Some of the older boys livened their lives by going to pubs and a few kept bottles of spirits. Having to hide the bottles in places where they were unlikely to be found added a certain zest to the gin which tonic could not match. One of the older boys I met had a master key which fitted most of the locks in the school. To prove to me that what he said was true, three of us broke into one of the official rooms of the school and I shared with them some of the excitement (and dread) of being caught.

Most of these activities take place within the closed world of the school and are rarely heard about outside. Minor acts of theft and petty vandalism are usually dealt with internally, where similar activities on the streets of Sunderland could result in custodial sentences. Public school headmasters dare not risk the possible effects on recruitment of bad publicity, and attempt to contain any problems if possible. On occasions, however, school-boy 'pranks' are conducted in the public eye. The three boys from Stowe, for example, who built a hoax bomb to greet Baroness Airey and the Duchess of Gloucester when they visited the school, causing a full-scale alert, found that their 'weird idea' was not the subject of internal discipline but brought short custodial sentences in a detention centre (*Guardian*, 1984).

In a boarding school with so many detailed rules it is easier for boys to make their lives more exciting through breaking rules than it is for most boys elsewhere. Activities which would hardly raise an eyebrow outside are treated with great seriousness by the school. Smoking is a case in point, for although it is unusual for any school to allow smoking in classrooms, at a state school any boy who wishes can easily smoke in leisure time. At most public schools smoking is strictly prohibited at all times, and is firmly sanctioned and could even lead to expulsion. In practice, however, the majority of boys at the two schools I visited were unimpressed by smoking. Only a very small number of boys smoked, the others refraining, not because of any school prohib-itions but because they saw smoking as being unhealthy, un-attractive and expensive. The few who did smoke were regarded as just foolish by most of their peers and were to an extent shunned because of their habit. Drinking, on the other hand, was a much more popular forbidden pastime, even amongst the younger boys. Only very few appeared to keep a regular supply of alcohol for their own use, but a considerable number seemed to occasionally buy or share a bottle. The attendant risks in this case were high, as expulsion could quickly follow a first or second warning. Expulsion was usually immediate if any other prohibited drug was discovered, the police usually being called in for anything other than cannabis, where headmasters would usually deal with the matter themselves rather than risk bad publicity. Again these instances are rare; the effects of the expulsion of four senior pupils at one of the research schools, for LSD and cannabis use, could still easily be felt the following term. The event was talked of in hushed tones and as a tragedy by both masters and most of the boys.

None of this is in any way exceptional in a group of some 600 boys aged between 13 and 18. The lack of criminal or seriously deviant activity in any sizeable proportion is perhaps more worthy of note than its limited presence. The vast array of rules boys can break enables them to make their lives more exciting while in practice only indulging in activities which outside the school world would seem insignificant. A 17-year-old being drunk in the world of Sunderland (or even Surrey) is thus totally unremarkable, but is, at least in theory, taken very seriously in public schools. Not surprisingly, there are cases where housemasters 'do not want to know' about transgressions. The house system, with its negotiated balance of control by housemaster and senior boys, enables housemasters to evade the implementation of rules if they so wish. They may well have a good idea of what is going on, but do not wish to be forced to expel their senior scholars or rising stars. They hope, and trust, that the other members of the house will be able to curb any real excesses.

That school rules were often seen as annoying nuisances which infringed one's liberty and were generally to be ignored if possible was indicated by some questionnaire results. Only 12 per cent thought that the majority of boys in the school kept to the rules and 42 per cent thought that most of the boys were actually 'anxious to get round the rules'. 41 per cent thought that being 'unconcerned about breaking the rules' was one of the things that made a boy popular. Generally, popularity was linked with being 'easy to get on with' (88 per cent), having a sense of humour (82 per cent), being generous (56 per cent) and being 'full of house spirit' (43 per cent). Being unconcerned about breaking rules was fifth out of thirteen statements.

It is inevitable within any school that there will be some boys who fare badly and are unpopular. Unpopularity was mainly associated with 'greasing up to masters', being 'unwilling to join in things', being 'interested mainly in himself', being a hypocrite or being conceited, and the small number of boys who may have some or all of these characteristics can find life very hard at boarding school. We saw in table 3.3 that the vast majority of boys either thoroughly enjoyed, or had a reasonably pleasant, time at the school. At the other extreme, however, a total of 6 per cent of the boys were either unhappy most of the time, disliked or really hated being at the school. There can be a variety of reasons for this reaction, but within this group is the small number of boys who have managed to become, for one reason or another, the 'butt of the class', or of the year in the house. These unlucky boys are to be found in any school. Turner (1983), for example, describes the way in which disliked or unpopular pupils are used by others as scapegoats to direct attention from their own actions and failings. Everhart (1983, p. 168) describes a similar process occurring in his American junior high school:

> Poor Larry, I often thought as we stood outside Marcy's English class every day after lunch. I wonder what he really thinks as Don, Dave and Steven continually harass him and purposefully single him out as the brunt of their sometimes almost inhuman jokes and ridicules. I never could see Larry as doing that much to deserve such persistent treatment. Yet Larry was considered a 'weirdo', and the way he and others like him were treated served to illustrate how some students were singled out and 'picked on'.

Once 'picked on' there is little that Larry or boys like him can do – each attempt to become part of the group is interpreted as further confirmation of 'weirdness'. But Larry could at least go home in the evening and prepare himself for the traumas of the next day away from his tormentors; not so at a public boarding school.

There were several boys who were tormented at the two research schools. Young teenage boys can be merciless in their criticism – especially those who, without someone else to take the role, might become the butt of the torment themselves. The worst case I experienced was Paul, a small, frail boy with traces of a slight physical disability. His family was affluent and secure, but his world at school was one of insecurity and isolation. I would continually see him wandering around the school alone, receiving jeers and the occasional mild physical assault from his peers. Some boys took pity on him, but to become too friendly would have been to have risked one's own position and image. Paul was physically weak and poor at sport, he enjoyed reading and stamp collecting. He was teased relentlessly. Aware of the problem, his housemaster had, on one occasion, made a special point of telling the boys in his house that such behaviour would not be tolerated, but this served to further emphasize Paul's strangeness, rather than alleviate his suffering. Public schools do hold some advantages for such pupils – ultimately parents are able to withdraw a boy from the school if he is unable to cope and find a more suitable school from within the diversity of provision in the independent system. Paul left soon after my research period but his role, no doubt, was passed on to others.

The possibility of removal from the school was not one open only to parents. Pupils, too, could arrange matters so that they could leave the school if they wished. At one of the research schools, a rather older boy, after a long period of unhappiness at the school, simply decided that he had had enough. He was found smoking a cigarette in the Masters' Common Room and was expelled as a result. He chose to go, and did so in a way that did not require any prior discussion or acceptance by his parents.

It is also worth noting from table 3.3 that 10 per cent of boys had been unhappy at first but had become happier later on. Part of this was due to initial homesickness, but bullying of younger boys by older boys also played a part. When asked an open-ended question about what they disliked at the school some 10 per cent of boys mentioned bullying. They wrote that 'older boys push you around' and that they disliked 'being pushed around by older boys'. Some wrote that they were bullied at first or teased. This does not imply, of course, that such bullying is worse in public schools than elsewhere. Indeed the number of boys mentioning bullying, some of which I observed, was actually reasonably small. The difference between the situation for these boys and those in day schools is again, however, that boarding school life means that those who are at the receiving end of bullying can never feel entirely free of its influence. There may be only three or four days respite for half term in a whole thirteen-week-long term.

The only single item that the younger boys disliked about the school more than the bullying was the fagging that they had to do. For some boys the two were linked, for it wasn't so much the officially sanctioned fagging that was condemned but the unofficial fagging. Some boys wrote that they 'were treated as slaves', others thought the whole thing ridiculous:

> The fagging is so tedious. People spend about half an hour looking for their fag to make them coffee, when in that time they could have made it themselves.

I saw evidence of this sort of fagging myself as older boys would 'ask' or 'instruct' younger boys to make coffee for them, or go and find something or someone. The extent to which such activities were acceptable differed between the houses, so that one senior boy told me that, only a little while before, he had been amazed by a friend of his in another house waking a young boy to make coffee for them both as they talked together (totally illegally) in his study in the early hours of the morning. Such extremes are now rare, and the once common fag call, where the last of the fags to respond to a bellowed call from a prefect was given the task, is now heard no more. Yet it is almost inevitable that older boys living with younger boys will somehow 'encourage' them to do minor tasks for them. Officially personal fagging may well have died, but in practice many boys still enjoy the labours of younger boys. Whether this is called 'fagging', thus making it something special and idiosyncratic within the public schools, or whether it is accepted as simply a fairly common adjunct to relationships between older and younger boys, is a political and ideological decision rather than one based on the actual experiences of the boys.

This is one aspect of a point that many of the boys continually tended to emphasize in conversations with me – they regarded themselves as just 'normal' teenagers. Only a very few boys outwardly revelled in and exploited the differences between their situation and that of pupils in state maintained schools – most did exactly the opposite. The days of cultivating a separate accent and flouting striped, coloured jackets and caps are now over, and the majority of the boys in public schools for most of the time wish to blend fairly anonymously with the crowd. They shared, and wanted others to know that they shared, many aspects of a youth culture which cuts across class lines.

It is here that the cultural production of these public school boys can be seen to be genuinely creative. The particular elements of youth and popular culture that were selected and incorporated within the individual cultural forms varied considerably. With some groups it was a keen following of football, while others craved motorbikes or collected the latest pop records. These boys were certainly not cut-off from the latest developments in fashion, music or media: they actively and selectively incorporated them within their own cultural forms. The consumer tastes of many of the boys were very similar to those of pupils in state schools, with the advantage that there was sometimes also the necessary purchasing power to enable the very latest in fashion to be complied with. Different groups and individuals selectively incorporated the various aspects of the wider youth culture to different extents, but there was no clear division between cultural forms as Willis found in his secondary modern school. Instead, here the cultural forms interweave and overlap, with a considerable degree of tolerance for particular styles that the individual might not follow. There are many reasons why this should not be too unexpected including, of course, the fact that a thorough-going, anti-school, counterculture would never be allowed to develop in these schools. The boys would be simply expelled. The potential range is thus narrower but the basic similarities between the boys are deeper than this.

For the vast majority of the boys these elements of popular and youth culture are grafted on to a solid core of understanding of how they view themselves as individuals. With a few exceptions, although there were many first generation pupils, the family backgrounds of the boys were inevitably fairly wealthy. For the most part their parents had to be seen as successful; people with a good future ahead of them and the ability to make choices about that future. Stemming from this, most of the public school boys shared, as a clear distinguishing mark which separated them from so many other teenagers, a view of themselves as people with positive futures. Their produced culture was based on a firm foundation of long-term ambition and long-term futures. Thus attending public school was viewed almost without exception as an important decision and one that the individual had a very large part in determining the success of. A good regular dividend on this investment in the future depended on an adequate non-financial investment for the few years at the school.

As we have seen, this does not mean that the boys did not enjoy their time at school or indulge in any activities that could be seen as oppositional to their long-term aims. What it does mean, however, is that the boys skilfully construct a cultural form which enables them to retain this solid core of understanding of themselves as people with a future.

Compared with the depth of this foundation on which the cultural forms are constructed, the differences appear minimal. Some of the boys may be part of a punk group while others may form part of a Mozart quartet, but eventually they all sit down in the same examination hall and know that what matters to them all is good O levels and A levels. Cultural production may thus result in a variety of cultural forms, but cultural reproduction is secured through fundamental ideological beliefs that are continuous with those of the boys' parents. While the boys may wish to have themselves thought of as 'just like any other teenagers', and the similarities may outweigh the differences, it is the differences that count.

4

Goodbye, Mr Chips – the schoolmasters

And the masters' hands were against him, and his against them.
And he regarded them, as a matter of course, as his natural
enemies.

(Thomas Hughes, 1857)

That pupils often see teachers as their 'natural enemies' is part of
the folklore of teaching. Various 'guides to survival' for teachers
in training repeatedly warn neophytes to take the threat of war
seriously and to make sure that it is they who win rather than the
pupils. Both Woods (1979) and Delamont (1976b) use the idea of
two battling groups pitted against one another to structure their
accounts of school life. Hughes (1857) sees it more as an aber-
ration on the part of Tom while he is going through a rebellious
phase, for the undergraduate Tom Brown, on vacation from
Oxford, is stunned by the death of Dr Arnold and returns to
Rugby to pray in gratitude for all he had learned while he was
there. It is unlikely that the real Arnold would have relished such
sentimental humbug, or that anyone would write about similar
feelings now, but undoubtedly schoolmasters do have considerable effects on boys' lives. In both the short and the long term a
good or bad master can make life in public schools either something approaching the best years of a boy's life or simply hell.

In this chapter I look at the sort of people who become public
school masters and the nature of their lives as schoolmasters. It
will be shown that commonly held images are now an inaccurate
reflection of the truth.

The traditional view of public school masters is that they form
an all-male, high status, academic élite. While in 1984 there were

some 500,000 school teachers in Great Britain, there were only about 10,000 schoolmasters in the 200-odd HMC schools. Just as the title public school emphasizes the distance between these schools and other schools, so the use of the term 'schoolmaster' emphasizes the difference between teachers in these schools and other teachers. The challenge to their élite status which used to come from grammar school teachers has subsided as comprehensivization of the state sector has taken place and grammar schools have disappeared. Traditionally, as great emphasis was given to the 'formation of character' for the boys, it was necessary for schoolmasters to be the social equals of the parents, and, characteristically, these schoolmasters had high and uniform social class backgrounds. In the tradition of Mr Chips (Hilton, 1934), schoolmasters are themselves public school products, boarding from age 7 in a preparatory school, then at 13 moving to one of the HMC schools. After three years at Oxford or Cambridge for a degree, they return, fairly swiftly, to their haven of intellectual endeavour.

Again, traditionally, they have had a high degree of commitment to their work and there is a low turnover of masters in these schools. Long service at a particular school is the essence of the system, for housemasters are appointed from within the school, often in strict order of appointment to the school. As we shall see in the next chapter, if a master wishes to take advantage of the comforts, prestige and power of being a housemaster, he is usually required to wait some ten to fifteen years in the same school before being given the chance, and then holds the office for a further ten to fifteen years. During the long wait he has to show himself 'suitable' by devoting himself to the school in teaching, sporting and cultural activities and by encouraging his own academic subject. In return for this dedication, schoolmasters receive a salary which is traditionally higher than those for teachers in state maintained schools, security of tenure is reasonably strong, and masters are allowed considerable freedom to teach in the way that they wish.

Some support for the quantifiable characteristics of the traditional image of a public school master was given by Kalton (1966), who was commissioned by the Headmasters' Conference

to make a statistical survey of all the HMC schools. The survey
was conducted in 1964 when there were 166 schools in membership, 56 being direct grant schools and 110 being fully independent. Kalton divided the independent schools into four groups –
either totally for day or boarding pupils or mainly for day or
boarding pupils. The schools within the Rugby and Eton Groups
would have been included in either the mainly boarding or
totally boarding categories.

Table 4.1 shows the proportions of staff with and without
degrees at independent schools. The figures for 1964 are from
Kalton's survey, and the figures for twenty years later are from
ISIS national statistics and from a count of staff at fifteen of the
Rugby Group schools where full details of qualifications of staff
were easily available. There were 952 full-time staff at these
fifteen schools in 1982. It can be seen that there has been very
little change in the overall proportion of graduates. What has
changed, however, is the type of graduate, in several different
ways.

Table 4.1 Percentage of full-time masters with degrees at independent
schools

	1964 Mainly day + mainly boarding	1964 All boarding	1964 All HMC schools	1984 All HMC schools	1982 15 schools
With degree	90	88	88	90	91
No degree	10	12	12	10	9

Data from Kalton (1966) and ISIS (1984)

Kalton's most outstanding finding in his survey of masters was
that 71 per cent of graduate masters at public schools had taken
their degrees at either Oxford or Cambridge. The proportion for
independent schools that were classified as either mainly boarding or all boarding was even higher as table 4.2 shows. In 1964
some 82 per cent of full-time staff in independent schools that
were mainly boarding had degrees from Oxbridge, and some 83
per cent of those in full boarding schools did so. There has been a

Table 4.2 Universities awarding first degrees of full-time masters at independent schools (per cent)

	1964 Mainly boarding	1964 All boarding	1982 15 schools
Oxford	41	38	32
Cambridge	41	45	28
London	5	7	7
Other	13	10	34

Data from Kalton (1966)

tremendous decrease in the Oxbridge influence over the last twenty years, for now only 60 per cent of masters at fifteen of the seventeen Rugby Group schools had received their first degrees at Oxbridge. The change is actually more dramatic than the figures indicate as most of this 60 per cent are older masters rather than younger ones. Several of the schools publish a list of staff in order of appointment to the school and where this is done a dramatic change can be seen about halfway down the list. The first half consists of masters with degrees from Oxford and Cambridge with the fact that these now elderly masters were once scholars or exhibitioners proudly proclaimed. The occasional degree from London or, perhaps, St Andrew's intrudes on the pattern. But after about halfway down the list, names of universities such as Birmingham, Leeds and Keele become more prominent. By the end of the list it is the Oxford and Cambridge degrees that are the exception and masters are shown as having received their degrees from a wide range of universities such as Wales, Sussex, Kent and Bradford. The non-university sector is also represented with degrees from Cranfield, Leeds or Leicester Polytechnics. Amongst those without a degree are certificates in Education from Shoreditch or Loughborough. The change is dramatic and widely found in the schools. It marks a distinct change in the employment policies of the schools and the acceptance, perhaps through lack of Oxbridge applicants, of staff without the traditional collegial socialization period.

There are other changes too. Kalton reports that in 1964 some 6 per cent of staff had some form of higher degree or diploma, including 2 per cent who had obtained doctorates. In 1982, within the fifteen Rugby Group schools surveyed, 13 per cent had higher degrees (not including diplomas) including 6.5 per cent who had doctorates. This is due in part to the general inflation of qualifications that has occurred, but there would also seem to be a clear drive towards obtaining staff with higher degrees. This is especially so in the sciences where it is not unusual to have three or four scientists with doctorates on the staff.

The presence of staff with two or more degrees makes the Oxbridge connection slightly less clear than table 4.2 indicates. If instead of just counting the university where the first degree was obtained, a count is made of any contact with Oxbridge, then the proportion rises: 33 per cent of the staff had obtained some degree at Oxford and 30 per cent had obtained a degree at Cambridge. The difference is small, but worthy of note. It must be remembered that academic degrees are not the only appropriate qualification for staff. Music, art and P.E. teachers may still be well qualified in their field, but not have a degree. In art and design many of the staff had a DipAd or DLC, while in music ARCM, FRCM and LRAM were common. Altogether there has been an increase in the qualifications of staff and a broadening of the types of qualification represented.

Another important change will be considered in more detail in chapter seven. There, the lives of female teaching staff in these schools are discussed, for in 1964 there were only 63 women among 6221 full-time staff but by 1984 there had been a tenfold increase to 929 out of 9316 (ISIS, 1984).

The modern public school master

Whilst at the two research schools, eighty taped semi-structured interviews were conducted with teaching staff. These staff were part of a stratified, pseudo-random sample, and eight of the eighty were actually women. To avoid the possibility of identification, however, the masculine pronoun is used throughout in this chapter. Tables 4.3 to 4.5 show the educational backgrounds

Table 4.3 Educational background: school

	Secondary Modern or Com- prehensive	State Grammar	Old Direct Grant	Private	Other HMC	Same HMC
N = 80	2	23	18	5	23	9
Per cent	3	29	22	6	29	11

Table 4.4 Educational background: day or boarding

	Boarding	Day
N = 80	36	44
Per cent	45	55

Table 4.5 Educational background: higher education

	Oxford	Cambridge	Non-Oxbridge	Higher degree	Teacher qualification
N = 80	25	21	34	10	44
Per cent	31	26	43	13	55

of the sample of masters. The exact numbers in the table are, of course, dependent on the particular sample interviewed, but wider study of other sources suggests that they are reasonably representative not only of the two schools involved but of the whole range of Rugby and Eton Group schools. The characteristics of the sample are in good agreement with national figures for Headmasters' Conference schoolmasters with regard to proportions graduating from Oxbridge, having higher degrees and gender. It is hoped that the sample members are fairly representative with regard to other uncheckable aspects also. Some of the material presented in this chapter has been discussed elsewhere (Walford, 1984) in connection with changes in professionalism for these teachers.

It can be seen from table 4.3 that there was a small core of 11 per cent of the masters who were teaching in the school where they had been pupils themselves. This lack of movement was not something they were usually proud of, and there was often a note of defensiveness in discussion of this aspect. For example:

67: Well, in that case, I'm a bad example, because I was educated here, and I suppose I always wanted to teach.

69: I was, in fact, a boy here. . . . I had no intention of coming here to teach at all. Quite the reverse. I thought that it was a bad thing to come back to your own school. I thought people were blimps who went back to their own schools.

A further 29 per cent had been educated at other HMC schools and, while some of these had an upper-class background and saw public school teaching as a natural progression in their lives, not every HMC boy was like this.

60: Well, my own background is not typically public school, let me say that. I came from a sort of . . . I suppose it would be called lower-middle-class background, certainly not more than that, and I went to a village school myself. I never went to prep school or even knew what a prep school was until much later. So I went to a village school, then I went to a grammar school and from grammar school I was one of the very early people to get the benefit of the 1944 Act, because I took a scholarship to go from grammar school to public school. My parents didn't pay a penny for my education – they couldn't afford it.

One of the unexpected findings was that only a minority of the masters in the sample had experienced boarding themselves as boys. Masters were often attracted to public schools as much by what they perceived to be the academic emphasis of these schools as by their desire to be involved in the total boarding community. Practically all of the masters from what used to be direct grant schools had been 'scholarship boys' rather than fee payers, and had been day pupils rather than boarders. One of the early 'scholarship boys' explained:

64: I was asked to take the job from my teaching practice school. I intended to stay for a couple of years, because . . . I was curious. I liked what I thought the life might be. As a sort of extension to Oxford in the way of a community and academic/social/sporting thing. I had a sort of image of the public schools – I suppose based on comics and films – a sort of gilded image. But I didn't think that I really belonged to the public school group. I very definitely wasn't like the rest of the staff – most of the staff then had been at public schools – boarding schools.

A common pattern amongst those from the state sector who had moved into public schools was a desire to be able to teach their subject away from what they saw as a less academic and more trouble-ridden sector. Some had taught in numerous state sector schools before making the change, almost in desperation. One described his last school as:

> 55: The worst of all of the comprehensives I've ever taught in. Terrible. . . . Teaching was just so unsatisfying and so unsatis-factory – and such a strain to the nervous system, because the discipline was so appalling. You were just there all of the time like a lion-tamer, trying to throw sops to the animals and at the same time trying to train them to do something. And it was just not teaching – there was no satisfaction in it.

Connell *et al.* (1982) call such teachers 'refugees' from the state system and it appears that they are common in England as well as Australia. Untypically, one teacher had made a startling move:

> 88: I knew nothing about public schools when I went there. It was quite a shock, moving from a secondary modern school to a public school.

While moving from a secondary modern school to a public school must be uncommon, there are many who move from other state schools to public schools. In the year 1983 there was a total of 925 new appointments (ISIS, 1984), representing about 9 per cent of the staff numbers. 285 of these were new recruits from university, polytechnic or colleges of higher education and 295 were from other independent schools including transfers between HMC schools. A surprising 202 came from teaching in maintained schools, representing 22 per cent of the new appointments at HMC schools.

Within the sample of eighty interviewed the closure of grammar schools was sited as a major aspect of their desire to teach in a public school, for example:

> 84: Well, I went to a grammar school and I must say that I enjoyed it there and, as a teacher, probably if grammar schools had continued I'd be teaching in one of those.

Another, in describing his life history, recounted:

> 68: So, by that time, I'd said that I liked the independent sector. I dare say I would have been looking for a grammar school job, and still might be, were there any grammar schools. Because there weren't, the independent sector – public schools – seemed to be the nearest approximation. And that's why I ended up in them – although I'm not in entire agreement with everything about them!

This last sentiment was surprisingly common. Many masters had tried teaching in public schools not because they had any great commitment to the idea of private education but simply because they felt that the teaching there might be more convivial.

The closure of the grammar schools was not, of course, the only macro-social pressure. We have seen that 13 per cent of these teachers had a higher degree and 6.5 per cent had doctorates. A decade earlier these people might have been expected to gain a lectureship at a university, but the stagnation and recent retrenchment within the universities had forced people to take jobs teaching in schools. (See, for example, Miller and Walford, 1985.) Some of the people interviewed not only had doctorates but had several years of experience as university research workers. The insecurity of a succession of temporary two- or three-year appointments had eventually forced them to look elsewhere for a permanent job. These potential university academics had little desire to teach in comprehensives. One explained:

> 12: I suppose I'm guilty of caricaturing some of the state schools now, when I say that I know so many people who are almost

distracted by the difficulties of just keeping discipline. It prevents them from teaching.

Not all of these masters had completely severed their university links. Some were still actively involved in writing and publishing research papers, but, as one admitted, he wasn't sure how long it would continue, given that there seemed to be less and less chance of gaining an academic post.

Many of the masters I interviewed made it very clear that one of the most important reasons for their teaching at a public school rather than a state school was that they wished to continue to be able to take an active interest in their subject discipline. Some aspects of the extent and effects of such teachers' involvement in the development of teaching curricula will be discussed in chapter eight; at this point it is sufficient to note that many staff saw the possibility of being at the forefront of curriculum development in their subjects as being one of the opportunities that teaching at a public school offered.

It was also seen as offering an ordered and disciplined atmosphere in which to teach. As one master cryptically told me:

11: You can actually teach your subject here – the boys aren't all swinging from the light fittings.

Here, practically all of the staff felt, it was possible to not have a daily battle with pupils about control or to spend lessons haranguing children into doing work. Pupils might not all be enthusiastic about one's subject, but it was possible to excite the few who were, and still have more than tolerable lessons with the rest. Even the lowest ability sets, where there were sets, were not usually seen as particularly troublesome. It should be remembered, of course, that common entrance examinations ensure that the range of ability is far narrower than in comprehensive schools and that even these lowest ability pupils would attempt O level examinations.

A further 10 per cent of the masters interviewed had become schoolmasters only after extended periods of quite unconnected work. This proportion is a little high compared with national figures, where in 1983 only about 3 per cent of new full-time staff appointments were from industry and commerce (ISIS, 1984). In fact, a slightly greater number of teachers in independent schools left to take up positions in industry than came into teaching from industry in that year. In the sample interviewed the range of occupations included international marketing, accountancy, banking, business promotion and restaurateuring.

Some of this last group of teachers were particularly keen to emphasize that their move to a public school was heavily influenced by the special features of a boarding school. Some spoke of the bliss of the long summer holidays where, for a period of about two months, staff were free of all responsibilities to the school. Some of the younger masters, in particular, regularly used this period to travel abroad, sometimes also managing to take another holiday at Easter or Christmas, which were also usually breaks of four weeks each.

Most staff felt that better facilities for their teaching and recreational activities were also available at the school than elsewhere. Science laboratories were usually well equipped and had laboratory assistants to help staff in the preparation for teaching. There were no problems of limited textbook or stationery budgets as boys, or rather their parents, usually bought books and stationery as an 'extra' on the termly bill. Staff were also keen to point out that they had use of a range of facilities which would be very expensive if used commercially. This was an especial advantage for sport orientated staff for they, and their families, had access to squash courts, tennis courts, physical fitness equipment, a swimming pool and, at some schools, even a golf course.

Music teachers in particular found that a public boarding school enabled them to find a teaching job quite unlike any available in the state sector. Schools differ as to the number of full-time music staff they employ. Some, particularly those near cities, will only employ one or two full-time and have a large group of part-time staff teaching the various instruments. Others will employ six or seven full-time musicians who are full members of staff. For these staff, these schools offer the chance for convivial teaching of reasonably keen pupils on a single or small group basis, plus the opportunity to build orchestras and various musical groups. They are usually encouraged to continue playing in a professional capacity, too, as long as this does not interfere with their teaching. The difference between their jobs and those of music teachers in state schools, teaching classes of thirty-five one or two periods a week, or being a peripatetic adjunct to numerous schools, was great.

On a financial level it is difficult to make comparisons between teachers in state maintained schools and those in public schools. Most staff interviewed thought that they were earning 'about the same' as they would in the state system or perhaps a little less. The state system has a series of different scales, each of which has yearly increments according to age up to a maximum. Teachers move to a different scale with a higher minimum and maximum on gaining a post of responsibility. In the public school system, however, each school has its own salary scale, which is usually advertised as being 'above Burnham'. They rarely, however, say which of the Burnham scales their salary scale is above. The basic scale in public schools is usually a very long single age-related scale of about twenty-four annual increments. Additional allowances are made for special responsibilities such as head of department and housemaster, but the number of special responsibility posts is lower than in most state schools. A further complication is that staff at public schools often live in accommodation in or near the school which is provided by the school. (Kalton, 1966, showed that, at the time of his survey, 85 per cent of masters at boarding schools lived in accommodation either provided by or rented from the school.) This has both the advantages of being easy and convenient for young masters setting up home, and the disadvantage, especially later, of having to pay rent rather than paying back a mortgage. Several masters were, in fact, buying their own houses elsewhere, usually in a cheaper area, where they went during vacations and to which they eventually hoped to retire.

There are a number of additional financial perks available which vary from school to school. Some are small like telephone rental being paid or free lunches during term time, but others can be of major significance. One such financial advantage is the special reduced fees payable for sons' education at the school.

At one of the two research schools masters whose sons were day boys at the school paid only a few hundred pounds for their tuition while if the sons boarded, which was not unusual, they paid only one-third fees. Often fairly similar arrangements were available for girls too, either through an allowance which could be used at a girls' school or at the same school if it accepted girls in the sixth form. Such generous reductions were sometimes significant factors in encouraging staff to come to the school and were often key items in ensuring that staff stayed. Once a son or daughter had started public school on these low fees it was difficult for staff to even think of moving to any other job apart from those few which offered commensurate benefits.

On the whole, though, staff were not simply interested in what the school could offer them but in what they could offer the school. While there were some for whom the boarding part of the school was an inconvenience which had to be taken against the other advantages offered, other masters had sought out a boarding school rather than a day school because they thought that this, in itself, would make their lives more fulfilled. A typical example was one younger master who told me:

> 33: I wanted somewhere where I could get more involved. Where I knew the people I taught outside the classroom as well as within, and, in some ways, more outside the classroom than within.

These masters chose to work in a boarding school because they did not want a nine to five job with almost complete separation between the work and non-work parts of their lives. They wanted the chance to get to know their pupils through sports and activities and through being involved in the pastoral and house system. As we shall see in the next section, there was usually plenty of opportunity for such involvement. What for some was a major burden of boarding school teaching was for others a major attraction.

In summary, we have seen in this section that the modern public school master is far from the traditional caricature. There is now a wide range of people teaching in public schools with a corresponding range of experiences, attitudes and expectations.

As such, there is now no clear discontinuity between the characteristics of this sample of teachers and the majority of teachers who teach in state schools. The two groups overlap considerably rather than being distinct.

Public schools as greedy institutions

From the outside, teaching in a public school is frequently regarded as being an 'easy life' or a 'soft option' compared with the lives of teachers in state maintained schools. After all, pupils are well motivated, classes are smaller, there are fewer discipline problems, there is good parental interest and support, facilities are good, surroundings are pleasant and the holidays are long. These and many more features of the job make it appear to be one that is highly desirable, provided the very existence of such schools does not conflict with one's personal political philosophy. The reality of life as it is lived by masters in public schools, however, brings out a number of important disadvantages which mar the idyllic image.

At the level of classroom teaching few would dispute that a class of 20 makes teaching far more easy and enjoyable than a class of 30 or 35, but what has to be remembered is that practically all of the pupils at public school will be taking O levels and the vast majority will continue with A levels. Boys begin at the school at 13 and usually start immediately on a two or three year course to O level. Every lesson thus becomes a lesson teaching examination classes. What is also often forgotten is that, while O level classes are practically always smaller than those in state schools, this may well not be the case with A level. At public schools the proportion taking A level is high, which means that it is necessary to have fairly large groups if the fees are to be kept at a reasonable level. In state schools the large numbers in the lower school compared with the small numbers in the sixth form mean that the schools can afford to run small A level groups. This is less possible where a high proportion of the pupils stay on, with the result that groups of twelve to sixteen are not uncommon. Thus at A level the number of students in each group is probably not significantly different from that in state schools. In terms of workload, however, it may be higher for teachers in public schools than in state schools, for a master in a public school may find himself with both a first year and second year A level set to teach, which is less likely in state schools. The overall workload, in terms of contact hours with examination sets, preparation and marking, may well be far higher than that for teachers in state schools.

John Burke (1983) has pointed out that a somewhat similar problem occurs in sixth form colleges. There, of course, all teaching is often at A level, and a typical teacher may have many sets, each with about twenty students. Keeping up with the marking of work thus becomes a major preoccupation and Burke found that some tutors were working an average of two to three hours per night Monday to Thursday on their regular class marking. On top of that, they had to make preparations for teaching individual lessons and keep up to date with their subject. With keen, interested students, if only a handful in each group, it was vital that they read widely in their subject area and continued to be knowledgeable about latest developments.

The demands of regularly set prep at public schools ensure that teachers there also have high marking loads. At A level in each subject it would be usual to set work to keep pupils occupied for at least a further five hours a week beyond lesson time and general reading. Much of this work would have to be marked individually and, moreover, it would almost always actually be completed. In the years before O level, marking can also be of horrendous proportions. A chemistry master might have a fourth year class for three periods a week and additionally set two three-quarter hour preps. Not only does this mean that marking rapidly accumulates, but also that teachers are not able to have an 'easy' period by telling pupils to 'write up notes' or 'write an essay', for this type of activity must be reserved for prep.

While teaching and related activities clearly occupy masters for many hours, this is but one part of their overall job for, unlike other teachers, they are expected to be teachers, counsellors, administrators and entertainment managers all in one. Advertisements for vacancies in public schools typically ask for well qualified university graduates able to teach their subject to the full age and ability range of the school, but then they often continue 'an interest in rugby would be an advantage' or 'ability to coach soccer would be an advantage' or, more inclusively, 'applicants must be prepared to play a full part in the boarding community'. Teachers of mathematics or physics are now almost invariably expected to have 'an interest in computing' or 'a knowledge of electronics', and even Eton asks for 'an academically distinguished graduate who enjoys teaching his subject and has wider general interests'. What all these euphemistic additions actually mean is that the school is not only interested in employing the best teacher it can find, but it also wishes that person to spend about an equal amount of time being involved with the many other formal extra-curricular activities of a boarding school. Teachers at public schools do not only teach their subject, but also referee football, coach tennis, umpire cricket and judge athletics. They organize films, are officers in the Combined Cadet Force, direct and produce plays, and oversee the chess club. Those involved with the house side (and that is the majority) also give out pocket money, check and counsel pupils' progress, stop the occasional pillow fight and act as father confessor. A public school master's life is a busy one.

Lewis Coser (1974) introduced the term 'greedy institutions' to describe a whole range of institutions which attempt to keep their servants completely dependent and try to demand exclusive and total commitment. His examples covered a range of individuals from eunuchs and royal mistresses serving greedy rulers, to domestic servants and wives serving greedy families, and to Bolsheviks and Catholic priests serving greedy institutions. In each case he sees a common seeking for undivided loyalty and the reduction of the claims of competing roles and status positions. More recently Sandra Acker (1980) has applied the idea of greedy institutions to the workings of universities. She argues that for a university academic to become successful it is necessary for him or her to research and publish and become involved in committee work and administration in addition to teaching. Such an 'overload' of work (Fogarty *et al.*, 1971) means that work spills over into what would otherwise be leisure time. While 'total institutions' demand total, undivided loyalty through the imposition of physical boundaries, greedy institutions are able to do the same, perhaps more successfully, through the maintenance of group norms of hard work and the expectation of availability to the needs of the institution at any time. One of the key aspects that Acker brings out is that the nature of academic work is such that it is never really 'done'. It is always possible to do more work, and the tendency, with those who wish to succeed, is to increase work output norms way beyond what could reasonably be expected.

Public schools, during term time at least, would appear to be even more 'greedy institutions' than universities. Not only is the nature of the work similarly such that it can never be 'done' or finished, but there are also elements of the total institution too. Thus preparation for a lesson could always be done better, and work marked more carefully and, at the same time, physical and time restrictions circumscribe the lives of the teachers in the same way as they do the lives of the boys.

All of the staff at public boarding schools will be involved with school activities which are additional to teaching duties. These include the organization of sports and activities in the afternoons and weekends as well as house related duties. While the major public schools do employ P.E. specialist teachers and it is not uncommon for there to also be a racquets or cricket specialist on a part-time or full-time basis, the majority of coaching, refereeing and umpiring has to be done by teaching staff. Staff are usually made well aware of these additional calls on their time before appointment so many of those appointed are themselves amateur sportsmen who view the ability to continue with their sports as one of the advantages of the job. It is lucky that most of them do, for they are likely to spend at least a couple of hours most afternoons on the sports fields. In summer those umpiring cricket may spend five or more hours three times a week on the square. It should be remembered that this does not just apply to one or two teams representing the school, but to two or three teams for each house. Even those staff with little sporting achievement are thus pressed into duty with the junior colts.

There are various other school activities which also have to be staffed by masters in their non-teaching time. This may be a trivial commitment of a few hours a week with debating or bridge, but it could also be a major responsibility such as voluntary service or Combined Cadet Force. In many schools voluntary service has grown into an impressive organization which visits old people, decorates homes, tidies gardens and helps handicapped children. The management of such an organization is far from being a trivial task and is again undertaken by one or two masters. Combined Cadet Force usually involves a greater number of staff, most of whom become officers. These officers are paid extra for the duty by H.M. Armed Forces, but they have to attend training and be prepared to spend weeks with boys on camp during the vacations in return for their extra pay.

House duties, on the other hand, which practically all still perform at one time or another, are usually unpaid for all but the housemasters themselves. Housemasters have ultimate responsibility for the running of their own house, but they need a small team of other masters to help them in their task. These may be called variously house tutors or assistant housemasters, but the tasks involved are similar, and there may be between two and five assistants attached to each house. Their main duties are to stand in for the housemaster on one or two nights a week to ensure that the evening's work and bedtime rituals are conducted properly but in good humour. The role is more that of another adult to talk to, rather than a policeman, but he must, of course, always be prepared to impose discipline should the need arise. House tutors or assistants are often involved with the regular checking procedures for academic work, and will have a group of boys in the house for whom they have some special pastoral responsibility. However, it is often the extra and unexpected house related duties that take the most time. The annual house play, for example, has to have someone direct it, someone to work at the lighting, stage and props and someone to organize the finances. While some of these tasks are done in conjunction with senior boys, the burden often falls heavily on house tutors. They are expected to enthuse about their house, support its boys when they compete, and be saddened when they lose.

The school thus acts as a very 'greedy institution' for most of the academic staff. During term time they have little time for anything else, and have to make a determined effort to be involved in anything other than the school. They find their time governed by the bell with few gaps to fit in friends or family. As one of the older masters told me:

3: This sort of school does make excessive demands on masters – especially the younger ones.

And, indeed, while new staff are briefed as to what to expect, some leave fairly swiftly once the reality is experienced. For, although the majority of staff at any one time may well have been at the school for more than a decade, this does not mean that the majority of people who become masters are also long-servers. There is usually a group of staff who only stay for one or two years, perhaps less, before finding that they are not prepared to tolerate the 'excessive demands' made on them.

Other than the housemasters, who we shall look at in the next chapter, it is the young bachelor masters who are expected to take the greatest interest in sporting and cultural activities. Most of the major schools provide semi-communal accommodation for these masters with meals provided. Even where separate flats are provided for these unmarried staff it is essential that meals are also available elsewhere, for they are simply too busy to buy food and prepare their own meals.

On marriage, or maybe just middle age, masters are able to move to houses provided by the school or their own homes. At this stage there is the chance of dropping the coaching of the first eleven and it being taken on by a younger and fitter man. Extra commitments certainly do not cease, but they may change in nature.

As one might expect, with sixty or so masters the sharing out of duties and responsibilities in a fair way is not an easy task. Some inevitably work harder than others and it is very difficult for a headmaster to force staff to do more than a certain minimum of extra chores if the teaching duties are conducted well. It appears, in fact, that it is becoming gradually more difficult for headmasters to find staff who are prepared to be academics, counsellors and entertainments managers all at the same time, and that the 'unfair' allocation of tasks is often a major cause of discontent. As another older master explained:

> 2: When I was first here I didn't do much sport. I didn't have to because there were a lot of keen people when I came. It's not so now – a new person would be pressed to do more sport.

There are several reasons for the change. One is the tension between wishing to appoint strong academic teachers and the needs of the school in other areas. We have seen that highly qualified graduates, with higher degrees and sometimes university research experience, are now quite common in the major public schools, yet these teachers are likely to see the main advantages of such schools as being their good teaching environment rather than the boarding aspect as such. They may thus be less prepared to be engulfed in extra activities. In the same way, the appointment of slightly older masters who have had previous careers in industry and commerce brings to the schools much wider experiences and insight into a range of careers, but these men may well have an established family and also be less willing than raw graduates to devote all of their lives to the school. Headmasters are, of course, aware of these problems when they appoint and are forced to balance the gains and losses in each case, but the pressures towards appointing masters with greater academic or business experience has thrown even more work on those appointed in the more usual way directly from university. A second reason for growing difficulties is that there are fewer opportunities elsewhere for masters in terms of promotion. Grammar schools in the state maintained sector are now few and far between, and even in comprehensive schools the falling total school age population has meant school closures and few new staff appointments. Masters in public schools are thus now not easily able to move and get promotion, and those who might have done so are likely to try to make their lives more congenial where they are by avoiding as many extra responsibilities as possible.

A third factor is that masters are reacting to the growth in the use of techniques of management akin to those in industry and commerce by headmasters under pressure from parents and economics. As schools have grown larger and the need for a tight financial grip has hardened, headmasters have found themselves drawn away from the classroom and teaching concerns towards the practice of management and the assurance of survival of the school as an organization. I have argued elsewhere (Walford, 1984) that this change in the relationship between headmaster and staff has shown itself in several ways, one of which is in the security of tenure of appointments. Surprisingly, appointments now seem to be less secure in these schools than in state schools, for while in state schools it is practically impossible to sack a teacher for anything less than gross misconduct, teachers at public schools are 'eased out' of their jobs for much less. Several of the younger masters I interviewed were genuinely concerned that their contracts might be terminated by the school, not because of their own inadequacies or failings, but because they foresaw a situation where it would be 'administratively convenient' to dismiss them due to other likely changes in the school. In another case pressure from parents and boys had persuaded the headmaster of one of the research schools to force out a master of long service. The case was complicated, but rested on implied but not proven inadequacies in teaching. The master left without another permanent job to go to, unable to make a protest for fear of never again being employed in an HMC school if he did.

The dismissal of a teacher in this way is an indication of the growing pressures on staff of public schools. The boys demand a consistent high level of performance from their teachers and, if it is not forthcoming, pressure from parents, if in sufficient quantity, will ensure that something is done about it. In Australia Connell *et al.* (1982: 89) found similar, if not more pronounced, pressures on staff in private fee-paying schools. They report one teacher as saying:

> The school's run by the kids, I mean, the level at which the teachers work – and they work very hard here – is controlled by the kids, their expectations. If you don't match up, you're out.

There, as in these British public schools, the pupils complain about any 'slackness' on the part of their teachers. They demand that their teachers have good discipline, set and mark prep regularly and are available to help them when required. It was evident from talking to boys at the school that the majority of them regarded the transaction as being a purely financial one. They, or rather their parents, were buying good teaching, good facilities and the chance to get good qualifications. Any deficiency in the 'goods' purchased would be the subject of complaint. An hour-long argument that I held with two 14- and 15-year-old boys emphasizes the extent of this feeling. They expressed considerable resentment that their teachers should be given two months' holiday in the summer on full pay and also have long holidays at Easter and Christmas. They argued that their fathers did not have such long holidays, and saw no reason why the men they were 'employing' should have longer holidays than the people who were employing them. None of my arguments about low pay, need to attract high quality staff, long hours worked by masters during term time or need for time to keep up-to-date with academic study convinced them. As far as they were concerned, if masters were being paid all the time they should be working for the school. They went on to suggest many ways in which they could do so, ranging from upkeep of the grounds to running summer courses for foreign students, the last of which they saw as particularly attractive as it would also bring in additional income to the school which would lower their own fees.

Many of the masters I spoke to, especially the older ones, rejected the extreme examination orientation that was now to be found in the schools. Not untypically one said:

> 47: I think that we are too examination ridden – it's difficult to get away from it, but we're now an examination mill. And parents' expectations when a boy gets accepted by the school are often quite unrealistic. . . . But, I think it's quite understandable when parents are paying out high fees. If the father's a businessman, he regards it as an investment and he wants the dividend in success for his son.

As the recession continues and unemployment even amongst graduates increases, so do the pressures on the schools from parents. Parents are no longer prepared to spend £4500 per year for their sons to 'run round fields half the time', but want as good teaching and facilities as their money can buy. As a consequence headmasters have been forced to act as managers and to take up a tougher stance towards their 'employees'. The masters, at the receiving end, have seen real changes in the expectations made of them and many now feel that they are being treated as 'workers' under the control of management, rather than professional colleagues working together for the common good. This has led in some cases, and is likely to lead increasingly, to a reluctance to allow the 'greedy institution' full dominance over their lives. Masters seem to 'need to be persuaded' to take on extra duties more than they used to, and are more prepared to say no if the demands of the institution are unreasonable. In this, as in so many other ways, there is a growing continuity of experience between masters in public schools and teachers in the state system. The pressures on teachers in the state system for greater accountability and the increased influence of parents, through parent/teacher associations and parent governors, may bring the nature of their experiences even closer together.

Pastoral and academic

Over the last decade or more the moves to comprehensive school-ing in the state maintained sector have brought with them an increased division of teachers into those who regard themselves as subject specialists and those who are more involved with the 'pastoral' aspects of the task. There has been considerable dis-cussion about the desirability, or more generally undesirability, of this development, those concerned arguing that pastoral work is better conceived as an integral part of all teaching rather than being the province of specialists (see, for example, Marland, 1974; Hamblin, 1978). However, often as a consequence of the creation of large schools through mergers, it has become common to create 'pastoral' posts to which the headteacher's authority can be del-egated in areas concerned with issues 'broader than subject per-formance'. Several authors have been explicitly concerned with the likely effects of such a division within schools. John (1980), for example, argued that the cohesion of the school had been adversely affected and that there was a growing gulf between curricular and pastoral systems, while Richardson (1973) claimed that the two areas pull teachers in opposite directions with the resultant possibility of confusion of goals for the school. More recent work by Redican (1985) has shown how, in two comprehensives each formed by the amalgamation of a grammar school and a secondary modern school, there had been a tendency for those with high academic qualifications to become heads of department and be more concerned with the academic side, while those teachers from secondary modern schools with less academic qualifications took on the pastoral responsibilities. What Redican shows, however, is that in practice those teachers on the pastoral side had systematically devalued the academic side and they had gradually moved from collating information about pupil learning, assessing pupil strengths and weaknesses and proposing remedies, to the 'supervision' of the work of the teachers. 'Pastoral' staff saw themselves, and other teachers saw them, as being both 'supervisory' and 'dominant' over those teachers concerned with academic teaching. Within these schools the 'pastoral' staff had been able to systematically and consistently create a position of superiority for themselves, where 'pastoral' issues were seen as more important than academic ones, and where decisions that affected subject teaching were being taken by teachers totally unqualified in that academic area. Most of the senior administrative and pastoral staff of Redican's two schools were poorly academically qualified, yet they had managed to seize control from the far better qualified heads of department and made major decisions as to promotion, appointments, finance, room allocations, teaching loads, and even examination entries for pupils. As one head of department summarized:

Heads of subject, like myself, are not consulted about appointments or about promotions of our own subject staff. Members of my department are given points of responsibility for administrative reasons and it is not clear for what and to whom they are responsible. . . . Why should they listen to me? Doing a little 'leg' work for the administration brightens their career prospects while working for me gets them nowhere.

(Redican, 1985)

Within public boarding schools the two sides of the school – academic and pastoral – are perhaps more clearly seen than in state maintained schools. There is a strong departmental subject structure with a head of department who is responsible for the organization of teaching of that subject throughout the school. Practically all of the staff are members of one department only and are thus responsible to their head of department for their teaching. While there is due consultation with the members of the department, the head of department ultimately decides on teaching syllabuses, on teaching group composition and on who teaches which groups. He has control of a budget for necessary supplies for which he alone is responsible and may have control over technicians, other support staff, and a specific suite of rooms, especially in the sciences. The pastoral side, on the other hand, is under the control of housemasters. Here, again, as we shall see in the next chapter, there is considerable autonomy of action and extensive responsibilities. Each housemaster will have access to a budget, will have authority over the use of an entire building or section of a building and will be *in loco parentis* to some sixty boys. In boarding public schools the pastoral task is a very real and demanding one, perhaps unlike the 'pastoral' side in most state maintained schools.

At first sight it would seem that the public school organizational structure, with its very clear division into two power blocs, must be designed for continual conflict. And conflict certainly occurs. At the financial level, for example, the demands for new scientific apparatus in the physics laboratories must compete with those for new carpeting for dormitories in the houses. The allocation designed for book buying for the school library is at the expense of a new shower. The services of a laboratory technician must be weighed against those of a gardener. This sort of decision making often involves partly concealed conflict as staff fight for what they believe to be in their own, or the school's best interests. As these decisions are part of regular planned communal expenditure the headmaster is able to deal with most of the claims through individual budgets differentially increasing with inflation. It is only infrequently that heads of department or housemasters will need to act as a group to get their priorities enforced. However, at times when new large capital expenditure is proposed the conflicts of interest can become more visible. This can be particularly obvious when the school is involved in appeals, which have taken on a major role in financing new projects in public schools. Here not only have the demands of various staff to be reconciled, but also tactical decisions have to be made as to the attractiveness of proposals to potential donors. An appeal for money to refurbish one of the houses is unlikely to be very attractive to industrial or commercial organizations which may be asked to contribute, but a new centre for craft and design, or perhaps engineering, craft and design, might well strike the right note. The need for new classrooms has to be balanced against the attractiveness to potential donors of a new sports centre.

In practice, appeals are now commonly for a range of new facilities rather than a single item. Various groups can thus find different parts of the package attractive. This can bring the conflicts within the school out into the open as masters fight to have their share of the spoils. It is worth noting that, while the pastoral and academic division is the major one in these schools, there are other groups making major demands. Those involved in sport, in particular in schools which force pupils to play almost daily, have an important power which can be exploited. Musicians and artists can also draw upon a wider range of supporting arguments than can teachers of pure academic subjects.

Not all of the demands are financial. Some of the most bitter and long-running conflicts can occur over time allocations and the demands made by the various aspects of the school on pupils' time. A common complaint from the academic side, for example, concerned Saturday morning school and the conflicting demands of sport. Although less true than it was, Honey's (1977) claim that to play sport with another school was an indication of acceptance of school status still has its significance. Public schools still largely only play sports with other public schools considered to be their social equals, which can necessitate several hours travel by coach for an away game. Away games on Saturday afternoon can thus mean loss of two or three periods of teaching on Saturday morning. As one master complained:

82: It is ridiculous that just before A levels they can be missing vital lessons and time just to go off and play cricket.

Saturday morning lessons are also particularly vulnerable to being cut or shortened by school events. Parents' meetings, gaudies or other special events can all cause the introduction of 'short lessons' on Saturday morning to enable activities to start earlier, much to the annoyance of some of those masters teaching at that time.

The house side of the school can also make demands on what would otherwise be pupils' academic time. House plays, for example, can mean missed lessons as the event nears, and preps can also be cancelled or, at best, only partially completed. Some of the heads of department also complained about the demands made by houses on the older boys to play their part in the organization and overseeing of younger boys. The position of head of house, in particular, was seen as a major responsibility which could be academically damaging. One master was prepared to quantify this conflict of demands:

73: If a boy becomes head of house you can be sure that it will mean a drop of at least a grade in his A levels.

Few masters would have been prepared to voice such doubts so strongly, but there were clearly conflicts of interest to be reconciled between the various school demands.

It can be seen that there are thus several similarities, with regard to conflicting interests of staff, between the situation in these public schools and the comprehensive schools studied by Redican (1985). But the divisions do not appear to be as deep, nor as disruptive, as was found there. In public boarding schools there is a much greater overlap of responsibilities amongst staff, with most staff being involved in a variety of aspects of the school life. All of the housemasters also do a major share of the teaching, usually still covering the full age and ability range. Most of the academic staff, including the heads of department, are involved in a similar way in the house system and in sports and other activities. Moreover, the traditional pattern has been that a good proportion of staff may become centrally involved in various activities at different points in their lives, so that someone who had been head of department might give that up on becoming a housemaster. It might also be possible, if still young enough, to return to head of department after being housemaster. In some schools it is still possible for masters to hold both of these posts at the same time. At public schools it has thus traditionally been the case that masters had experience of both 'pastoral' and 'academic' responsibilities. Conflicts would still occur, but the shared experiences meant that it was unlikely that major diversification of goals would develop.

The shift towards a greater academic emphasis and the appointment of very highly qualified academic staff is beginning to change this delicate balance. Several of the highly academically qualified staff I talked with were not interested at all in the boarding aspect of the school and had no desire whatever to become housemasters. They saw a clear career path through the academic side of the school, and were hoping to eventually become head of department at a similar school. One older teacher explained:

> 11: I think that now when you come as a junior master, after you have found your feet, you can decide in principle whether you want to go up the academic side or the house side – teach boys or subjects – there are generally those two paths.

We have already seen that some of those members of staff rather less well academically qualified, but still usually graduates, have been under increasing pressure to become involved in sports and activities. The seeds of a dangerous division within the teaching staff are being sown, and masters now seem more likely to see their future career lines as either being on the academic or the pastoral sides rather than on both. The push towards academic qualifications and the appointment of highly academically oriented staff has meant greater pressure on the rest. In the two comprehensive schools studied by Redican (1985) those masters on the pastoral side, with poorer qualifications, were able to construct a position of dominance for themselves over their more academic colleagues, to the detriment of academic work in the schools.

In public boarding schools there has been traditionally a balance between the power and authority of the various sides of the school, which was facilitated by the interlocked and wide ranging nature of the responsibilities of individual masters. If a greater division of responsibilities was to occur, the pastoral staff might be able to assume a position of dominance in a similar way to 'pastoral' staff in comprehensive schools. This would be a disaster for public schools, which can now only survive through their academic achievement record.

5

The medieval baron in his castle – the public school housemaster

The Doctor looked up from his task; he was working away with a great chisel at the bottom of a boy's sailing boat, the lines of which he was no doubt fashioning on the model of one of Nician's galleys. Round him stood three or four children; the candle burnt brightly on a large table at the further end, covered with books and papers, and a great fire threw a ruddy glow over the rest of the room. All looked so kindly, and homely, and comfortable, that the boys took heart for a moment, and Tom advanced from behind the shelter of the great sofa. The Doctor nodded to the children, who went out, casting curious and amused glances at the three young scarecrows.

'Well, my little fellows,' began the Doctor . . . 'what makes you so late?'

(Hughes, 1857)

In Tom Brown's time Dr Arnold was not only headmaster of Rugby but housemaster of School House too. As such he was directly *in loco parentis* for all of the boys in the house. When Hall, East and Brown arrive back late, dirty and exhausted having tried to follow the hare-and-hounds designed for boys three years their senior, they are sent to Dr Arnold. There, in the doctor's own library on the 'private side' they disturb him from time with his young children to make their excuses and eventually, on this occasion, be forgiven.

Then, as now, housemasters learn to accept regular intrusions by the boys in their care into their private lives. During term time housemasters have little time that they can truly call their own, for at any time they can be called away to tackle house problems. In this chapter we look at what life is like for these housemasters.

Medieval barons

> We are rather like mediaeval barons, each with his own castle. And the Headmaster is the King.

The analogy is a good one, perhaps better than the housemaster who suggested it realized, for it hints at the constraints of geography and tradition and, at the same time, points towards the complex web of reciprocal responsibilities, allegiances and obligations which exist between pupil, housemaster and headmaster.

Practically all of the major public schools divide their pupils into mixed age, hierarchically organized 'houses'. The term is used to signify both the collectivity of fifty to sixty boys and accompanying staff, and also the physical buildings in which these boys will spend a major part of their five years at the school. As with so many aspects of the public schools, while there is much in common, the details of the organization and structure of houses differ from school to school.

For example, some of the schools with few day pupils integrate them into the boarding houses, while others provide separate houses for the non-boarders. Some of the schools which accept sixth form girls also attempt to integrate them into the boys' boarding houses, while most, as numbers have grown, have built separate houses for the girls. The size and number of the houses also vary. Thus, for example, Harrow and Oundle each have 11 boarding houses while Cheltenham has 6, Clifton 7 and Shrewsbury 8. In all these cases the houses stand as separate physical structures – castle-like – and defended by surrounding garden. This is not always so. At Stowe, four of the nine houses are contained within the eighteenth century palace of the Dukes of Buckingham and Chandos. At Wellington most of the fourteen houses, called in-college dormitories, are part of the original main college building. Here, as at Stowe, the boys eat communally rather than in their separate houses.

This difference is generally one of historical origin. In the schools of ancient foundation, boarding houses developed as an independent and profit-making activity. Usually it would be the rather poorly paid masters who would provide food and accommodation to pupils within their own houses and they were paid directly by parents for this service. Gradually, of course, schools began to take over the ownership of these houses in an attempt to regulate pupils, masters and profits. None of the major boarding schools now has privately run houses, but in many schools housemasters have managed to retain considerable independence of action and autonomy.

The economic gains of mass catering have meant that many schools have gradually moved from a house-based to a school-based eating system. But some have resisted the pull of centralization, feeling that eating together as a house is an important act of building up house identity. Uppingham, Repton and Charterhouse, for example, all still have a system whereby the housemaster and his wife are responsible for all the domestic arrangements for some sixty boys. At Oundle there is an interesting compromise, in that a central refectory serves several of the houses – but each house has a separate dining room. Even where boys eat in one large dining hall, there is still often the attempt to retain a house orientation through house tables.

All of the schools agree on the importance of the house and housemaster, and we have seen that it is within this unit of about sixty boys that each new boy will make his major friends. For much of his life, some forty weeks a year, he will have to thrive or survive within the confines of the rules and regulations, traditions and oddities of his particular house, under the control of his particular housemaster. Each house is different for, while over the years there have been moves towards standardization and centralization within all the schools, the physical allocation of boys into separate buildings under the charge of a housemaster has meant that housemasters have been able to retain considerable independence from the headmaster. Each house provides a unique environment which, like a castle, is closed to uninvited guests and regulates itself with its own set of rules, traditions and precedents. The pupil's first loyalty is still usually to his house rather than to his school, and battles with other houses are fought, not with swords and shields, but with football boots, cricket bats and even the mighty pen. The winners proudly take their trophies and shields back to the house hall for ceremonial display. As each baron knows his ultimate loyalty must be with the king, so, too, the housemaster's ultimate loyalty must be with the headmaster, but there is still considerable independence within the house itself.

The job of a housemaster

During my time at the two research schools I interviewed twelve masters who were also housemasters and asked many others about their feelings about becoming a housemaster. The sample of twelve was not intended to be a representative sample of public school housemasters generally, or even from these two particular schools, but they are not atypical either. In this discussion, as elsewhere, I have tried to emphasize the common elements of experience rather than the idiosyncratic.

It was an unusual privilege to be allowed to visit so many of the houses and to interview housemasters, for while the houses are not totally impregnable fortresses, neither were they widely open for general inspection, even by other masters at the school. At the end of my research I found myself in the rather strange position of knowing more about the inner workings of some houses than masters who had been at the schools for decades.

In the last chapter we saw that work in public schools could be very intrusive upon leisure time for masters. For public schools retain elements of the 'total institution' (Goffman, 1961) as well as being greedy institutions. Not only are there physical boundaries between the inmates and the outside world, but also there are symbolic boundaries. For the masters there is no physical coercion enforcing their stay, rather it is the developed loyalty and commitment to the institution that is the key. In Coser's words:

> Greedy institutions aim at maximising their assent to their styles of life by appearing highly desirable to the participants.
> (1974: 6)

Perhaps even more than for a headmaster, the job of housemaster demands total commitment, for being *in loco parentis* for some sixty boys at a time over a period of ten to fifteen years is not to be taken lightly. It is much more than a full-time job, for while some of the day-to-day responsibilities can be shared with house tutors, matron and wife, the ultimate responsibility for the welfare of those boys is his alone. He must deal with problems big and small. He not only checks each boy's academic progress, advises on examination choices and liaises with parents, but also gives out pocket money, encourages involvement in extra-curricular activities, punishes for smoking and occasionally is forced to expel.

Most boarding houses are physically divided into 'the private side' and 'the boys' side', with what is often called a 'green baize door' between. In the period following the Second World War it was still the custom that the housemaster very largely kept to his side of the house, and the boys to their side. On the boys' side the highly structured, hierarchical prefect system theoretically ruled the house, but in practice often degenerated into brutality and squalor. While it was claimed that such a system encouraged leadership and responsibility, its major asset from the house-master's point of view was that it made his work very much less demanding and enabled him to be irresponsible.

While there is still considerable diversity in managerial styles, there has clearly been an overall movement towards a closer, more caring and concerned role on the part of the housemaster. During the 1960s and 1970s, in particular, it became obvious that parents, boys and masters were no longer prepared to tolerate the brutality and unhappiness that the old system almost automatically engendered. Housemasters went through the door into the boys' side and tried to remove initiation rites, personal fagging, fag calls, beating and so on, and in doing so they made their work not only far more rewarding but also far harder.

It is an indication of the independence of each housemaster within his house that this is not all ancient history. One house-master that I interviewed, taking on a house as late as the mid-1970s, was faced by a resentful head of house who told him after a couple of days that 'the traditions of the house are that the housemaster does not come into the boys' side'. This house-master, along with the vast majority of other present day house-masters, had changed this tradition, along with numerous others, initially through close supervision but eventually by encouraging the growth and development of rather more positive traditions.

But the door between the two sides of the house opens both ways, so that most housemasters now find, and indeed encour-age, boys coming through to the 'private' side of the house. To become a housemaster is to move yourself and your family into the public arena, for most housemasters now regard themselves as 'on duty' the whole time. Clearly this must be so in emerg-encies, but in practice the needs of the greedy institution tend to take precedence for much of the time.

Most of the housemasters I interviewed seemed to rise at about 7.15 a.m. in an attempt to grab a few moments peace before the boys start knocking at the door. He sorts the mail, checks that the boys are all up and out, and if boys eat in the house will often take breakfast with them. Most housemasters teach a fairly full time-table during the day, and in spare periods check around their house for breakages or damage, write letters to parents, show prospective parents round, deal with innumerable problems and even do some teaching preparation and marking.

Lunch, practically always with the boys, is followed by the daily queue, where any boy who needs pocket money or special permission for a visit, or who has been reprimanded by another master, or who just wants to talk about something, knows he will get his turn. It is one of the many times during the day that the housemaster will attempt to keep in touch with what each of his sixty boys is doing. During that time he will praise for a good score at cricket, blame for looking untidy, praise for a good essay that another master told him about, question about a lost tennis racquet, or perhaps offer congratulations on one of the sixty birthdays. Trivial, but the essence of the job.

If it is a games afternoon the housemaster will usually try to watch some of every game in which his boys are involved.

67: I think that whatever they're doing you've got to give them a bit of support. . . . if our chaps were playing games, I would go out and watch. . . . I would try to turn up at any matches where any of our chaps were playing. And, I suppose I might watch some things just because I wanted to watch them, but I just feel . . . it's terribly important to be able to comment on it afterwards and to be able to recognize that what they've done is good.

This was not just idiosyncratic. Another housemaster, in discussing his style of running the house, explained in a similar way:

56: You're tramlined into doing certain things by the job, so that 80 per cent of the style is the same from House to House. We must go through their reports, and their assessments at regular intervals because that's just part of the tradition – what's expected. One always watches as many conceivable activities as one can get time to do – heavily games orientated, but one also goes and watches the music competition for the musical boys' sake, and one catches the art exhibitions and goes to the workshops. You try to see the total life of the boy.

And it was certainly true that on most afternoons the house-masters could be seen watching cricket or tennis, rarely watching the whole of a match but moving on after a little while so that they would see and be seen by as many boys as possible. Boys clearly expected their housemaster to take an active interest and would complain if he did not appear to.

The housemaster's day continues with tea, call over, and later on prep. All are occasions when he can again talk and listen to boys. Housemasters are usually officially 'on duty' for about four out of seven nights each week, the others being covered by house tutors, and this period is generally spent in 'wandering around' the house chatting; the apparent triviality of this activity belies its importance. By about 10.00 p.m., the younger boys are in bed, but many housemasters continue with the job. One who didn't rather apologetically explained:

56: Now the area where I think some housemasters are better than I, often by a long chalk, is after that. It's 10 o'clock at night, some of them are still on the job – prepared to go round and drink coffee or invite in for a drink of beer the senior boys, and have extended conversations. But, quite frankly, at 10 o'clock onwards . . . I tend to switch off.

Not completely, however, for at any time a senior boy may still knock and ask, 'Please sir, can I have a word with you?'

69: Even if I have guests in for dinner, I go if they want me. If you aren't there or if you don't immediately drop what you are doing when a boy says 'can I talk to you?' then that moment is missed, because whatever it is that he's plucked up courage to ask or he's decided to place his confidence in you – which is a compliment. And if he comes to you when he needs it – and you are the lifebelt and you catch the lifebelt off the water and say 'come back in ten minutes' – that moment is gone. Guests can get on eating by themselves – but the boy's particular need is then.

Placing them first in time is what I mean by being a father figure. You can tell by the pitch of the voice. If the pitch of the voice suggests anxiety – then I would always leave guests to spend half an hour to help.

The idea of being in some ways a father figure to the boys occurred several times during the interviews. After a similar discussion, one bachelor housemaster explained:

17: I think everyone likes being a father figure. I mean, it appeals to me because I'm not a father anyway, and one has these instincts, as it were. It certainly . . . I can see exactly the sort of thing in my colleagues who are fathers, but get exactly the same satisfaction of being able to organize the 'big family' of the house or, more superficially, being able to help individual boys who are in some ways up against it.

But ironically, this commitment to the house was often at the expense of the married housemaster's own family. One explained, for example:

67: At the beginning I used to spend more time on the boys' side in the evenings, which I don't think was a good thing as far as [my wife] was concerned. We had small children, and she bore the brunt of a certain amount of neglect at that stage. She would say that I put the job first, second and third, and the family definitely after.

Another housemaster, in talking about the problems that he had felt with his young children, expressed it as:

9: The fact that a father can't be their father, in the sense of not having the time, is again one of the tensions of the job.

During the term time a housemaster has very little time indeed to be with his wife and family, for their home is to a large extent shared with sixty boys. Then, during the holidays, after his wife and children have learned to be without him, they suddenly find that he is with them almost too much of the time. I was told of several cases where the demands of the job had clearly been a contributory factor to the breakup of a marriage.

Who are the housemasters?

The job is clearly a tough one – not without its rewards of course, but a job which requires a very special sort of man. A successful housemaster needs patience and stamina, quick-wittedness and concern and, perhaps above all, a sense of altruism which is prepared to let the affairs of sixty boys dominate ten to fifteen years of his life. It means loss of privacy and being constantly in the public eye. What sort of men allow themselves to become so engrossed in the demands of the greedy institution?

Yet here is the paradox, for it is not the few who are chosen but the many. The average public boarding school with which we are concerned has about 600 boys, 60 staff and 10 houses. Masters have an average teaching life of about forty years and the housemasters are in office for ten to fifteen years, with the average declining rather than lengthening. This means that well over half of the masters in the school are either housemasters at the present time or can expect to become housemasters in the future. But further, some of these sixty will be people who teach in the school for only a few years before moving on to something else entirely, and others will move out of the system into the state sector. It would seem, then, that the major criterion for becoming a housemaster is merely that the man has stayed the course. It is not so much a question of what sort of men take on this job, but rather of how the greedy institution can make the job desirable to so many men.

It is of interest to outline the careers of the men who were housemasters at the time I interviewed them. There were twelve in all and, because they were older masters, they resembled the 'traditional' picture of a public school master more than did the bulk of the masters in the school. Of the twelve, eight had boarded as boys, and had done so in schools very much like the schools in which they now taught. Some had, in fact, returned to the schools where they had spent their schoolboy days. Three of the housemasters had gone to HMC direct grant schools as day boys, two of which had boarding houses as well as catering for day boys. One of the housemasters had spent his early years at a state grammar school.

In general, the family background of the housemasters had not been particularly wealthy, but comfortable. Two of the direct grant schoolboys had got there on state scholarships, and some of the scholarships for the masters from boarding schools had been awarded on the basis of need as well as individual merit. The range of occupations of fathers ranged from a naval officer to a farmer, and parsons were also in evidence, their boys profiting from the reduced fees often available at that time to sons of Church of England ministers.

Ten of the twelve had gone to Oxford or Cambridge for their degrees, but only four had followed this by taking a teaching qualification. It must be realized, of course, that all careers and life histories are constrained by the particular historical context, thus all of these men did National Service for two years either before or after their university courses. Usually they became officers. These experiences, not insignificant in themselves, also had the effect of delaying the start of their teaching careers. Most thus started teaching in their middle twenties. A few had spent some years either teaching in another school or doing something completely different beforehand, but most of the twelve immediately started teaching in the schools where they were now housemasters.

A closer understanding of these careers can, perhaps, be grasped by way of an example. Mr Crispin is a composite of several of the housemasters interviewed.

Born in 1932, the son of a country parson who had himself been to public school, at 9 Mr Crispin was sent to a local preparatory school which had slightly reduced fees for the sons of parsons.

He managed to win a minor scholarship to one of the major boarding schools where he started at 13. He still regards these next five years as amongst the happiest of his life. He enjoyed the freedom that being away from his rather restrictive parents gave him and got involved in as much as possible of the school life. He was a good sportsman, eventually getting into the first eleven at cricket and playing more minor roles in the rugby. He took part in school concerts too, playing the oboe. He became the head of his house and a school prefect, was not academically brilliant, but a 'good all-rounder'. On the strength of this he managed to get a place at Clare College, Cambridge to read history. He delayed entry for two years and did his National Service in the army, gaining a commission fairly quickly. His second year was spent in the Suez zone – still British then – which he still remembers well.

At Cambridge Mr Crispin threw himself into the college life. The college was about the same size as his public school and had a very similar male and sports orientated atmosphere. He thrived, doing rather better at cricket, where he got a blue, than history, where he just managed an upper second. He spent a year teaching at a prep school, before being appointed to his present school, a post which he didn't actually apply for, but was asked to consider by the then headmaster.

He was 24, and still unmarried. He moved into bachelor accommodation which was run by the school on lines not dissimilar to an officers' mess. Meals were provided communally for the dozen or more young bachelor masters. For the next seven years he taught history, refereed football and umpired cricket. He organized a brass band and an expedition to Nepal. He was quickly grabbed by one of the housemasters to act as a house tutor. During the vacations he travelled abroad and spent time at his parents' home where he re-met a girl from his childhood and married at 31.

The couple returned to the school and moved into a nearby cottage owned by the school. His wife enjoyed the life too, taking full advantage of the tennis and swimming facilities at the school. They had two children, a boy and a girl. With their young children they spent a year in the USA on exchange with a teacher from an independent school on the East Coast. After five years of married life, at 36, he was asked to take over Green's House, which he did two years later on the retirement of the previous housemaster. Their son is now a pupil at the school in one of the other houses, where Mr Crispin pays very much reduced fees as a concession for sons of masters.

Why become a housemaster?

In practically all of the major boarding schools the 'gift' of a house to a member of staff is entirely at the headmaster's discretion. Yet in practice, the weight of tradition is so great that the headmaster does not have very much flexibility. Most headmasters appoint new housemasters approximately according to the order in which names appear on the masters' list or, in other words, according to the length of service that a man has completed in that particular school. Masters moving from another school usually go to the bottom of the list along with new graduates. The broad expectation of most masters is that if they stay at the same school long enough then eventually they will be offered a house, and most of them, as they see their name creeping up the list over the years, come to want to take on this responsibility.

There are always some exceptions, of course, where men make it clear that they are more interested in running an academic department or are not prepared to sacrifice their own family. But these are few – most men ultimately, at least in the past, have found that they want to do the job and would feel 'passed over' if someone below them on the list was asked first.

There used to be a very strong tradition in public schools of bachelor housemasters and headmasters. As Coser (1974) argues, celibacy is a very good way in which a greedy institution can ensure that it is served completely by its servants. The Catholic Church still insists on celibacy for its priests so that nothing can distract or divide attention from the flock. Indeed, before the Second World War, many housemasters and headmasters of public schools were not only celibate but also ordained priests. But the decline in the numbers of bachelor masters and general changes within society have meant that, in a number of these schools, bachelors are now beginning to be 'passed over' when it comes to their turn to be appointed as housemasters. One reason for this is financial – wives can be invaluable in the work they do in running the house, and are not generally paid for it – but it is probably also – or even mainly – due to fear of homosexuality or just 'oddness'. Of the twelve housemasters I interviewed, four were in fact bachelors, a somewhat high number overall. As one of the bachelors explained:

> 67: Some parents particularly want their sons to go to a married housemaster. This is a prejudice – which may be a perfectly proper prejudice in favour of a house which is part of a family . . . Others say they want a bachelor housemaster because . . . they say if a man has got a family he's going to have less time for my son.

What is interesting is that where bachelors are not now being given houses they often very much resent it. The job is regarded as a just reward for being at the school for a long time.

Clearly they are correct in assuming that there are some fairly substantial rewards associated with the job. Pay, for example, is considerably increased. We have seen that accommodation, which in these schools is very often owned by the school, varies according to rank and the length of time the master has been with the school. The move to housemaster means a move to often quite luxurious accommodation which is provided usually entirely rent and bill free. But, even including these undeniable perks, one housemaster estimated that overall he would be just as well off if he were a headmaster of a medium-sized state school. The appropriateness of this comparison can be seen by the fact that, before the decline of the grammar schools, there was often a steady drift of housemasters or potential housemasters into such headships.

The main rewards are not, therefore, financial. If a housemaster were coolly to take into account the number of hours worked it would become evident that the rate of pay is not very high. What, then, are the inducements? Housemasters say that, although it is hard work, they often enjoy it immensely. They talk quite simply of the joys of seeing new boys change over the years under their control, of meeting again a boy who left a couple of years before and thinking 'wasn't he a really nice chap' and hoping that some of that was due to their influence. In the words of one of these housemasters:

> 7: There's an enormous amount of satisfaction to be gained from seeing not necessarily the good boys doing well . . . but the chap for whom academic life has been a trouble, and he's done well – that's an immense satisfaction. There's an immense satisfaction, I think, in seeing them all get their just rewards.

They enjoy the responsibility too, and the independence of 'running their own show'. In talking with a master who was due to be appointed as housemaster within the next couple of years I asked him why he wanted to take on the job. He replied:

> 16: Well, I basically enjoy running things. I like to be in charge of things – I enjoy it more than doing things, if you like, for other people. And I think that if I can't run a whole school, which I probably won't get the opportunity to do, and influence the school with your own ideas and your own thoughts, then the next best thing to do is to do it with a house. And it will be tremendous fun.

Becoming a housemaster was also a way in which they could achieve promotion, while remaining at the same school and retaining friendships that they had built up over the years. They also recognized, of course, the prestige that the job carried within the school and the increased power that they would have within the school hierarchy. To return to the original analogy, in many ways it was as if they were being offered a peerage and a castle, if only temporarily. The 'king' had honoured them with the possibility of being a baron – who could refuse it?

It was quite clear that few of the older masters refused the offer. For them, their socialization process was such that it was almost unthinkable. It is worth considering, again in their historical context, the careers of these teachers in an attempt to see why this is so.

Men entering public schools as teachers are selected by those institutions because the headmaster believes that they have the potential for absorption within the organization. We have seen that the headmaster looks not only for academic ability but a whole host of other abilities which indicate that the man will fit, and will be amenable to the socialization processes that occur to masters within these schools. At the time these men were first appointed, headmasters were concerned to appoint 'all round' men, preferably with experience of public boarding schools themselves. Thus most of the sample of twelve housemasters interviewed had boarded as boys at public schools. Even as boys, whether they wished to emulate it or not, they had felt the weight of power and prestige of their own housemasters and could not avoid learning something about the job.

Many of these housemasters had moved from boarding school, to an Oxbridge college, to national service and back to a boarding school. Practically all of their lives had been dominated by single sex, hierarchical, institutional living. A major part of their lives had been played in the public eye, in institutions which were small enough for most people to be known by name, rank and reputation, and in which privacy was a rare and maybe not particularly valued luxury. A key factor to survival in these sorts of institutions is an acceptance of the necessity for a hierarchy and respect for the particular occupants of the positions in that hierarchy. Thus, for most of these men, the socialization process began at 13 or earlier when they went to boarding school and continued for the next decade.

The experiences of national service and the officers' mess were also key socializing episodes in these men's lives for, when they were first selected by the school, as young bachelors, they usually spent five to ten years in a situation which can be seen as an extension to that period. During these years of close daily contact with other masters with similar experiences, the acceptance of and accommodation to the needs of the institution could take place. The man who had not boarded as a boy could also be socialized into acceptance of the school's view at this time. This new man could, along with the others, learn what boarding was about by taking on a job as house tutor, but it is most likely that the camaraderie of the extended officers' mess was of major importance. Here a common idea of 'what it was to be a master' could develop, and the idea clearly included the probability of eventually running a house. In answer to a question about why he had wanted to become a housemaster one man's first response was simply and ingenuously 'All my friends had become housemasters.'

In many ways the situation is almost an ideal type of the sort of society and stratification structure envisaged by Davis and Moore (1945). In their highly influential paper on principles of stratification they seek to explain in functional terms why it is that societies need to be highly stratified. They argue that hierarchy and inequality in the distribution of rewards are functional necessities, as each society must somehow distribute its members in social positions and induce them to perform the duties of the positions. The theory has been highly criticized when applied to societies at large (for example, Tumin, 1953) but within the micro society of these schools, especially as they were when these men were younger, this aspect of the theory can be seen to have some validity. Rewards in the form of finance, comfort, self respect, ego expansion, power and prestige all accrued to housemasters and worked, together with the socialization process of growing expectations, to ensure that few refused the offer of a house once it was made. The socialization process and the reward structures worked together such that, once the initial decision to teach in such a school was made, it became almost inevitable that career progression to housemaster would occur. Looking back on the careers of these men it is as if the short period living alone with wife and small children is the anomaly. It is this period which interrupted their normal pattern of communal, hierarchical and institutional living. To take on a house was a return, albeit in a new role, to what was known and accepted.

We have seen already, however, that there have been changes in the nature of the experiences of masters now being appointed to these schools. While following through life histories of the housemasters can tell us much about how their career patterns occurred, it cannot tell us much about how careers may develop for masters who are at present at the beginning of their teaching. Life histories must be seen in the context of the particular historical situations in which people find themselves, and in this case the experiences of single sex Oxbridge colleges, national service and extended periods of bachelor schoolmastering were no doubt of fundamental importance. However, many of the new masters being appointed to these schools have not passed through these institutions. Masters are being appointed who took their degrees at non-Oxbridge universities – and even Oxbridge colleges are now co-educational. National service ended many years ago, and an increasing number of masters are marrying at a younger age or even before starting to teach. It would be reasonable to surmise that, not having been part of a ten or more year socializing process, these man will probably see less appeal in the job of housemaster. One might expect that these younger men might take a rather more calculating attitude towards the offer of house-mastership, weighing the advantages and disadvantages, and finding that they prefer the somewhat greater freedom and independence that they can retain as an ordinary master or head of department. In some of the less prestigious HMC schools there are already signs that difficulties are occurring, as some are beginning to advertise specifically for housemasters rather than making appointments from within the existing staff. Girls' independent schools have been doing so for many years. In the future it may be that these Rugby and Eton Group schools, too, will find a shortage of suitable and willing men and will be forced to readjust the reward structure or the responsibilities to ensure that no castle is without its baron.

Housemastering style

In his account of the changes that have occurred in the organization of the inner workings of state maintained schools Ronald King (1983: 168) argues that 'older pupils have become more reluctant to act as agents of control in the traditional way'. The tradition to which King refers was, of course, not of particularly long standing in the state sector, but was borrowed from the public schools where it had a more distinguished lineage. Although the prefect system was not actually 'invented' by Thomas Arnold at Rugby, he is usually given credit for shaping it into a tool for 'building character'. His cure for the bullying and bestial behaviour prevalent in public schools during the eighteenth and early nineteenth centuries was simply that of putting senior boys on their honour, and thus making the potential bully an official disciplinarian (Wilkinson, 1964). Perhaps strangely, it had the desired effect, and the public school system of the twentieth century incorporated a prefect system as an essential part. But King's observation of changing attitudes amongst pupils in the state sector could also be made about boys in public schools. Older boys are far less willing to spend time either disciplining younger boys or organizing the domestic chores of the houses. The prefect system in public schools is also no longer what it was.

There are several reasons for the change. Most masters I spoke to linked the initial movement with the wider social changes of the late 1960s and early 1970s. At that time the public schools were forced to make considerable changes all round, and became far more liberal and tolerant institutions. The older boys were less inclined to wish to act as disciplinarians for the school because of their liberal moral stance towards what the school stood for. They themselves were questioning the values of the school and bringing about changes, and were thus unwilling to act on behalf of a system which they largely regarded as having a considerable number of errors and weaknesses. More recently, however, it has not been moral reasons but pragmatic ones which have led to a de-emphasis of the prefect system. The increased need for high academic qualifications for entry into universities, higher education and employment has meant that pupils are less interested in spending time on house matters and feel that their time might be better used in academic study. This is a further reflection of the increasingly calculating and instrumental attitude that pupils and parents have towards public schools. They see high involvement in house activities as unlikely to be of benefit to themselves in the long run, and recognize that the days when being a head of house compensated for poor A level grades have now gone.

This does not mean that, in practice, time which would have been spent in prefectorial duties automatically is spent doing academic work. For some, it is the more immediate gratification of girl friends that fills the void, while others just 'doss and fester' – the key is that increasingly boys now ask 'what's in it for me?' and find that the answer is 'hard work and very little else' in the case of being a prefect. It should also be recognized that, strangely, this does not mean that boys do not wish to become prefects. They acknowledge that, other things being equal, the boy who has been a prefect has a competitive edge over those who have not, or, perhaps more accurately, the boy who has failed to become a prefect is looked upon suspiciously and is thus at a disadvantage. Boys still wish to have the label, but generally are only prepared to do the minimum to ensure that they keep it once it has been given and maintain a reasonably favourable image with their housemasters.

This instrumental attitude on the part of boys has meant that the housemaster's task has broadened. In the words of one of the masters, in the late 1960s and early 1970s 'the green baize door opened, and remained open'. The division between the 'house side', where prefects ruled a tightly defined hierarchy of power and privilege, and the 'private side', where the housemaster lived in luxurious, ignorant bliss, has now declined in importance. Housemasters are now more likely to directly organize the boys' side, check the studies, discipline wrong-doers and take the evening roll-call. The prefect system still exists, and it would be very difficult for the houses to function without it or something similar, but it is now not so all embracing, and no longer do prefects take full responsibility for the younger boys.

To indicate the broad direction of change, however, is not to say that each house and housemaster is at the same point on the continuum. Nor does it mean that housemasters all adopt a similar style of working – in practice they vary widely in the ways they carry out the job. Some are still fairly distant, formal figures, acting as much as possible through their head of house and prefect system, while others have taken over most of these responsibilities themselves, especially where they have taken over a house which has degenerated under its previous housemaster. Style also differs according to the length of time the housemaster has been in control. As one explained:

> 30: Any housemaster has, I think, however good he is and however bad his predecessor has been, a problem in the first three or four years, because the children who have got used to the man before, have got used to his way of doing things, find it extremely difficult to make the change. . . . They behave like children of parents who get divorced.

But not only do boys have difficulties initially, so do the masters:

> 84: . . . coming into a boarding house was something of a nightmare initially – it was so frightening – one was basically terrified of making a mess of it.

But once the first few years have passed, initial fears have subsided and most of the boys in the house are ones that the housemaster himself has selected for entry. He can begin to relax and modify what might initially have been an authoritarian regime. He settles down to his own way of running the house and his own style of management, influenced by the general ethos of the school and what the other housemasters do, but being able to have considerable independence as well.

Although the headmaster sets out clear rules of behaviour for pupils, which are supposed to be enforced consistently and fairly by housemasters, it is doubtful if any housemaster actually does so. At one level this flexibility in rules enforcement is openly negotiated between housemaster and individual pupils.

> 9: A boy may say, can I do something, can I do this, that or the other, and he and I know and we explicitly agree that it is not within the normal framework of the rules. . . . For example, Saturday night, it might be to a function that is taking place beyond the bounds area and I say, 'look, you know the reason for this rule, it's your own safety', because people have been molested – a chap was thrown through a plate glass window a

few years back. That's the sort of thing I'm aware of, I say as much to the boy concerned. . . . I'm breaking the rules, but he knows I am. And the boy usually responds to that.

The time at which boys must be back in their houses can also be adjusted on special occasions by this process of direct negoti-ation, in exactly the same way that children can negotiate with their parents about what are supposed to be fixed rules. Inevi-tably this leads to differences between houses in the way in which rules are enforced and the severity of punishment for infringement. There is even greater variation with regard to the condoning of activities that the housemaster 'did not know about'. While some housemasters tried hard to catch smokers on finding any tell-tale signs, some practically laying traps to catch them, other housemasters were prepared to let one room, perhaps one of the toilets, become an unofficial smoking room. Again, while some housemasters would be on the lookout for drinks and intoxicated boys on Saturday evenings others would prefer simply to ensure that they were far enough away from any possible noise and disturbance to turn a blind eye. If pupils are caught by housemasters, there is still flexibility. It may be the school rule that all cases of drinking by boys are dealt with by the headmaster but, as one housemaster indicated, 'One doesn't like washing one's dirty linen in public'. Housemasters use their dis-cretion to deal with individual boys and incidents in a way that they believe will best help the boys and the house, which results in differences between the houses and differences in the same house at the various stages of the housemaster's career.

Housemasters admitted that their styles of working had usually changed during their period in control. The first few years had been the most difficult, as they had attempted to make changes and build a house ethos to their liking. After a few years there was less contestation and, in some ways, less challenge. As one new housemaster argued:

94: Once you've got anything running in the way you want it to run, then there is a tremendous risk of the thing getting boring if you're not careful. But I don't think it will happen in a house – you have so many varieties of individuals through, at any

time, that you will continually be faced with different problems to try to sort out.

More established housemasters agreed:

30: The moment you think it's any good, the moment you say
'Oh, it's all going beautifully, everyone's getting on well with
their work, getting on with each other' there's always a disaster
tomorrow. And you expect adolescents to go off the lines.

19: The other point that is always made clear to me is that, you
know, you don't get complacent. When things are going well in
the house, you can be sure some crisis will occur.

Another told me:

40: You can never do any good in these strange communities
unless things go wrong. One of the things I say to parents when
they come to the new boys' tea party, at the beginning . . . I say
'don't worry if your son does something dreadful . . . things
tend to go on between 13 and 18'. It's much better that they
make pigs of themselves with me, when I'm paid to cope with
it, than they get to university or their regiment or their firm and
do it there. They get the worst of it out of their system here,
where it doesn't basically matter because it's part of the game.

Connell *et al.* (1982: 156) argue that, for headteachers of private
schools, charisma is now at a discount, and headteachers who still
try to operate in this way can be regarded as 'an anachronism, and
something of an embarrassment, by the parents'. My data on headmasters in HMC schools is far too slim to enable any generalizations to be made, but for housemasters the charismatic and
slightly eccentric style of leadership still has a place. The number of
masters and housemasters in this category does seem to be declining, but they do still seem to have considerable success with boys,
especially the younger ones. A little arbitrariness and individuality
makes a break from the general orderliness of life in public schools.
As one, whose reputation was widely known, explained:

30: I think I'm unpredictable, which must be very phasing for
them at times – but at least it's not dull. They usually know

what sort of things upset me, but sometimes things that they don't think will upset me, upset me.

I think that I have a sort of 'spiel' in the house and the classroom that outsiders would say – well, you know, that bloke on the Radley programme . . . Goldie. I'm not like Goldie, but I'm a bit like Goldie, because I'm a bit of an actor at times. I do it, partly to protect myself, because if you *feel* everything there'd be nothing left.

Most of the housemasters played down any charismatic qualities and organized their houses in terms of 'fairness' and 'care'. They argued that the main thing is that the housemaster 'had to be himself', for a housemaster to try to erect an image and character that was not his own would be bound to lead to failure over the ten or fifteen year period. One mid-term housemaster summarized his style:

19: I think that the whole skill of the job really, you know, is running the house in such a way that the boys think they are running the whole show, but actually, behind the scenes, you're doing the right moves to make it run smoothly – obviously you can make mistakes sometimes.

As their period as housemaster draws to a close there is an almost inevitable change in the housemastering style. The housemasters who were reaching the end of their term readily acknowledged that they had decreasing energies available, and their control and knowledge of what occurred on the other side of the 'green baize door' became more distant. The initial ideas and changes had either been put into practice or had failed and the last few years were largely seen as a time to keep the boat steady before a new captain took over.

In most of the interviews with masters and housemasters I asked near the end the simple question, 'Where do you see yourself going?', which always produced thoughtful and often intensely intimate replies. The quick response was often 'nowhere' or 'downhill', but it was always qualified and explained further.

Some of the younger housemasters still saw the possibility of a further transition, as one explained:

67: I've tried for headmasterships before, but it's very difficult and I know how competitive it is at the moment. I've served under four different headmasters now, but being just at one school for the whole time will be a big disadvantage.

Most of the older housemasters had either stopped trying to become headmasters or had never had this in mind. For them the next transition was to be the first on the downward spiral, and for some it was something that they were clearly concerned about.

56: I'm fifty now and I'll be fifty-four at the end of my time here. What do I do? Do I sit here for another six years? I think I would try to get away somewhere else, but knowing me, I'll probably stay. I think it will probably be a bit frustrating. I've had a very full life here and I really don't know what I'll do, or where I'll plug my extra energy.

The impending downward transition was not always viewed with concern – for some it was taken as the next logical step in their careers.

79: It will be a much quieter life than I've had up until now. I'm fifty-two now and I'll leave the house in two years' time. I suppose I'll have six years really. I don't want to become a headmaster, they don't have much contact with the boys, and I don't like admin either. I think I'm a Mr Chips really.

The character of Mr Chips was one which these older masters viewed sympathetically. Theirs had been lives that had been lived for the most part in one school in the same way as had the fictional Mr Chips, and in some ways they, too, still wished to retain some contact with the school after leaving their houses and final retirement. One of the housemasters who had himself spent his schooldays at the same school exemplifies these feelings to an extreme:

41: It doesn't worry me yet – any more than getting old worries anyone. I'll have three years left of teaching when I leave the house and then I'll probably retire here. I'm a bit of a Mr Chips I suppose, but then you can't really expect me to move. [The school] will have been my life from thirteen.

6

Girls in a male world

Unlike the other chapters in this book, this chapter does not begin with a quote from *Tom Brown's Schooldays*, for not only are there no passages which might be suitable, but the only reference to girls at all is the brief mention of Tom's sister that appears at the head of chapter three. For Tom Brown, or perhaps more realistically for Thomas Hughes' sanitized Tom Brown, girls simply do not exist. They are certainly not to be seen at Rugby and neither do they make any significant appearance in the world outside. Hughes presents an almost totally male world at Rugby and sociologists have tended to do the same when writing about public schools.

The major interest that sociologists have had in public schools has been concerned with their role in the reproduction of élites in society. So, as we noted in chapter one, the work of Stanworth and Giddens (1974), Boyd (1973) and MacDonald (1980) for example, has looked at the composition of various different élite groups in Britain and traced university and public school links. Receiving one's education at a Headmasters' Conference school or, in particular, one of the Clarendon nine schools, has been shown to be a very common characteristic of members of these powerful groups. Women and girls' schools were not included in these studies simply because at the time women had only a limited direct stake in these power groups. The majority of members of the élites was, and still is, very largely male, and at the time when these men were at public boarding schools their future wives were being educated in girls' boarding schools which, apart from a few notable exceptions, were more concerned with 'the making of a lady' (Blandford, 1977) and success through marriage than with encouraging individual success for women. The traditional lack of links with the universities and the professions has been a key element in restricting the title of public school to boys' schools only. The general consensus has been that girls' schools are not to be taken as public schools.

The emphasis on élite reproduction has meant that there are relatively few sociological studies of girls' private schools. For example, the series of studies conducted under the direction of Royston Lambert (Lambert and Millham, 1968; Lambert, Hipkin and Stagg, 1968; Lambert, 1975), whilst being concerned with all types of boarding education, only considered boys' and co-educational schools, the study of girls' boarding schools being relegated to the rather less well known work by Wober (1971). Apart from this we only have the interactionist work of Delamont (1976a and b; 1984), the semi-autobiographical work of Okely (1978) and the impressionistic work of Lamb and Pickthorne (1968). A similar emphasis on boys is evident in the more histori-cal introductions to the public schools, for example, Honey (1977), Simon and Bradley (1975), Gathorne-Hardy (1977) or MacDonald Fraser (1977). Girls are mentioned, but in contrast to the boys and more or less as an addendum.

The studies that we have show that public schools have tra-ditionally been involved not only with the reproduction of class relations but with the reproduction of gender relations too. In fact, it might be argued that girls have been excluded more completely from high status positions than working class boys, for while there were always paths through to public schools for a limited number of working class boys, all girls have traditionally been excluded from these routes.

The situation, however, is rapidly changing. Pressures both internal and external to the schools have forced remarkable changes on the public schools. As John Rae (1981) recounts:

In the early sixties no public school was co-educational. There were independent co-educational schools, the best known of which was Bedales, but it was precisely because such schools admitted girls as well as boys that they were regarded not as public schools but as experimental and outside the main tradition. In 1979, sixty out of 210 schools in the Headmasters' Conference admitted girls and of these twenty-six had gone fully co-educational from the age of eleven or thirteen.

This was actually an underestimate, even for 1979, for by 1980 official figures showed that 100 schools admitted girls either at sixth form only or throughout (Conference, 1981). Full details of arrangements are difficult to obtain but recent information indicates that of the 220 HMC schools in Great Britain and Northern Ireland listed in Devlin (1984), 63 were fully co-educational and at least 69 admitted some girls at sixth form level only. The total of 132 means that *most* HMC schools now have girls – a startling thought for Thomas Hughes and his followers of a sanctified, sexless Rugby.

The introduction of girls

We have seen in chapter one that there is a considerable diversity between the schools in the HMC. There is a similar diversity in current provision for girls. The major difference here, however, is whether the school is now co-educational throughout or whether it only admits girls at sixth form level. Examples of the former include Cheadle Hulme (which has been co-educational since its foundation in 1855 and so until recently was excluded from membership of HMC), Alleyn's, which became co-educational on the ending of the direct grant in 1975, and Bristol Grammar School which has only recently become co-educational. Of the second type, where schools only admit girls at sixth form level, examples include Felstead, where all the girls are boarders, and Prior Park, where all of the girls are day girls although the school is predominantly boarding. Even in some schools which have remained for boys only there are sometimes girls in the same classrooms. At Malvern, for example, 'girls from the neighbouring girls' independent schools may study some or all of their A level subjects at Malvern College', and even Eton is prepared to occasionally allow girls from the local schools to attend on a part-time basis and allows daughters of masters on the staff to attend full-time for A level courses. It is worth noting, however, that none of the Clarendon schools has yet become fully co-educational, and only four of the nine admit girls regularly to the sixth form. Of the twenty-nine schools in the Eton and Rugby group, only one is fully co-educational and thirteen admit girls to the sixth form.

Table 6.1 shows the number of boys and girls in HMC schools since the start of the Independent Schools Information Service annual statistical survey of schools in 1974. Unfortunately, considerable care has to be taken in the interpretation of these figures. They are not directly comparable year to year as the number of schools in HMC varies as some headmasters leave membership and new headmasters are invited to join. A further problem is that a new system of collecting information was introduced in 1982 which, while eventually giving fuller and more accurate information, has led to a slight discontinuity between 1981 and 1982. Figures for 1982–4 have been calculated to include pupils from 11 upwards only. There is a growing tendency for HMC schools to also have a linked 'prep' school, but these changes are not shown except for the 11–12 age group.

In spite of these problems the general trends are clear from the table. Girls now take 11.7 per cent of the places in the HMC schools. There has been a considerable increase in the numbers

Table 6.1 Number of boys and girls in HMC schools

	Number of schools	Boarders		Day	
		Boys	Girls	Boys	Girls
1974	207	46,208	1195	63,295	2330
1975	208	46,307	1392	64,810	3448
1976	208	45,836	1818	65,966	4130
1977	210	45,420	1973	67,871	4871
1978	210	45,244	2228	68,992	5033
1979	208	44,849	2752	69,175	5980
1980	209	44,155	3086	71,063	7003
1981	214	43,937	3467	72,788	8212
1982	208	42,454	3693	69,702	9038
1983	217	43,270	4129	72,238	9614
1984	221	41,901	4478	73,438	10,786

Data from ISIS Annual Surveys

of both male and female day pupils, the number of day girls in 1984 being about 4½ times what it was in 1974. There has been a corresponding drop in the number of boy boarders. Without wishing to imply causality, or even the direction of causality from these figures, it is worth noting that the decline in the number of boys is almost balanced by the increase in girl boarders. While the boys' schools have expanded overall, a rather different picture is found from the girls' schools. Figures for schools in membership of the Association of Governing Bodies of Girls' Public Schools (GBGSA), while this organization is not as prestigious as the HMC, can act as an indicator. From ISIS statistics, over the period 1974–84 the number of girls in GSA/GBGSA schools aged 11 and over fell from 92,406 to 83,405 even though the number of schools rose from 223 to 247. In 1974, 30,424 girls boarded and 61,982 were day girls, while in 1984 there were only 22,420 boarders and 60,985 day girls.

A small part of the increase in girls in HMC schools is clearly due to changing membership of the HMC schools such that headmasters of co-educational schools have been elected, but the majority of the increase has occurred in schools where the election was originally made as a boys' school. The independence of this group of schools is such that the process of the introduction of girls has not been uniform and is not easily described. Each school has responded in an individual way to the pressures and possibilities of its own history and circumstances. In a few cases the change was made very suddenly, such as at Hutcheson's Grammar School where the separate boys' and girls' grammar schools combined in 1976, or Morrison's Academy where a similar thing happened in 1979. The more usual pattern was to introduce girls slowly, usually in limited numbers in the sixth form. Depending on circumstances, individual schools have either maintained their restriction to sixth form only, or at a later date introduced girls at all ages. Only a minority took the more adventurous step of introducing girls at the entry age without 'experimenting' with girls in the sixth form first.

Of the now fully co-educational schools, Alleyn's is perhaps a fairly typical example. The school, which traces its history from 1619, admitted a few girls into the sixth form in 1971, and then opened entry to girls aged 11 in 1975. At Oakham 'girls were first accepted into the sixth form in September 1971; they proved so successful that full co-educational throughout the age range 10–19 followed in 1972. Four new houses (two boarding, two day) have been built for girls in the last three years' (Burnet, 1978). Of the sixty-three fully co-educational schools, thirty-two are all or mainly boarding and thirty-one are day or mainly day. Of the boarding schools it is only at Bedales that the girls outnumber the boys. The average ratio is nearer one girl to every two boys; in some schools it is one girl to ten boys. In addition, several of these schools only take day girls, while practically all of the boys board.

The schools which admit girls to sixth forms only show a similar diversity. Some schools such as Marlborough and Westminster have been able to attract seventy to a hundred or more girls and advertise them proudly, while others have only admitted very limited numbers. Those schools within cities have, of course, been able to expand day girl provision with greater ease than the geographically isolated schools. Such schools as Stowe and Repton, which are rather isolated, initially developed a system of girls boarding in the homes of married masters. Both schools have since developed new girls' houses and expanded numbers. On the other hand, at Bloxham girl boarders still benefit 'from the proximity and warmth of family life' by boarding in the houses of masters or friends of the school. At Forest School a new girls' school was built in 1977 which has a separate teaching staff, but the sixth forms of the two schools are combined.

Schools also clearly have different attitudes towards the introduction of girls. Brentwood and Hymers, for example, make little mention of girls in their prospectuses, yet both admit girls in the sixth form. On the other hand, Ardingly and Sevenoaks, for example, advertise their girls well and include numerous photographs containing girls in their prospectuses. Overall, there is a considerable heterogeneity and the position of many schools is in flux.

Reasons for the introduction of girls

It is, of course, impossible to discover *post facto* the pressures within these schools and the reasoning that led to the introduction of girls. Any replies to questions now would be bound to be influenced by the teachers' experience of teaching girls within the school, and would thus be complex rationalizations. It is possible, however, that some useful insights can be gained by interviewing teachers at a boys' public school which has not yet admitted girls, but has seriously been considering the possibility for a number of years.

The research reported in this section thus draws upon interviews conducted in the school which did *not* have girls in the sixth form. Interviews were conducted with thirty of the staff in this school and the majority of the remaining staff members were talked to informally.

It would be possible to argue that the opinions and attitudes of staff at a school which had not admitted girls would be fundamentally different from those of staff at a school which had admitted girls, for precisely that reason. However, in this case I do not believe this to be true. The school has toyed with the idea for over a decade and although I have classified the school as boys only, there have been some girls who have joined third year sixth scholarship groups by 'special leave of the headmaster', where the girl's own school was unable to offer facilities. A few years ago some general studies periods for the sixth form were shared with an independent girls' school, but the high cost of 'bussing' over quite large distances has meant that this has now been discontinued.

The issue of co-education was thus a live one at the school under study, and it is informative to examine the opinions of the staff. As might be expected within such a large staff, I found a variety of opinions expressed as to the desirability of the school becoming co-educational. Comments ranged from the evasive:

17: Ah, now really I'm not the person to talk to about this. I have not kept up with it I'm afraid. You'd better go and talk to . . .

and the direct

18: I'm dead against it. This is a boys' school, and always has been. The whole atmosphere of the place would completely change if we let in girls.

to the more favourable

> 20: I must admit I would prefer it if there were girls in the school.

and

> 22: I certainly think that having a mixed school would be a vast improvement.

It is also worthwhile to consider some of the masters' rather wider comments about the disadvantages of the school from the boys' point of view. For example,

> 30: I think those who don't have girlfriends, and a lot of them do now, may find it very difficult after being here, having relationships with girls – very difficult indeed. But then, perhaps I am speaking for myself. I found it very difficult when I left school, and then suddenly the whole thing seemed to click. . . .
> I would like this place to be co-educational in many ways. Because so many are gauche with the opposite sex.

Or,

> 22: I would certainly like a mixed school, because it's been my experience that the girls' influence on the boys improves their manners no end.

And,

> 20: I think that one disadvantage of this type of school is that they are always in the presence of males. And I think that's . . . I'm not really sure that's healthy . . . it's not always good. . . .
> I always feel that it's a shame that we can't have . . . the girls can't have lessons with the boys . . . (*even if it's just general studies which is perhaps not as critical as the rest of the subjects*), but I think it would be nice, and they therefore wouldn't feel so concerned about getting to know girls.
>
> (Emphasis added)

Many of the staff interviewed thus saw single sex education as a distinct advantage for the boys. Some were concerned about the school's possible effect in encouraging homosexuality, but more were simply worried about the boys' lack of social skills in relating to girls. Girls were seen as an advantage because of what they could offer the boys, whether this was in terms of improving manners and behaviour, a chance to practise social skills or the implified provision of more acceptable sexual partners.

In questions about the advantages of the school and about the school's aims, practically all the staff interviewed gave replies within a framework of offering opportunities. They spoke of excellent and diverse academic and social facilities being available, and boys being able to develop their full potential at the school. They spoke of the wide range of cultural and artistic activities and opportunities offered for self-development of a full rounded person. For example:

> 3: The school aims to do the best it can for every boy who comes here. It aims to enable the boy to fulfil himself in every way he can. Whether it be the academic, or sport, or art, music, whatever. By the time he leaves he should finish being competent at something.

Yet none of the staff interviewed used a similar sort of rhetoric or argument in the discussion of the introduction of girls. This is not, of course, the same as saying that none of them were interested in offering opportunities to girls as well as boys, but that this was not the sort of argument that was at the forefront of their thinking. Opportunities were offered to boys, and girls fitted into this framework by providing further opportunities for the boys' general education rather than being offered opportunities for themselves.

From the limited information gained from this case study it thus seems unlikely that educational and social arguments by themselves would be sufficient to put into practice what was seen as a major change within the school. It is necessary to look at other pressures for change.

Pressures for change

It would appear that pressure for change, to a large extent, originated outside of these schools rather than inside. In this context it is necessary to review the changes that occurred in the national, political and economic climate of the time in question.

The early 1970s saw a rate of inflation which was unprecedented. Only a very few public schools have foundation income, so there was a direct need to either pass on increases in fees to parents or become more efficient. According to Rae (1981):

> For all independent schools the critical years were between 1974 and 1976 when fees felt the full impact of inflation, particularly as it affected teachers' salaries. In the year September 1974 to September 1975 the percentage increases in fees for the different types of independent schools were:

HMC major boarding	HMC small boarding	London day schools	Direct Grant day schools
32.91	35.29	52.66	62.84

> This was way above the rate of inflation for that year of 26 per cent as the schools had to cope with the Houghton increases.

Increased efficiency meant that schools became more cost conscious. They began to look at economies which could be made by increasing the scale of the operation, and many schools at this point started working towards a small expansion of numbers. But expansion was not necessarily needed for the whole school. Expansion of the sixth form only was seen as a useful contribution. There were several influences here. The majority of boys in public schools take both O levels and A levels; it is the exceptional boy who leaves after his O level work. Nevertheless, an increasing number of boys began to do so during the 1970s. Part of this was due to increased costs. Parents found that they could no longer afford the increased fees, and 16 was not too disastrous an age to change the school of the boy, either to a cheaper school, to day instead of boarding, into the state sector, or even into work if it did not seem that the boy would achieve very high results. During this time also the state sector at A level, though not before, was beginning to look more attractive to both parents and boys. The introduction of sixth form colleges appealed to parents in giving a wide range of courses in an academic atmosphere without payment and also appealed to boys by having fewer restrictions and the presence of girls. Public Eye (1981) and Bowen (1983) both chart the growth of ex-public school pupils in sixth form colleges. In 1984, for example, some 2500 pupils left HMC schools after GCE/CSE examinations to continue secondary education in the maintained sector. In the less cost conscious atmosphere of the early 1960s the losses had been absorbed, but now headmasters and governing bodies became aware that some effort should be made to take in more pupils at this level.

This was also in line with the growing emphasis on the academic side of the school. Parents and boys now demanded a greater choice of A level subjects. Restricted choices of subjects which were a consequence of small sixth forms were no longer seen as adequate. Greater choice necessitated larger sixth forms which meant looking for new student markets.

The deepening recession of the late 1970s and early 1980s brought new pressures on the schools. For some schools the problem was no longer one of expansion, but one of simply trying to keep the numbers up to previous levels. This was especially so for one particular group of schools – the direct grant schools. For them, 1976 presented a very specific problem in that the Labour Government of the day, in line with its election manifesto, started to phase out the grant. This was clearly a major problem as direct grant schools, by definition, had at least 25 per cent of their pupils on free places. Many had more than this – some had well over half their places given to pupils who would probably not be able or willing to pay fees once the grant was withdrawn. For those schools which opted to become fully independent, there was thus a very necessary desire to look for new student markets in order to survive. Of the sixty-three HMC schools that are co-educational throughout, thirty are ex-direct grant schools and twenty-six of these can be classified as day only or mainly day. The vast majority of these first became co-educational very soon after the start of phasing out of the direct grant. These day schools, which served the local community and anticipated a considerable fall in boys entering at all levels, expanded their market by offering places to girls of all ages. Some like Bristol Grammar started with the sixth form only, almost as an 'experiment', then went fully co-educational throughout, while others such as Portora Royal made a once and for all change, taking girls into their intake year and working through.

Females or foreigners?

While changing attitudes towards boarding may have had an effect in reducing the total number of boarders, the HMC predominantly boarding schools were feeling the pressures mainly at A level. Some were concerned with the fall in boarding boys as such, while others were just concerned with numbers whether they boarded or not. There were two different markets that the schools could encourage according to the individual school's needs – females or foreigners.

In table 6.1 it has already been shown that overall there has been a considerable decline in boarding for boys since 1974. Table 6.2 shows, however, that the decline for boys with parents resident in Great Britain and Northern Ireland was even greater

Table 6.2 Number of students with parents overseas in HMC schools, 1974–84

	Number of schools	Students with parents overseas	
		British national (excluding HM forces)	Foreign
1974	207	5626	2591
1975	208	5959	2971
1976	208	5755	3572
1977	210	5875	4112
1978	210	6575	4614
1979	208	6424	4653
1980	209	6447	4573
1981	214	7576	4563
1982	208	5848	5123
1983	217	5680	4173
1984	221	5833	4389

Data from ISIS Annual Surveys

as there was a sharp increase in the number of boarding students from overseas. Again there is an unfortunate change in method of calculation between 1981 and 1982, so it is best to look at the years from 1974–81 as one sequence, then a new sequence from 1982–4.

It can be seen that from 1974–81 an additional 4000 places, the vast majority of which were presumably boy boarding places, were taken up by pupils with parents overseas. It would seem that some schools, at least, were expanding overseas students to balance their books. That the schools saw females or foreigners as clear alternative survival strategies was apparent from many of the interviews conducted at the case study school.

For example, when asking one senior member of staff whether there had been any moves to go co-educational, he told me:

12: Yes, it's been discussed a great deal. Indeed, I was on a committee which discussed it for about eighteen months. And we saw a lot of the advantages, provided you went co-educational right from the start. I still think that people like (headmaster of a major school), who put his hand on his heart and said that the finest thing that he did was to have girls in the sixth form, is a bogus charlatan. Because all he took girls into the sixth form for was to make up his numbers of boys who had left after O level. Well we do the same by taking in Nigerians and Asians and various foreign students. . . .

But you see a school like this nowadays, when people are cost conscious, is going to have a leave after O level. Not because we don't like the boys or because they are useless, but because they've probably reached their ceiling, and they're not academic boys. And so, simply as we've got to make the place pay (not necessarily make a profit, but pay) then we can't have empty places in the sixth form. And it would also unbalance your school to have it bottom heavy. We've got about the right balance here now. About half are post O level and half pre.

He, and a number of others, saw the introduction of foreign boys as a less traumatic change than the introduction of girls would be. This solution also, of course, had the additional advantage of greater flexibility. There is no minimum number of foreign students that is necessary for the smooth running of the school, whereas a certain minimum number of girls must be instituted for viability. Foreign boys do, however, present their own problems, as one housemaster recounted:

> 17: Some come at 13, but a lot come after O level at the age of 16 probably. They are a mixed bag, some of them are extremely bright and very hard-working and others don't quite make it – they can't adapt. Their English may not be quite good enough anyway. And it doesn't necessarily always work too well. But taken on the whole, if you can generalize, the foreign boys do quite well, because they are more hard-working than the English boys.

Another housemaster gave a rather different emphasis:

> GW: Have you taken many foreign students?

> 19: I've taken foreigners into the lower sixth, to make up my numbers there. The headmaster likes to bring in about ten boys a year into the sixth form. He feels we should take those boys who maybe the parents have sent them to, for example, the local comprehensive school, and it can't offer the particular A level combination they want . . . or maybe they're overseas people. He feels that we should take some in. . . . But, they're difficult to integrate; boys who arrive at that stage. They're really hard work.

He then described particular cases where it had been 'hard work' for him, as a housemaster, to get the boy to be accepted by the other boys and to fit into the school. For this, of course, is a major problem within a boarding school. Boys are gradually socialized into the rituals, hierarchies and responsibilities of being in a house during their time there. Sixth form boys have an important part to play in the efficient running of a house, and it is important that all of the boys share in these responsibilities when they are living in the houses.

While foreign students can give much to schools, they can also cause problems within the community when introduced at sixth form level. Girls may be less likely to do so because it is expected that separate boarding facilities will be provided for them; they are not expected to fit totally into the existing house structure. A further advantage of opening a school, whether only at sixth form level or at all stages, to girls is that they can be accommodated with the minimum of expense, since the local market can be tapped. Overseas students have to be boarders, which might necessitate considerable investment in new buildings.

I have argued elsewhere (Walford, 1983a) that a number of similarities can be drawn between some aspects of the introduction of girls into these schools and the position of women as employees in capitalist industry. These parallels can be seen in the idea of a dual labour market as developed by Doeringer and Piore (1972) and Bosanquet and Doeringer (1973). In outline, they identified two types of internal labour market, structured by employers for the efficient working of industry. Employers draw upon a primary labour market where specific skills can be developed within a stable labour force which is well motivated and committed to the firm. In addition, however, they require a secondary labour market which can easily be made redundant, is mobile, needs little training and can be recruited quickly on the open market, to iron out the peaks and troughs of production in the most efficient way. Madeleine MacDonald (1981) summarizes:

> These 'labour market strategies' adopted by employers to improve the efficiency and stability of the enterprise, utilise for their success the existing social prejudices or ideologies such as racism and sexism.

Barron and Norris (1976) developed these ideas and argued that in Britain this secondary labour force was predominantly female. Women acted as a reserve army within industry, being a relatively cheap source of flexible labour. While recognizing that there are problems with this analysis (e.g. Beechey, 1978; Rubery, 1978; and Bruegel, 1979), it can be argued that *in the initial phases* many boys' public schools developed a 'dual student market' which in a number of ways has parallels with the dual labour market developed by employers. The various economic pressures on boys' public schools in the 1970s meant that they were forced to become more efficiency conscious and, for some, the exploitation of this secondary student market was a logical consequence.

A key aspect of the secondary student market was that a flexible source of students was provided. Efficient use of plant and teaching personnel requires that the members of the secondary student market are dispensable or easily removed. This could be achieved by admitting girls in the sixth form only so that the school turnover period is relatively short. For example, girls initially were often admitted to study for the particular subjects in which the school had vacancies for that particular year. In several schools girls were only accepted after the boys in the fifth form had made their A level choices, so that only girls whose choices 'fitted' were accepted. This meant that over-supply in terms of teaching of English, for example, could be remedied by admitting girls for this subject. A reduction in the number of English staff, on the other hand, could be swiftly accommodated by not admitting girls in that subject in the next year. Girls had the further advantage that they tended to wish to study subjects which were less attractive to boys. Girls could thus be useful in terms of balancing the numbers of students in different subjects in a way that foreign students would not.

The crude exploitation of the secondary student market must be seen in most cases as a transitory phenomenon. While some schools are still using girls to fill specific vacancies in a curriculum designed for boys, most have now passed beyond this so that, while there is still discrimination in that sixth form girls usually have higher entry requirements than boys from within the school, the permanence of a female presence in most of the schools is no longer in doubt. It is interesting to make comparisons again with foreign students in this respect for, while schools still usually keep their overseas admissions rather quiet, the presence of girls is becoming something about which a number are quite proud.

Who the girls are

One of the problems with the 'secondary market' model for the introduction of girls is that it implies rather too much cold calculation on the part of the schools. In fact, there is little evidence to suggest that organizations such as public schools, or even individuals within them, spend very much time setting out objectives and planning strategies to achieve them. Change more often occurs in a pragmatic, piecemeal fashion in response to particular events, rather than the full effects having been considered and evaluated in detail before any change is made.

This was certainly the case with the second research school studied in which, by the time of the research, girls were an established presence. I found that the first girl at the school had been accepted a decade or so previously, almost as a local good-will gesture as her own school had been unable to offer the range of A level subjects she desired. A second girl had been persuaded to apply to 'keep her company'. Both were day girls and few special facilities were provided. Gradually, however, the numbers grew, and a not insignificant factor was the pressure from staff to have their daughters receive a public school education at a reduced rate in the same way that other masters' sons received one. Boarding facilities were eventually provided, and girls now form a sizeable proportion of the sixth form. This pattern of expansion is not unusual, and shows the unplanned nature of the decision; indeed it is not clear at what point a 'decision' was really made.

In the Eton and Rugby Group schools, thirteen of the twenty-nine now accept girls in the sixth form. The second research school was one of these thirteen and evidence about girls' experiences within predominantly boys' schools is thus largely drawn from this school. There are problems regarding generalization here, for it is likely that there is greater variability from school to school in the experiences of girls than in the experiences of boys, for schools differ considerably in the extent to which girls have been integrated into the life of the school and the ways in which this has been done. At Stowe, for example, there is a girls' house but it offers only day facilities. Boarders live with masters' families in the school grounds or nearby villages. They have their main meals communally with the boys. At Rugby there are two houses for girls where boarders sleep, but both boarders and day girls are also attached to one of the boys' houses for their main meals. At Repton an impressive newly built house for girls provides not only accommodation in single or shared study bed-rooms, but also meals and other facilities.

Competition for places for girls is high. A survey conducted in January 1982 showed that few of these schools had difficulty filling their sixth form places. Of the sixty-nine schools in HMC taking girls at sixth form level only eighteen were already full for September 1982. Most of the remainder, although not having allocated all places at that time, were careful to emphasize stiff competition for places. Most required at least five O levels at A or B grades, good reports from headteachers and often a good pass at a special selection examination and interview. Whether or not the school was 'full' in January was thus dependent on adminis-trative deadlines rather than lack of applicants. Only a very few schools showed signs of eagerness and shortage of applicants. Within the Rugby and Eton Group schools accepting girls at sixth form level, entry lists appear to be long. The case study school regularly rejected twice the number of girls as were given places, and spent a whole day in an intensive interview selection process. Where such difficult decisions have to be made a girl would be well advised to ensure that her parents had produced a brother for her, for there is a common practice, which Wellington makes explicit, that all other things being equal, 'priority is given to sisters of boys already in the school or due to enter the school and to girls whose present school cannot offer the A level courses they wish to follow'.

The final clause of the last quote is an indication of a smoulder-ing truce in a long, and sometimes bitter, dispute between the HMC schools and girls' schools. For the girls' schools have been far less successful in attracting boys than have the boys' schools in attracting girls. In 1984 there were only twenty-nine boys aged 11 and over in all the GSA/GBGSA schools, and HMC schools are well aware that while the introduction of girls may have made survival more sure for some of their members it has been at the expense of some of the girls' schools. Indeed, the threat to girls' schools is illustrated by the case of Campbell College which in September 1979 started to admit girls into its sixth form. Girls' grammar schools in the same area of Belfast challenged Campbell College's right to admit girls, and in March 1982 the High Court ruled that the school should return to admitting boys only (Fair-hall, 1982).

It is important to consider why it is that the boys' schools have been so attractive to girls and not vice-versa. The arguments here can be seen as the result of asymmetries within the system which reflect the different historical roles of independent schools for girls and boys. One of the staff who was closely involved with the girls in the sixth form at the research school summarized the girls' reasons for changing schools as:

24: Because most of them are sick to the back teeth with the schools they're already in.

GW: As simple as that?

24: Not quite – but nearly. Quite a few of the girls have been at their girls' school since they were 8 – until 16 – it's a long time. They just feel they can't stand it for another two years.

My questioning of girls at the school was in strong agreement with this generalization, for the most common first answer I received was that they wanted to get away from their old school. Girls' schools, at least the ones that most of these girls had been to, were seen as boring, petty, restrictive and isolated places that they simply wished to be free of. While some had, indeed, been at their previous schools for half of their lives there was usually a lower and upper school with a break between them at 11, and quite a few had changed schools then. However, this age change differs considerably from 13, which is the normal age of entry to a boys' public school. The majority of the girls interviewed felt that after four or five years they were simply ready to move on. They also felt that the presence of 11-year-olds in the school meant that there were automatically more restrictions on them too, even when they grew older. The ethos of the schools was seen as too childish for 17- and 18-year-olds. Historically, of course, most girls would have left their schools at 16 anyway and not con-tinued with academic work. The development of A level courses within the schools has meant that the age range of pupils within the schools is now remarkably long.

Clearly, however, this was not the only reason for moving to a boys' school. When talking with the boys about the girls they frequently divided them into two groups – those who were there for study or sex. The girls interviewed tended to agree with this, giving the two alternatives about equally, but practically all, in fact, hoped to combine the two. For some it was the perceived better facilities and teachers that were given highest priority while for others it was the presence of boys themselves. The differing statuses of the two systems are again reflected here. It is not entirely unknown for 16-year-old boys to feel some attraction towards girls, especially those one or two years younger than them, yet the independent mixed schools which were formerly girls' schools have not been able to attract very many boys even from single sex boys' schools. The boys and their parents would probably have seen this as moving to a lower status institution, while the girls clearly saw their move as one to a higher status institution.

Some of the girls were quite explicit about this, and said that they hoped to be able to benefit from the traditional HMC links with Oxbridge colleges. Until very recently it has always been more difficult for a woman to enter Oxbridge than a man, simply because there were far more places for men than women. The majority of colleges with foundation income had been for men only. During the 1960s and 1970s this gradually changed as new mixed colleges were first established and then the male colleges gradually altered their statutes to allow women also. It is clear that a major reason for this change in admissions policy was that once some colleges had become co-educational the remainder found that the academic level of their intake declined relatively. Oriel College was the last Oxford male college to bow to the pressure in 1984, leaving Magdalene College, Cambridge as the sole surviving all-male Oxbridge college. Several of the girls interviewed hoped that they would stand a better chance of entering some of these previously male colleges through attendance at an HMC school. This desire on the part of several girls to enter Oxbridge was not an insignificant feature of the school's acceptance of them. For the number of pupils sent to Oxbridge is one of the most important, and the most public, ways in which

HMC schools are ranked. Highly academic girls in the sixth form can be added to the success lists of the school to encourage future parents to send their sons and daughters.

The opportunities that the HMC schools offered were not just in academic areas. Many of the girls spoke about the better facilities in art, music and sport as well. I was told stories of girls' schools where everything closed down for the weekend and even the tennis courts were locked. The girls, however, still stayed at the school, making weekends periods of long boredom. The standard of provision in their present school was seen as far higher and far more available for their use.

Table 6.3 A level courses followed in HMC schools and GSA/GBGSA schools in 1984 in percentages

	Boys HMC	Girls HMC	Girls GSA/ GBGSA
Science and maths group only	35.9	24.1	24.7
Non-science and maths group only	37.5	50.3	48.1
Mixed A levels	26.6	25.7	27.1
Total no.	31,417	4863	15,895

Source: ISIS, 1984

Two somewhat contradictory claims have been made about the subject choices of girls. On one hand, the perceived better facilities of the boys' schools in areas such as science might be expected to mean that there would be a large proportion of girls taking A levels in the science subjects. On the other hand, it has been argued that, at least initially, schools welcomed girls in part because their traditional female choices of non-science subjects would bring about greater overall balance in the numbers of pupils taking various subjects. Some indication of the relative importance of these two claims can be gauged from table 6.3, which gives the A level courses followed by boys and girls in HMC schools in 1984. For comparison, the choices of girls in GSA/GBGSA are also given, but care needs to be exercised in any direct comparisons for the proportion staying on for A level is much smaller. Many girls leave after O level to go to maintained schools or, of course, these HMC schools to take their A levels. It can be seen that girls accounted for 13.4 per cent of the A level students in HMC schools, and that over half of them took non-science and maths subjects. The proportion of girls taking science and maths subjects only is far less than boys in the same schools and, interestingly, slightly less than girls in girls' schools. While individual girls may well have been choosing to go to HMC schools because of perceived better science facilities, overall proportionally fewer girls followed maths and science courses (including biology) than in the GSA/GBGSA schools. It is, however, worth pausing to remember that, due to the smaller proportion of girls taking A levels in girls' schools, this still means that HMC schools were teaching some 23 per cent of the female scientists from these two groups of schools.

Of greater interest are the comparisons that can be made in terms of subjects studied in higher education. Table 6.4 shows the subjects studied at either degree or HND, BEC or TEC level at universities and colleges in 1984. Only 2.6 per cent of girls from HMC schools entered engineering or technology compared with 17 per cent of the boys in the same schools and 3.2 per cent in the girls' schools. A similar pattern is found in the area of science where girls from HMC schools are less likely than either boys, or girls from girls' schools, to enter university to read for these subjects. More girls from HMC schools do, however, enter medicine, etc. Overall, it would seem that HMC girls' choices of subjects to study at college are likely to be more traditionally female than those who remain in girls' public schools. Again, care needs to be exercised in the interpretation of these figures.

In particular, many girls leave girls' schools to take A levels elsewhere, either in state schools, sixth form colleges or in other independent schools. There are no figures for the destinations of these girls. However, what figures there are certainly do not negate the calls from a number of feminists for the retention of single sex schools. Jennifer Shaw (1980; 1984), for example, argues that single sex schooling for girls is an important way in which girls can benefit from a positive collective experience which can act to encourage success in academic areas other than

Table 6.4   Pupils leaving to take higher education in UK or overseas in HMC schools and GSA/GBGSA schools in 1984 in percentages

	Boys HMC	Girls HMC	Girls GSA/ GBGSA
Engineering/Technology	17.0	2.6	3.2
Medicine, etc.	6.9	8.1	7.7
Science	19.8	15.4	18.7
All other subjects	56.2	73.9	70.5
Total no.	11,126	1524	5221

Source: ISIS, 1984

those which have been the traditional strongholds of women. From the evidence in table 6.4 it is clear that the girls' schools have not been very successful in their attempts to encourage girls into science, engineering and technology, assuming such attempts have been made, but what is also clear is that the HMC schools have not been successful either. The idea that girls in HMC schools would be encouraged and more able to develop careers in science and technology does not appear to be correct.

The experience of girls

In the second research school I was able to talk with an opportunity sample of girls both individually and in small groups, sometimes with boys present but usually not. As with the experiences of the boys in the school, it is not possible to make generalizations which cover the reactions of all the girls, but it is possible to bring out a few views which were widely voiced.

Obviously all of the girls knew that the school they were entering would be male dominated, but to 'know' this was different from experiencing it and practically all of the girls expressed initial shock at the reality. Even the few girls who had experienced co-educational education before had difficulties with the male ethos of the school. The overall difficulty was perhaps best expressed as 'you're always aware that you are different'. They claimed that boys, masters and other staff usually treated them in a way that made it obvious that they were female. They didn't necessarily object to this, but it meant that they could not easily 'fade away into the background'.

They felt that when in the public areas of the school they were always on show, and that boys would notice what they were doing, who they were with and what they were wearing. These perceptions undoubtedly had truth in them and it was not just boys of their own age who watched their every move. On the questionnaire completed by third and fourth year boys the question, 'what would be the best thing that could happen to you at school this year?', brought forth a not insignificant number of replies which related a range of sexual activities with named sixth form girls. While in one of the houses with some of the boys, I was told that one particular dormitory was popular because it overlooked some of the girls' bedrooms. I was shown the binoculars and asked to look for myself. Some of the girls found the weight of being the object of so many boys' sexual fantasies difficult to deal with at first, but they had developed successful strategies to reduce the problems of advances from giggling 13-year-olds down to manageable proportions.

All the girls interviewed who had been to girls' schools agreed that the school was less restrictive than their old one, but they also agreed that they were not given as much freedom as they wished. A particular gripe from the boarders was virtually being 'locked in' after about 9.00 p.m. In this they were officially treated in more or less the same way as the boys, but the school tended to be more careful with the enforcement of rules for the girls in this respect. They, again like the boys, joined a large number of spurious school clubs and organizations just to get some evening social life. Some of the few girls who had been at state schools found the restrictions particularly painful.

There was still, however, a good number of occasions when boys and girls could meet socially. One room was semi-officially set aside during fixed hours for 'cuddling' and recognized by staff as such. The girls, of course, had a far wider choice of partners than the boys, and some of the girls were keen to exploit this advantage. One I spoke to had 'five boy friends' in her first year. The record, I was told, was eight. No boy could hope to break this record.

Terminology is difficult where a group of people live on the same campus and may see each other every day, but clearly there is a difference between friends who are boys and 'my' boyfriend. The general estimate was that about a quarter of the girls never had boyfriends as such while they were at the school. About another quarter 'tried very hard' and had a succession, while the majority had, for a period, been going out with someone. Most of the boys were either from their own year or the year above, but it was not unusual for a special relationship to develop with boys in the year below as well. To go much lower than that was regarded as taboo, and I was told several times of one girl who had broken it by 'going out with' one of the 13-year-old boys. I was told there had been a very small number of pregnancies, which had been 'dealt with' by the quiet removal of the girls.

The greater maturity of the girls meant that, unless this sort of disaster struck, the girls were usually better able to deal with the pains of breaking-up relationships than were the boys. With both, the pain was more severe because it was lived out in the open, everyone knowing that it had ended. It was often especially painful to male pride to be passed over for someone else who you knew well. So much so that several of the sixth form boys felt it would be better for them if the school did not accept girls. It broke up friendships between boys, caused them to not work as hard as they should and was simply 'not fair' as the girls, being in the minority, could make all the choices.

Restrictions with regard to boys were not the only ones complained about. Several of the girls felt that they ought to have been able to control their time more than they could. They resented the official fixed times to work, and the relentless pressure of the bell. They also resented the degree of everyday, trivial activities that the school wished to be informed about. Not having full control of their own money aggravated some in particular.

The girls also found the experience of being taught in the school different from what they expected. Some found themselves in sets with perhaps only one or no other girls. They felt that male staff often did not know how to treat them, on the one hand being very polite and singling them out for special female treatment, and on the other, simply ignoring them and expecting them not to mind being called 'boys'. This last point was an interesting one, for I noticed that many of the masters would talk about pupils as 'the boys' even when they clearly were including the girls in their comments. Announcements were made at meetings at which 'boys' were given instructions and it was left to the girls to deduce whether this instruction was directed towards the female 'boys' as well as the male ones.

The girls interviewed were also not always as impressed by the quality of the teaching as they had expected to be. Several pinpointed staff who they felt were not really good enough, and here there was general agreement between the girls and the boys who answered questionnaires. The particular subject areas were, of course, peculiar to the particular school, but the uniformity of the areas of complaint may mean that headteachers would do well to pay more attention to the feelings of even young pupils about staff.

The main difference between the experiences of the boys and the girls at these schools relates directly to the girls only being at the school for two years. Many girls agreed that by the time they had really begun to understand the place it was time to start working seriously for their A levels. They could enjoy the school for what it offered them, but the experience was too transitory for them to make, or even want to make, any impression on it. The boys, on the other hand, spent five years at the school, gradually working their way up the school hierarchies. They were gradually socialized into the school, and either identified with it or reacted against it. The girls' relationship with the school was much more pragmatic and instrumental. They had calculated the pros and cons of the move from their previous schools and wished to ensure that they made the most of what the school had to offer.

Girls do make a difference in the schools. They are able to play female parts in plays (and bake cakes for boys' birthday parties!) They 'civilize' the boys and enable them to learn how to act with the opposite sex. They may raise the academic level of the school, encouraging the boys and gaining Oxbridge places for the school. But they do not fundamentally change the ethos of the school.

Admitting girls for two years only, in the sixth form, is very different from going fully co-educational. As one of the masters stated:

> I wouldn't like to see the whole school co-educational. . . . You either do it by reducing the number of boys you take in and if you do that in a school this size . . . you instantly change its nature, undoubtedly . . . or you do it by making the school larger which also changes its nature.

On my first day at the school I was asked what sort of thing I was interested in.

> GW: I'm interested in the changes that have been occurring in public schools.

> 43: Well, you've come to the wrong place then haven't you?

> GW: What about the girls. Aren't they a large change in the school?

> 43: Girls. I haven't really noticed them yet.

But perhaps it is best described by quoting the information given by Cranleigh School:

> Founded in 1865 as a boys' boarding school, it continues to follow that pattern, which the presence of girls in the VI Form has adorned but not fundamentally changed.
>
> (Burnet, 1982)

7

Women in a male world

The housekeeper comes with strong salts, and Tom soon recovers enough to sit up. There is a smell of burning; she examines his clothes, and looks up inquiringly. The boys are silent.

'How did he come so?' No answer.

'There's been some bad work here,' she adds, looking very serious, 'and I shall speak to the Doctor about it.' Still no answer.

(Hughes, 1857)

Tom Brown's Rugby may well have been a world where girls did not exist, but women certainly did. Faced with a 'dying' Tom, after his sadistic roasting in front of the fire, the housekeeper is the first adult that the boys run to for help. Her job was a vital one then, and still remains so. This chapter is concerned with documenting what life is like for the range of women who are now part of these public schools.

The variety of different roles open to women is now far wider than it was in Tom Brown's time. In particular, the introduction of girls has meant that there have had to be related changes in the composition of the teaching staff as well. Women have begun to enter the inner sanctums of the Masters' Common Room, and it is to this aspect that we first turn in this chapter.

Table 7.1 shows that there have been considerable changes. When Kalton (1966) surveyed his 166 HMC schools in England and Wales he found that of 6221 full-time staff only 63, or about 1 per cent, were women. By 1984 there were a total of 10,245 full-time staff in the 221 schools with women now occupying about

Table 7.1   Teaching staff in HMC schools, 1984

	Graduates		Non-graduates		Total	
	Men	*Women*	*Men*	*Women*	*Men*	*Women*
Full-time	8510	697	806	232	9316	929
Part-time	321	423	161	274	482	697

From ISIS (1984)

9.1 per cent of the posts. However, in 1982 (the latest data available) all of the heads or acting heads were male.

At first sight it might seem as if the proportion of female teachers in the schools (9.1 per cent) might be fairly closely related to the proportion of girls (11.7 per cent). Such a comparison is, however, misleading, for many of the female teachers are at HMC schools which are still for boys only. This is particularly true for staff teaching art and music. The 9.1 per cent of female staff are spread unevenly throughout the 221 schools, some having none, one or two, even where girls are admitted, while others have many more. At Bedales, for example, more than 20 per cent of the staff are women, but then Bedales is one of the few HMC schools to have roughly equal numbers of boys and girls.

Exact details of the subjects taught by women are not available, but some indication is given by the published data which are divided into the categories of graduate maths, science and other teachers. Women account for 7.7 per cent of graduate mathematics staff, 5 per cent of graduate science staff and 8.5 per cent of other graduate staff, but 22 per cent of the non-graduate staff are women. It would seem likely, and a check of prospectuses supports the idea, that female teachers are more commonly found in low status subjects than high status subjects. The introduction of girls, for example, usually necessitates the appointment of a female PE specialist. Women are also commonly found amongst the art and music staff of the school.

There are further indications of the tendency for women to occupy the lower status positions within the teaching staff of these HMC schools. None of the schools has a headmistress instead of a headmaster and I have not yet found any school where a woman is head of an academic department. The main high status position for women is housemistress of the girls' house where there is one, but even here the status of the house-mistress is not always on a par with the status of housemasters of boys' houses.

It is worth trying to make some comparisons with girls' private schools. The GBA/GBGSA is again the most convenient group of girls' schools with which to make comparison. Here, in 1982 (the most recent data available), of 209 heads or acting heads, 26 are male, there are many male heads of academic departments and 11.8 per cent of the full-time teaching staff are male. This, it should be noted, is in schools where less than 1 per cent of pupils are boys.

Tables 7.1 and 7.2 also give information on part-time teaching staff in HMC schools. It can be seen that 59 per cent of the part-time teaching staff are women. In addition, for graduate staff, on average, women teach more hours part-time than men, while with non-graduate staff the hours worked are very similar. There are several possible explanations for this. Firstly, it is again likely that women are concentrated in the low status subjects such as music and art which are often taught by part-time staff out of normal timetabled periods. Secondly, it may well be that there is greater reluctance to move female staff from part-time to a full-time appointment in academic subjects, a feature which would be reflected in the greater number of female part-time staff and the greater number of hours worked by those women with degrees.

Table 7.2 Teaching hours of part-time staff in HMC schools, 1984

	Graduates		Non-graduates		Total	
	Men	*Women*	*Men*	*Women*	*Men*	*Women*
Number of staff	321	423	161	274	482	697
Aggregate number of hours per week	2606	4478	1467	2456	4073	6934
Average hours/member of staff	8.12	10.59	9.11	8.96	8.45	9.95

From ISIS (1984)

There may be, of course, many good reasons for any reluctance to appoint female staff on a full-time basis within a traditional HMC school. Within the boarding schools especially, teaching staff are expected to play a large part in out of lesson activities, whether these be supervising sports, organizing clubs and meetings, becoming officers in the Combined Cadet Force or being house tutors and housemasters. Headmasters clearly wish to be sure that female staff are able and willing to offer some comparable skill or interest outside the classroom before making a full-time appointment. Teachers are appointed to specific academic posts, but the headmasters make it clear that 'other interests' are not only preferred but required, and that staff are 'expected to take a full part in the life of a boarding school'. Within the HMC schools which only admit boys or admit girls at sixth form level only, it is felt, whether rightly or wrongly, that women may be less able to offer traditional out of lesson-time activities.

Female teachers' experiences

It is very difficult to make generalizations about such a diverse range of schools as are included within the HMC. Each school has its own character and traditions, and, obviously, the experiences of a female teacher entering a fully co-educational school with many other female teachers will be very different from the experiences of a new teacher in a boys' only or restricted co-educational school.

However, as only one of the schools in either the Eton Group or the Rugby Group has so far become fully co-educational there is perhaps more interest in the last two categories. The ethnographic fieldwork, it should be remembered, was conducted in one of each of these types of school. Both of these schools had only a very small number of female teaching staff, so that new teachers entered a very male orientated and dominated society. In this section I shall consider only the full-time staff in an attempt to try to separate feelings of marginality caused by part-time work from those related to gender.

In talking of her initial experiences of joining the school, one woman stated:

> 70: I was surprised really that I was surprised, but that first staff meeting – you know, there's just no doubt about it – it was grey as far as I was concerned. Because they were all men.

While new female teachers obviously realize at an intellectual level that they will be entering a male world, the experience is still often traumatic. The younger female teachers, in particular, often found themselves far more isolated than they had expected.

> GW: What sort of reaction have you had from the other staff?

> 16: Very mixed. Some have quite accepted me as a colleague. Some have definitely treated me as a woman and some, I appreciate, are not too fond of females in the masters' common room. They've never been rude, never awkward, but I just feel they're used to a male situation. Fair enough – it doesn't worry me. I don't impose myself.

Another teacher replied to a question about what she had found unexpected at the school:

> 62: The staff. I didn't expect them to be quite as stuffy as they are. I thought they might be shy, but I didn't expect them to be quite as difficult as they were, and quite so lacking in social graces. . . . I expected the men to be very polite and terribly correct, and they weren't. They just didn't speak at all! They didn't speak at all. You know, you'd say 'Hello' to someone and they'd just walk straight past you. Now they're a bit less frozen. They do nod to you, say 'Good morning' or 'Good afternoon' and that sort of thing, but I still feel isolated.

Not all the women found it quite as bad as this. One, for example, was keen to emphasize the divide between the friendliness of the community on a social level, and the distance that she experienced as a teacher as such.

> 58: What I really found difficult was trying to get myself accepted as a colleague rather than just as someone who would be available to make coffee. . . . People would feel that 'she could help' but not initiate.

Social isolation, however, was a common theme for many of the female teachers, as was their desire to try to reduce this isolation by some expansion of the number of female staff at the school. One of the problems is that public boarding schools are small communities in themselves and often develop a 'village' atmosphere where everyone knows exactly what everyone else is doing. In such a situation male staff, especially the bachelors, become somewhat reticent about being seen to be too friendly with any of the female staff. Boys' boarding schools are traditionally male dominated, with men occupying all the positions of power and authority. Living in such a community means that, quite literally, some of the masters do not know how to react to female teachers. They lack the 'social graces', are 'shy'. One female teacher said, wistfully: 'I'd like the single men to be a bit more fun – a bit more normal'.

It is important to note that all of the women quoted so far stated that things had got better. They had not encountered outright hostility, but perhaps what might best be described as 'fear'. They had all found that they had gradually become more accepted as they had shown that they were not likely to disrupt too greatly the established order. I heard stories of women who had tried to make changes, but they had since left.

The difficulty of trying to find a niche or identity within the school was a further common problem. One of the women explained how important out-of-lesson activities like sports were to the school and to the teacher's standing and acceptance by the community. She explained:

> 58: I really must admit that one of the things I don't like about it is that I don't see how I – how my 'unique selection of talents' – can be utilized in a place like this, because there isn't much I can offer that people want.

Identity is sometimes a problem at a rather more basic level too. The male teachers invariably call themselves school masters or assistant masters; but while 'master' implies more than an ordinary teacher, the term 'mistress' implies rather less than an ordinary teacher. Many schools simply ignore the problem and officially use the term 'assistant masters' to include women teachers. But the power that language has to reproduce and reinforce sexist ideologies has been widely recognized, not only by academics (Spender, 1979) but also by the female teachers themselves. One such had written in the suggestion book of the Masters' Common Room:

> That this room should be called the Teachers' Common Room or else the Masters' and Mistresses' Common Room.

to which the comment had been added:

> Why?

This woman has since left the school.

Living in the school grounds where movements could be seen by boys and masters had initially presented particular problems for two young single female teachers whom I interviewed. They felt that their ability to lead ordinary lives in their own time was hampered by the school. They had felt it necessary to make elaborate arrangements to ensure that their male friends who wished to stay for the weekend were not seen by either boys or masters. One told me of an occasion when she had got off a bus with her male friend near the school and they had walked on opposite sides of the road to her flat rather than endure the stares of boys or masters. They knew that boys took a keen interest in everything they did, and believed that to be seen with different men would have caused them considerable difficulties in their teaching.

Not all of the female staff found acceptance by the community quite such a problem. It would seem, for example, that a fair number of women teaching at the schools gain acceptance, and indeed initially gained their jobs, because their husbands were already teaching at the school. This was particularly true of the part-time female staff teaching academic subjects, and sometimes a full-time post was obtained after having taught at the school for many years. It is important to note that the taking on of female teachers itself was not a revolution but a gradual progression and adaptation. Part-time female staff have been teaching music and art at HMC schools for decades, but they were rarely regarded as being members of the Common Room because of their triple burden of being female, part-time and teaching low status subjects. Art and music staff, whether male or female, are still classified separately in several school staff lists. It was just a small step from part-time music staff to ask the wife of one of the masters if she could 'help out' a little by teaching an academic subject part-time and this step has been taken by many schools, again often some decades ago. These women could be accepted by masters because they had already been accepted as masters' wives.

It would seem that this intrusion of women into the male world was usually accomplished with very little antagonism or anxiety. Presumably wives of masters presented no threat to underlying patriarchal relations within the schools. They had been accepted as wives of colleagues first, and only secondly as colleagues themselves. It is worth noting that even here, where a woman had shown herself to be 'acceptable' to the school through part-time work in an academic subject, the path to full-time work was not smooth. I was told several stories of the detailed, delicate and sometimes contested negotiations that had been conducted before the transition to full-time status could be effected. Schools are clearly still undergoing changes in this respect, and we can expect that, having now gained a foothold, the position of women will gradually be strengthened, especially in schools which accept girls.

Some of the women in the research school which did have girls in the sixth form were well aware of what they saw as a special responsibility here. They felt that their presence in the school as teaching staff was very important for the development of the girls. One argued, for example, that:

> 55: The girls are academic girls, and they should not have an image all the time of the woman who is a housekeeper or the woman who is on the domestic side, they should also have in front of them the image of the woman who is a more dominant personality, or in a more dominant position, or more respected position perhaps I should say.

But, of course, the number of female teaching staff is so small that the impact they can make is restricted. At the moment, it does not seem that the presence of women teachers is likely to lead to major changes. Indeed, those women who remain in the schools, be they full-time or part-time, do so largely because they are prepared to accept the schools for the most part as they are. While questions of gender and gender reproduction may now have greater prominence than before, few of these women would consider themselves as feminists and most are seeking moderate changes rather than radical reorientations.

Non-teaching women in boys' public schools

So far this chapter has concentrated on the position and experiences of female teachers, but in doing so there is a danger of missing the central role that women play in these HMC boarding schools. For we have seen that, although there has been an increase in the number of female teachers in these schools, women have mainly only entered teaching positions of low power, prestige and influence, and their role has been of marginal importance to the schools. But while these women may be marginal within the 'male world', other women are of central importance within the 'female world' of the public school.

It is important to remember once more that many of these public boarding schools still may be largely described as 'total institutions' (Goffman, 1961). They are total in that they provide everything that is deemed necessary for the pupils and exert control over pupils' activities day and night for periods of up to three months. Such provision and control requires an army of domestic, administrative and other personnel. It is in these areas that women have a vital, yet largely unnoticed, part to play and they have done so for decades. The dimensions of class and gender cut across non-teaching jobs in these schools. Most of the domestic cleaning staff are part-time and women, as are those who prepare, cook and serve food in hall or houses. Women sell snacks, ice cream and sweets in the 'tuck shop', or the latest paperbacks in the bookshop. They act as matrons in the houses and as nurses in the 'San'. On the other hand, the groundsmen are always men, who spend long hours mowing the cricket square to perfection or ensuring that the flowers near the headmaster's office are suitably impressive.

Other men find themselves in maintenance work as plumbers or electricians or as 'removals men' doing a multitude of odd jobs requiring heavy manual labour. In the school offices the headmaster and bursar are always male, but the secretaries are always female. However, while there are clearly both high and low status jobs for both men and women, it is the women who are usually to be found in the subordinate jobs and who are more likely to be part-time and more poorly paid. In addition, of course, practically all of these jobs for women are within traditional stereotypes of female service and nurture.

One of the key jobs for women in the traditional areas of service and nurture is the matron or housekeeper. We have seen that there are considerable differences between schools with regard to domestic arrangements for pupils, but all of the schools 'like Rugby' divide the pupils into houses under the supervision of a housemaster. There are very few female influences in the house – the matron is the most important. Her job is formally that of supervision of the domestic side. She deals with laundry and lost shirts, she dispenses aspirins and sticking plasters. Of greater importance, however, is her informal role as someone who is both outside yet inside the system and with whom the boys can talk. Usually matrons live in the house in a small flat, which is often closer to the boys' side of the house than is the housemaster's accommodation. Housemasters recognize the importance of this informal role. Ideally, most would wish to find a woman as matron who is able to exploit this position such that she will discreetly deal with minor personal problems of the boys but will pass on to the housemaster, in confidence, any more major problems. In this way the matron acts as a second pair of eyes for the housemaster.

It would seem that Dr Arnold's housekeeper, as quoted at the opening of this chapter, was not particularly good at this aspect of her job. Her direct questioning was unable to elicit the required information about the roasting and she made it clear that such information would be conveyed directly to the housemaster. In talking to both matrons and housemasters at the two research schools I came to realize the delicacy and importance of the matron's role in looking out for potential trouble and gaining information about problems that have occurred. As with all relationships, a balance is negotiated over time, and matrons are usually able to adopt a more liberal and understanding role than the housemaster. The matron may thus deal with minor problems herself or sometimes let the older boys deal with them. Officially the housemaster is thus ignorant of some infringements of rules, but unofficially he may well still be told by the matron.

Most housemasters thus look for a matron who has had experience with children and with whom, quite simply, he and his wife feel they will be able to live. Most are middle aged – definitely not too young. Very nearly all are single women, the ideal probably being a widow whose children have recently gone to university or married. To be doing the job 'for something to do' rather than just for financial need is also recommended, and indeed it would seem that several of these women do have limited private means and come from clear middle or upper class backgrounds.

Not all of the housemasters had managed to find their ideal matron, of course, and for some a succession of matrons had proved to be one of the major problems of housemastering. For this job, like that of housemaster, is very much a full-time job; the matron is really on-call day and night even though officially there are some days and some nights off. Ill or worried children tend to ignore official timetables.

The other main female influence in the house is the housemaster's wife, and it is worth considering the role of wives in the running of the school in some detail. As a general rule, wives of masters become increasingly important according to the status of the husband. The demands made on new and junior masters by the school are such that, ideally, wives should not exist at all. Public school masters tend to marry late. There are still many who enter the schools as bachelors directly after university and spend the first few years practically totally involved with the school. It is these younger masters who dominate in sports coaching and organization, who take groups of boys hiking or on holiday during the vacations. Their timetables are often full seven days a week. However, though they are given very little time during term to do so, they are expected somehow to have found wives by the time they are due for a housemastership.

We saw in chapter five that there used to be a tradition of bachelor housemasters in many HMC schools, and, indeed, there are still quite a number now. But the tradition is changing, and headmasters are taking the opportunity, on retirement of unmarried housemasters, to extend and improve accommodation such that married men can take on the responsibilities. This is partly, of course, a reflection of the decreasing number of unmarried masters but there is also the feeling that bachelors are now beginning to be positively excluded. One master described the position for headmasters in the following terms:

> 21: There's a very comical bias in the promotion system for headmaster, which says that they must be practising Christians, either genuine or in appearance, and they must be married.
>
> I think it is a most deplorable state that the public schools have got themselves into. And it's very curious that they have, in curricula and in developing the Arnoldian triple pillars of Chapel, Scholarship and Games into what public schools are now, they've gone back into this entrenched Ayatollahesque insistence, first of all on the Christianity, which I think fatuous, and the marriage thing, which is just dangerous.

He added that this was equally true for housemasters, and that, though there were some bachelor housemasters at the school in question at the time, he was sure that the headmaster would never appoint another.

This reluctance to appoint unmarried masters as housemasters is not simply due to fears of homosexuality or 'oddness' (although undoubtedly that is an influence in response to parents' perceptions), it can be seen as an indirect result of the increasing need for financial economies. Especially in schools where boys eat in their own houses, an unmarried housemaster requires a housekeeper in addition to a matron. Someone has to organize the domestic staff of the house, prepare menus and costings, and in some schools even go and buy food for sixty in nearby supermarkets. Beer has to be bought for the house bar, repairs and decoration have to be organized, someone has to take telephone messages, and someone has to be prepared to step in and 'make do' if any of the other staff are away. If the cook is ill or has a day off, someone else has to ensure that sixty boys are fed. Not only are such people increasingly difficult to find, they are also expensive. A married housemaster, on the other hand, is appointed to the job with the implicit and sometimes explicit assumption that his wife will take on these responsibilities. Neither do her responsibilities end there. Housemasters have a continuous flow of visitors in the form of parents and prospective parents of boys in the house, old boys, teachers and visitors from other schools, visiting speakers and even sociologists. House-masters' wives are expected to be welcoming to guests and largely deferential to their husbands. This is not to suggest that these women are totally dependent – many are not and have full, independent and active lives both in the school community and outside. But the housemaster's wife must expect that her home will be open to a wide range of guests, and she will know that, while usually only expected to offer coffee and biscuits or drinks, there will be other times when she will be expected to put on a full dinner party and accommodate overnight guests.

More directly, the housemaster's wife will know that she will have to share at least part of her home with sixty boys. A division is obviously made between the house side and the private side, but a boy can at any time go through the 'green baize door' for help. If her husband is not available or if it is a 'domestic' problem, she knows that she is expected to deal with it.

Wives of housemasters thus represent an almost classic example of wives who are highly likely to become incorporated into their husband's work. In *Married to the Job*, Janet Finch (1983) discusses the ways in which women's lives are directly affected by their husband's work, and also the ways in which they can become drawn into that work as subsidiary, subordinate and usually unpaid workers. She describes a wide range of occupations, from clergy to merchant seamen, and locates five features of the way in which work is organized which have special importance for both of these aspects. She concludes that incorporation is most likely to occur where the husband has (a) flexibility of working hours, (b) the possibility of work being done at home, (c) work which is highly socially valued or has strong moral overtones, and where the husband is (d) self-employed, and (e) living in an institutional setting. Four of the five criteria are clearly satisfied by the job of housemaster, and indeed, even the fourth one, that of self-employment, used to be the case a few decades ago and traces of the related independence of action still persist. It is no wonder that wives of housemasters find themselves so involved in, and their lives so structured by, their husband's work.

This does not mean, of course, that other wives, or even the occasional husband, of members of staff, are not incorporated into the work of these schools. Wives, whether married to house-masters or ordinary masters, often give much of their time to the school. It is, in fact, the exceptional wife who does not support the school in some way, even where she is in full-time paid employment elsewhere. In most schools wives usually attend the major events of the school's calendar, whether these be speech days, school plays or music festivals. They often 'help with' make-up and costumes for plays, sell tickets, support football or cricket teams, and provide refreshments for boys and visitors. They, too, have a succession of visitors to their houses to whom they are expected to play hostess, and, in addition to finding coffee and snacks, they occasionally also provide another listening ear for boys.

It has been shown already that public schools are very 'greedy' institutions as defined by Coser (1974). There is no clear line to be drawn between work time and non-work time, and the demands of the institution tend to extend such that non-work time is reduced to a minimum. What can be seen here is that public schools are not only greedy with respect to their direct employees, but also with respect to spouses. The social pressures on wives in such communities are such that there is a tendency for their lives too to become dominated by affairs of the school.

This is not to say that such activities are necessarily undertaken unwillingly. Certainly, some wives did object to the school's expectations that they should be prepared to act as unpaid employees. Some took outside jobs or became involved in outside activities specifically to reduce these pressures. In other cases the excessive demands of the schools were cited as contributory factors in marital breakdown. However, the majority of wives of masters and housemasters generally accepted that they were expected to play a part in the school. For many, especially some of the housemasters' wives, this role was seen as extremely fulfilling both because of the contact with pupils and because they were able to work alongside their husband and contribute to his career. It is possible to see many wives as having invested in what have been called, after Goffman (1963), 'wife of' careers, whereby fulfilment is obtained through the husband's career and the benefits attached to it, rather than through the woman's own separate career. Indeed, the social world of the school has much to offer, especially in terms of cultural and sporting facilities. Wives often make good use of the school's swimming pool, tennis courts and similar facilities during the pupils' lesson times, and informal sports 'clubs' are a regular part of life.

Even in these informal activities, however, the social networks appear to be influenced to some extent by the formal positions of the husbands. The wife of a head of department has a potential edge over the wife of one of the members of that department, for example. A clearer distinction is seen in the career transition from master's wife to housemaster's wife. Here, a fairly distinct change in the way of life and patterns of activities demanded mean that there are corresponding changes in the informal networks and the way she is treated by others. Part of this is due to physical movement of the family into the house, away from nearby friends and neighbours, and also to new time constraints imposed by the regime of looking after some sixty boys. The greater isolation of housemasters also seems to affect their wives, for they appear much more likely to associate with other housemasters' wives than with wives of ordinary masters.

The final career change for 'wives of' is that from housemaster or head of department to headmaster. This career change is only achieved by a few and it is clear that the wife can play a vital part in assuring that last career transition. The achievement of a headship and subsequent success in that headship must be seen as a team effort. It seems that the appointment procedure for headmasters almost invariably includes an occasion at which his wife can be 'vetted'. She, after all, has to be able to take on a wide range of responsibilities, and be prepared to do so. The headmaster of a public school is very much a public figure and so, perforce, is his wife. She must accompany him to dinners and social occasions and be able to converse with and entertain a wide range of important and well-connected people. More importantly, there must be no trace of any scandal. Even moderately 'inappropriate' behaviour on the part of the headmaster's wife could be newsworthy enough to reach the national newspapers and affect the standing of the school. It is thus not surprising that governing bodies wish to meet and at least informally interview the wives of applicants for headmaster.

Differentiation and consolidation of gender

It can be seen that women play vital roles in most HMC public boarding schools, whether partly co-educational or for boys only. Over half of the HMC schools now admit girls either throughout the school or at sixth form only, and this partly accounts for the increased numbers of female teaching staff in these schools. However, female teaching staff are not new – women have been teaching part-time or in low status subjects for decades, and it is still the case that, although there are exceptions, most women teachers have only marginal power, status and prestige. The women with status and prestige in these communities, if we can conceive of it in these terms, usually derive it from their marriages to men with power, status and prestige.

But, although partly unacknowledged, women play a vital part in the organization and running of these schools. They are to be found as domestic and secretarial staff and in other roles where service and nurture are emphasized. In general, the women's jobs are largely oriented around the servicing of men and boys and are under the overall supervision of men.

None of this, of course, is particularly unexpected, for it is well accepted that public schools have traditionally been as concerned with the reproduction of gender as with the reproduction of class. The schools traditionally have a masculine atmosphere, both in the sense of being for boys only and in the sense of all positions of power and prestige in the school being male.

It is worth considering in some detail the effect that women in their various roles in the school may be having on the development of conceptions of gender held by pupils. The terms 'gender differentiation' and 'gender consolidation' have been used elsewhere to describe the image projected by school science textbooks (Walford, 1983b). Gender differentiation is the process by which individuals of different gender are separated from one another, which at a simple level, for example, might be the division of a class into boys and girls for specific activities. Gender consolidation, on the other hand, is concerned with the process of the transmission and reification of traditional male and female gender roles, which may well be a dated caricature of present-day gender possibilities. The two dimensions overlap, of course, but it is instructive to consider the present position of women and girls in boys' public schools with regard to these two aspects.

Gender differentiation, which was very strong indeed, is undoubtedly decreasing. Quite simply, where boys and girls used to be educated in totally separate schools, now girls are being admitted into boys' schools and are sitting in the same classrooms. However, gender differentiation is not an 'all or nothing' criterion and individual schools retain different degrees of gender differentiation even where they are co-educational. In some, girls still live and eat in separate houses, while in others they do at least eat with the boys. All of the schools have at least some rules which are specifically for girls and 'visiting times' between the sexes, for example, are often carefully controlled. Sports and other activities are also often gender specific. At the level of teaching staff, too, there has generally been a weakening of gender differentiation as more female staff have been taken on as full- and part-time teachers. Overall it is an area where there has been considerable change, and where more is likely due to continued struggle.

This does not seem to be the case with regard to gender consolidation. All of the adults in the community act as potential role models for the pupils in the school. In girls' boarding schools there is a wide range of potential models for girls. Here, women are found in positions of real power and prestige as headmistresses, heads of department and housemistresses. These women hold their positions through their own individual abilities as women and thus, in a number of ways, could act as positive role models for their female pupils. This is not so in the HMC schools. Here practically all of the positions of power and prestige are held by men and if women have any prestige at all it is mostly through the reflected glory of their husbands. It is their relationship with, and subservience to, their husbands that gives them prestige. Thus, housemasters' wives have prestige through their husbands, and the headmaster's secretary through her special relationship and knowledge of the headmaster.

The strange thing is that it seems that many of these roles may be becoming more, rather than less, traditionally female. One of the consequences of increased economic stringency is that there are now fewer domestic servants in the schools. Where twenty years ago a headmaster or housemaster could call on a servant to bring the afternoon tea to guests, it now often falls to his wife to perform such functions. Class and gender interact again, for we see that where once it was possible for men to be supported and served by the lower class, they are now increasingly supported and served by the 'lower gender', regardless of class. The female academic staff, in addition, are likely to be women who defer to men – those women who do start out on the long hard battle against male authority tend to be eased out fairly quickly. In the main, the women in the school exhibit traditional female characteristics and do not greatly challenge traditional male or female gender role stereotypes. The result is that gender consolidation may be getting stronger rather than weaker.

Quite clearly, the roles that are adopted by most women in these schools reinforce sexist, familial and heterosexist norms. Sara Delamont (1980) argues that most schools are very conservative in the nature of society that they present. Teachers feel required to officially support and propagate a view of morality, the family, and sexual relationships that is far less liberal than the view held by the majority of society, and which they might not themselves hold. This is certainly the case in public schools where the roles that women play in the school are far more restricted than those in the wider society and where they are restricted in their ability to openly question the norms of the school.

As a final word, however, it must be noted that the picture is not static. Schools are increasingly becoming potential battle-grounds for the gender struggle. There were more than a few women and men who, in these tightly knit communities, were trying to make changes. Some of the wives of masters explicitly rejected the idea that they should merely have a career of 'wife of', and were developing careers of their own, either outside of the school or within. Female teachers were beginning to take a more aggressive stance towards their own potential career development in the schools. And, of course, the presence of a fair number of intelligent and thoughtful sixth form girls was having the effect of questioning taken-for-granted assumptions about gender. The introduction of an increasing number of girls and women into these schools does potentially make the schools' role in the reproduction of gender inequalities more problematic. As these changes occur it is almost inevitable that more of the terrain will be contested and that these schools will be unable to maintain their present male sexist ethos.

8

Examinations and
the formal curriculum

The master of the form gave out at fourth lesson on the previous day the subject for next morning's vulgus, and at first
lesson each boy had to bring his vulgus ready to be looked over;
and with the vulgus, a certain number of lines from one of the
Latin or Greek poets then being construed in the form had to be
got by heart. The master at first lesson called up each boy in the
form in order, and put him on his lines. If he couldn't say them,
or seem to say them, by reading off the master's or some other
boy's book who stood near, he was sent back, and went below
all the boys who did so say or seem to say them.

(Hughes, 1857)

For Tom Brown the curriculum was almost totally concerned with
the classical literature. Every day the boys would be expected to
write a Greek or Latin verse on a given subject and to learn by
heart some extracts of verse by ancient poets who had rather
more talent in this area than the average schoolboy. For centuries
the teaching and learning of classics dominated the work of
public schools – very little else was thought worthy of the time of
gentlemen.

Historically, it is clear that the public schools had a major part
to play in encouraging an anti-industrial and anti-practical attitude. Wiener (1982), for example, argues that the public schools
of the nineteenth century actively aimed to 'civilize' children
from the new commercial and industrial middle classes away
from holding what were regarded as somewhat vulgar 'capitalist'
values about the importance of science, technology, business and
commerce. Many of the new public schools of the last century

were specifically founded with the general intentions of providing an education to the sons of the new middle class which would make them acceptable to the old middle class, and this required a clear distancing of the sons from the source of their wealth. For a time, it was thus necessary for there to be 'a direct relationship between a school's social prestige in the community and the extent to which it is classically based' (Campbell, 1970). But this emphasis did not last long for, as entry to universities and occupations became increasingly bureaucratized, competitive and open, it became necessary to ensure that public school boys had their share of a much broader range of curriculum options. The curriculum is no longer dominated by classics and has not been so for many years. Far from being outdated and reticent to make changes, many of the public schools have been at the forefront of curriculum development and have been the driving forces for the acceptance of new subject areas and teaching methods.

As we shall see in the second section of this chapter, the notion that public schools are still inherently anti-science and technology is particularly inappropriate, for in this area the pressures for change have actually mainly come from public school masters, who have been very influential in the acceptance and subsequent shaping of science education in schools. The curriculum in public schools has changed dramatically from the days of Tom Brown.

The formal curriculum within public schools, however, can only be seen in the context of a complete educational system which embraces preparatory schools, public schools and universities. Although far from all pupils eventually go to university, the entry requirements of universities, in particular Oxford and Cambridge, act as severe limitations on possible change within the schools. Thus as long as Oxbridge demanded knowledge of Latin as an entry requirement, as it did until the 1970s, Latin was automatically taught in the major public schools, and while Oxbridge still demands knowledge of at least one foreign language, French or German will still be taught. The public schools, in turn, set their own entry requirements for boys coming from preparatory schools, to ensure that adequate tuition is given in the required subjects. This is usually ensured through the use of the Common Entrance Examination, to which we now turn.

Preparatory schools and common entrance

The Common Entrance Examination to independent schools is one of the strangest examinations in Britain's peculiar examination system. It can only be taken by boys who have already applied for admission to an independent senior school, usually an HMC school. The examination is common in the sense that it is set and administered centrally, and the examination papers are the same for all candidates and based on an agreed syllabus. But at the marking stage of the examination there are few common elements, for each senior school marks separately the papers of its own applicants.

The procedure is that parents decide which school they wish their boy to attend and make an application to that school. Usually, after an interview, the boy is offered a place subject to 'passing' Common Entrance Examination at a 'satisfactory standard'. The examination itself is held three times a year in February, June and November. As boys usually take the examination in the term before starting public school, the majority take it in June, when it acts as a final school examination in the prep schools. Boys actually take the examination in their own prep schools, or possibly in a nearby prep school for those boys in the maintained sector at the time. The completed examination scripts are then sent to the various schools to which the boys have applied and are marked by the masters at the separate public schools. Each school is free to decide its own pass mark.

Compulsory papers are taken by all boys in English, mathematics, French, science, history, geography and scripture and there are optional papers in Latin, Greek and further mathematics. There is a clear and close similarity between this subject list and that of a normal public school boy's entry list for O levels. The similarity is reflected in the examination papers themselves, which look very much like O level papers, and in the fixed examination timetable covering most of a week, with an additional test in oral French some weeks before. Boys spend about nine hours on the ten compulsory papers. During this relatively short time they have to tackle a wide range of questions from factorization and geometry in mathematics, to essays on Sir Robert Walpole or

King Henry VII in history. In English they might write on 'My kind of music' or 'a frightening situation', while in science they describe how to make a simple barometer and use it to measure atmospheric pressure or answer questions on photosynthesis. In scripture and religious knowledge all of the questions are based on the Bible and may ask the candidates to describe the trial and death of Stephen or explain why Jesus taught in parables, while in French there is guided composition based on pictures and a short read-out story, and questions to be answered in French on another French passage.

In short, it is a gruelling experience for most of the boys, and many still remembered it as the time when they had worked hardest in their lives. It made the last term at their prep schools one of worry and work. It is not clear, however, just how justified all this anxiety actually was for most of the boys at the research schools. I was able to obtain considerable information on entry procedures for one of the two schools, and it was clear that the boys might have had a more pleasant and relaxed time at the end of their prep school careers had they also had access to this information.

For the main entry in 1982 there were about eighty candidates, from twenty-seven different prep schools, who took the Common Entrance Examination for this research school. The 'official' position is that the school has a fixed pass mark which does not vary from year to year. In the event about twelve boys achieved marks below the official pass mark, but only two were denied admission. One boy who gained an overall mark some 9 per cent below the pass mark was still admitted and the two who failed had marks which were much lower than this. 'Special factors' and 'additional information' had been taken into account with the boys who were not too far below the line, to enable them to be given places. In the end, the number of boys passing the examination and thus being admitted to the school very closely matched the planned intake numbers for that year.

The right of each individual school to set its own pass mark is not the only oddity, for each school's marking of only the scripts of pupils who wish to be admitted to that school means that the comparability of marks between schools is also suspect. There is some attempt to cross-check marks between schools by a small sample of scripts being double marked, but it is difficult to do this well without considerable effort. Thus, although marks are often allocated specifically for particular parts of questions, a school may mark papers 'hard' or 'softly'. A 60 per cent score may be significantly easier to obtain at one school than at another. Further, individual schools can give different weights to the marks from various papers in arriving at the total score for the examination. Some schools, for example, might give very little weight to the scripture and religious knowledge paper, while others might value it highly. The optional papers, which are taken by some boys but not others, add further confusion.

I was able also to examine the waiting list for future places at the same research school and the position accorded with Devlin's (1984) view that 'generally the era of putting your children's names down at birth for certain schools has passed'. For the main entry of 1982, for example, only 17 per cent of the names had been entered more than four years before the year of entry sought; 35 per cent had been entered in the year preceding year of entry, and 16 per cent had only been entered in the same year. The times when it was necessary to make sure early on that a child's name was on a school's list have now certainly gone for this particular school and the general impression that I gained was that the position was similar in all but a few of the most prestigious schools whose names were household words. This research school took no account of the date of entry of names in its selection procedure.

The degree of flexibility in entry procedures noted above should not be taken to indicate that these schools are not highly academically selective. After entry all of the intake year at one of the research schools is given a simple test of verbal and mathematical and diagrammatic/spatial abilities. In 1981 the mean mark for that group of pupils was exactly the same as the grammar school norms on which the test was standardized, but with a slightly greater standard deviation. On the basis of this test it would seem that practically all of these boys would have obtained grammar school places if they had been available in the state system. The mean and standard deviation of the marks had remained relatively steady for several years.

Curriculum development

As public schools have a clientele of mainly academically able boys, the involvement of masters in curriculum development has been largely with courses designed for this ability range. Thus, one might expect that the development of new ways of teaching Latin might originate from within the public schools, as indeed it did, but public school masters have been involved with far more important and influential developments as well. Moreover, in some of the major subject areas public school masters have led the way, and have been key people in proposing new methods of teaching established subjects and in the promotion of new subject areas. Often ideas that germinated in the public schools have subsequently spread into the state sector. Advanced level business studies, for example, was pioneered at Marlborough and Sevenoaks, but has since spread widely. Engineering science A level was developed in HMC schools. Public school masters have also played major parts in the development of mathematics courses such as SMP and other forms of 'new mathematics'. Cooper (1983) argues that the independent schools, being well-resourced institutions and maintaining a high degree of contact and interchange with university personnel, are well placed to respond to any university-led demands for change. This was one aspect of their involvement in the School Mathematics Project, which has since been widely adopted in both independent and state schools.

Perhaps the most pervasive influence of the public schools on curriculum has been in the area of science teaching. I have argued elsewhere (Walford, 1985) that public school masters have, until very recently, written a disproportionate number of school science textbooks which have not only followed existing syllabuses but have also modified and stretched what is to be counted as valid knowledge in that area. The influence of the public schools in this area can be seen most clearly, however, through the role of public school masters in the Association for Science Education.

The Association for Science Education (ASE) is the largest and most influential subject orientated teachers' organization in Great Britain, its 17,000 members forming a network of twenty

British and one overseas regions. The association has numerous activities, which include regular meetings and events in each of the regions, an annual conference lasting four days and hosted by a university, and an annual education conference. It has strong links with the Institute of Physics, the Royal Society of Chemistry, the Institute of Biology and the British Association for the Advancement of Science. It has numerous committees which formulate policy and produce statements on science education, and it has been extremely influential in initiating curriculum change and in helping to direct the path of change within science education.

There is as yet no definitive history of the ASE, but the work of Waring (1979) and Jenkins (1979) enables an outline to be constructed. The historical roots of the association lie with the Association of Public School Science Masters which was established in 1902 to try to promote the status of science within the public schools. This was at a time of great educational ferment, and it emerged as one of the first organized pressure groups for school science education in the country. It became the Science Masters' Association in 1919, when entry conditions for membership were widened to include all graduate science masters in secondary schools. Membership was extended once more in 1946 to include all secondary school science masters and in 1963, following an amalgamation with the Association of Women Science Teachers, the ASE was formed and women were included. The AWST had itself been founded in 1922, had been smaller and less influential than the SMA but had shared the journal *School Science Review* with the SMA for some forty years before amalgamation.

The historical roots of the ASE have meant that until very recently there was a public school dominance within the committee structure and active membership. The influence of the public schools appears to be decreasing, as there is now an awareness of the effects of such a dominance within the association. However, of the sixty-six members of ASE committees giving a school as an address in 1981 (ASE, 1981) no fewer than twenty were from independent schools. In addition, the editor of the ASE's major journal, the *School Science Review*, has, since 1966, been A. A. Bishop of Harrow School. In practice this means that changes in science education almost without exception involve the ASE, and this has, until recently, meant heavy involvement of public school masters. Of the trial schools for Nuffield A level physics, for example, seventeen out of fifty-eight schools were independent.

There are a number of reasons for the considerable involvement of public school masters in curriculum development. One is, quite obviously, the type of academically well qualified graduate teachers that are employed by these schools. They are likely to be active members of subject group organizations, and retain and broaden a network of contacts with other teachers, university staff and educationalists. These contacts can act to encourage greater involvement. One science master I interviewed who had written several textbooks explained how his first book had been the result of a contact first made at Cambridge. They had been contemporaries for their degrees there, and both had entered teaching. After a few years, the other man had become science editor for a major publisher and had asked him if he would be interested in writing a textbook for them. He had replied that it:

> 15: was a bit much for me, and that I wasn't really experienced enough at that stage to be able to produce everything . . ., I had been teaching for about ten years, but I wouldn't regard myself as experienced in all branches of the subject. So I said I would contact the other members of the department and see how they felt about doing a joint one.

The resulting book was highly successful. Other masters, too, had similar experiences of being invited to write or contribute to books. Once some members of the department were involved, others often felt able to do the same. As another author explained:

> 28: [textbook writing] becomes one of the things that . . . em . . . not one is expected to do to make one's career, but something that doesn't seem unusual.

A further advantage that these teachers have over most state school teachers is a greater degree of autonomy and freedom of action. At a simple level, the far longer holidays are such that there is time not only for recovery from the arduous term but also for other projects. A good space of free time in which to write makes the prospect of writing a textbook far less daunting than it would be for someone who has to squeeze all of the writing into evenings, weekends and odd week holidays. Autonomy is also far greater within the school time. Individual teachers and especially heads of department often have a very high degree of autonomy over the way they teach and what they teach. This was indicated by one head of department who explained to me how the school had become one of the trial schools for a Nuffield science A level:

13: I think it was probably about a couple of years later, there was a meeting at Leicester University which was organized by [. . .] to which I was invited as head of department. This was about the first time that I had got together with other people in the same position and talked about how one should be teaching a subject. [The speaker] talked about this, and then, at the end of his talk, I just went to him and said 'Are you interested in having more schools to try this out?' He said, 'Yes, if you would like to join in, please do.' So we joined in the second year of the school trials – there had been some involved for the first year before we really became aware of this.

GW: It's interesting that that could be your decision as head of department to go into the trials like that.

13: Yes, we had a headmaster at the time who was prepared to take what the heads of department thought as something that he was prepared to do. He would back their judgement. . . . Of course, I asked him whether this would be all right. . . . He said 'Certainly, go ahead.' He felt that it was a good thing to get into.

Here we see a headmaster encouraging staff to develop new teaching methods. He was prepared to tolerate the uncertainties of a new course and new examination and probably new calls on financial resources in order to ensure that his staff could be at the forefront of teaching in their field. No doubt there was also the expectation that their being a trial school would act as a good advertisement, as would any book and publications which might result, but the headmaster clearly showed that he trusted the head of department's judgement in the matter.

There are indications that headmasters may not be as tolerant now as they were at the time just considered. This is partly due to the fact that the days of large centrally produced curriculum developments have gone; there is neither the finance nor the desire to develop new teaching methods and areas in this way. The large scale core-periphery model has largely been replaced by a model of much smaller and locally based initiatives, such as Secondary Science Curriculum Review, which may or may not link back to the centre and produce textbooks and materials. There is less direct prestige in being involved with such subjects. However, a more important restriction is that public schools are now less likely to be prepared to take the risk of developing new courses and examinations. The increasing clarity in the relationship between parents and school, where parents see themselves as primarily buying academic success, means that headmasters are less able to take any risks. Parents might complain if they felt their sons were being used as 'guinea pigs' in experimental courses. In the short run, the fear of something going wrong and pupils not getting the grades they might otherwise have got in a more stable and established course, might now override the educational benefits to both pupils at the schools and others elsewhere once a new course has been developed.

Such short-term considerations, while logical in terms of pupils and parents of pupils taking examinations at the time, may be to the disadvantage of public schools in the future. For the close contact of public school masters with the process of shaping subjects and their examinations has, without doubt, been to the overall advantage of pupils in the schools. At a surface level these advantages are seen in teachers' knowledge of the exact weightings given to parts of questions, and of the type of answer expected at each point. Someone in the process of writing a textbook is likely to be able to explain the material well, and be keen to understand individual learning difficulties. But the advantages occur at a deeper level, too, for academic subjects are not 'out there' waiting to be boxed and brought into school. Rather school 'subjects' are changing bodies of knowledge which develop through social

interaction between the various individuals and groups concerned with each area.

There have recently been several studies of the history and
development of school subjects (e.g. Goodson, 1983a and b; Ball,
1983) which have shown that the view that subjects are defined
and derived from fixed 'forms of knowledge', as suggested by
Hirst and Peters (1970) and others, is no longer tenable. Rather,
as Musgrove (1968: 101) argues:

> Within a school and within a wider society subjects as com-
> munities of people . . . [are] competing and collaborating with
> one another, defining and defending their boundaries,
> demanding allegiance from their members and conferring a
> sense of identity on them.

In rather different language Cooper (1983) has argued that 'subjects' should be seen as 'a set of segments, or social movements,
with distinct missions, or perspectives, and material interests'.
What counts as subject knowledge thus develops through
relations of conflict and co-operation between the segments, those
segments or individuals with the greatest power being able to have
a larger share in the shaping and refining process.

Within school science, for example, a key area of conflict has
been, and still is, the extent to which science teaching should
prepare a technological and scientific élite or should be available
to serve the needs of the majority. The official and semi-official
announcements have been many and varied and certainly not all
in the same direction, but, in practice, science education in
schools has tended to emphasize the function of training an élite.
Michael Young (1976: 51) argues that science teaching

> began and continues with its main purpose to maintain the
> supply of future scientists. This has two interrelated, and in
> effect self-justifying, outcomes – the mass scientific and tech-
> nological ignorance of a people in an increasingly technologi-
> cally dominated society, who see themselves as dependent on
> experts in more and more aspects of their life, and a community
> of scientists who see the knowledge which they are responsible
> for producing and validating as *necessarily* not available to the
> community at large.

Young sees the nature of science as taught in schools as abstract, dissociated from its applications and social implications, and acting to reproduce the class determined divisions of labour. Workers largely remain ignorant of dangers to which they may be subjected within the workplace, and unable to question manufacturing processes and procedures. They are forced to rely on academic 'experts' in these areas and thus lose control of their workplace environment and their working conditions. In their work they may 'learn enough technology to supervise and repair complex machines but will never learn about the social relations of which the designing and manning of machines is a part' (1976: 53). In a similar way Hine (1975) has highlighted the political non-neutrality of school science and argued for an integrated approach which would combine elements of physics, chemistry, history, economics and sociology and which would allow greater criticism and comment from pupils. This redefinition of the science curriculum might steer the subject away from its role in the reproduction of class relations towards a more emancipatory role.

Such a broadening of what counts as scientific knowledge might also help to reduce the sex bias that is to be found in science, for it is clear that the traditional emphasis of science teaching has been such that not only does it help maintain the current class structure, but it also helps to maintain present gender relations. Science is dominated by men at all levels, and traditionally physical sciences have been regarded as 'boys' subjects' at school. In examinations, for example, nearly four times as many boys enter physics O level as do girls. A detailed examination of the content of school physics helps to explain this difference, for it reveals that physics has been constructed and is taught in such a way that girls are eased out. Studies of school textbooks have shown that physics and chemistry are overwhelmingly presented as boys' subjects (Kelly, 1979, 1981; Walford, 1981). Illustrations, questions and general content use boys and men as examples far more often than girls and women. In addition, where girls or women are used they are highly likely to be shown engaged in stereotypical female activities. The consequence has been that girls have had little to identify with in school science and have not joined the scientific élite.

That physical science subjects within schools developed and are structured in this way, such that they help maintain both class and gender relations, is in no way surprising. Public school masters, who have traditionally served an all male élite group, have been dominant in writing textbooks, curriculum development, political policy making, and in the running of the Association for Science Education. It would be surprising if the subjects had developed differently. It is not, of course, that public school masters or the ASE intentionally structured school science in this way, rather, it is that the 'principles, the ideas, the categories' that conform to and support unequal productive relations will be 'naturally generated out of those productive relations themselves among individuals and groups' (Apple, 1979). What is considered to be appropriate school knowledge in any subject area, and the principles used to select and value it, are not neutral, but stem from current productive relations. The world of the public school is one in which inequalities of class and gender can be easily neglected, and public school masters have merely reflected the world as they see it in shaping and defining, through the ASE and their individual work in textbook writing and curriculum development, the nature of school science.

Science is just one area of many where public school masters have played a major part in structuring the school subject. It is also clearly not an insignificant area in terms of the number of pupils from within the schools taking the subject. In 1983, 45 per cent of entrants to university from Headmasters' Conference schools were in science, medicine, engineering and technology, showing that science and engineering have become a major career path for public school pupils. The figures for boys alone are some 2 per cent higher. The involvement of masters in such activities has thus clearly been of considerable long-term benefit to those who wish to purchase a university place for their sons through these schools. But, as has already been suggested, there are signs of change which may mean that public school masters will be less influential in the future in shaping the curriculum. Forces both within and outside the schools are causing public school masters to become less central to new curriculum developments.

Within the schools, as already indicated, increased parental pressure on examination success has made masters and head-masters less willing to take any possible risks with new courses. Parents are concerned that their own sons and daughters achieve success, not that future children will benefit from better courses in the future. Outside of the schools, the move to comprehensive education has caused a rethink in what should be taught and in teaching methods to which, it is widely felt, public school masters have little to contribute. Although most public schools would be claiming to be teaching a wider ability range than the majority of the grammar schools in the maintained system, their experience is certainly not with mixed ability teaching or with the full ability range, and their teaching experience and expertise is being seen as increasingly idiosyncratic. Under the bipartite system there were clear similarities with the teaching require-ments of public schools, such that public school masters were able to have an influence on the teaching and subjects in grammar schools as well as their own. However, changes in subject patterns and teaching that have occurred recently have been designed mainly to deal with teaching throughout the ability range, and offering some form of certification to the majority. Public school masters have been far less able to have any influence here, and may find that the nature of both O and A level teaching is gradually changed as these examinations accom-modate to new demands from the state system.

External examinations

Academic qualifications at the appropriate level are now essential for entry into universities, other forms of higher education and the professional occupations. Examination results have thus become one of the primary indicators by which public schools have come to be judged. O and A level results, and the pass rates and grades achieved, have become key factors in the image of a school presented to parents and the outside world, and to parents in their choice of school. The numbers of pupils going on to university, especially Oxbridge, and other institutions of higher education are something which, if they are high, is advertised widely.

All of which is rather strange, for the 'output characteristics' of a school in terms of examinations and university success are more dependent on the 'input characteristics' of the pupils in terms of ability, motivation, 'cultural capital' and financial support than they are on anything internal to the school. Put bluntly, if the scholarship boys at Winchester, who have a minimum IQ of 140 (Wilby, 1981), did not continue to university, then there would be something very wrong indeed with the school. The 'quality' of the school in terms of the effect of its teaching on examination performance can only be estimated if there is information about the abilities and characteristics of pupils on entry as well as the examination results. The school that sends twenty pupils to Oxbridge each year may well be doing badly rather than well.

Unfortunately there is very little information available that makes any attempt to relate these two types of data. The most recently available data is that of Halsey, Heath and Ridge (1984) whose results will be considered in the final chapter. Meanwhile, it is sufficient to note that a large number of examination passes in itself is not necessarily a sign of an academically successful school. We need further information to make that judgement.

There is, however, considerable information available on the extent and range of examination success. Schools in the Rugby and Eton Groups typically offer about twenty subjects for examination at both O and A level, although not necessarily the same subjects. The range is from the standard English language, physics and history to the rather more esoteric occasional entry for Dutch, general classics or maths for biologists. At A level subjects such as economics, politics and ancient history may be introduced and the rather more distant languages dropped. In the latest examination results available to me from one of the research schools the pass rate for O level varied from 33 per cent for the hard core of difficult cases who were attempting English with an 'easier' Board to 100 per cent. The majority were well into the 70 and 80 per cent mark. A similar pattern was found with the A level results, but here over half of the subjects achieved pass rates of 90 per cent or more.

Again, however, such figures seem to tell more than they really do, for they do not give information on the numbers of boys who were advised not to take the examination. Most boys will be taking eight or nine O levels and three A levels, but some will take fewer in order to give themselves a higher chance of passing some. The figures also do not indicate the numbers of pupils who leave before taking examinations.

In 1983, 59 per cent of leavers from HMC schools post O or A level went on to some form of higher education. Of the 22,000 leavers 42 per cent went to university. Looking at these figures in comparison with those for state maintained schools shows that 'more than a quarter of school leavers who go on to degree courses at universities and institutions of higher education came from independent schools' (ISIS, 1984). At Oxbridge the proportion is even higher. At Oxford, for example, in 1983 47.1 per cent of the acceptances were from independent schools, even though only 38.7 per cent of the applicants were from these schools. These figures probably underestimate the influence of the independent schools, for the growth of sixth form colleges, which claimed some 9 per cent of places, now often have strong contingents of independent school pupils who transfer from public school to sixth form college after O level, and enter university from there after A level (Bowen, 1983).

Good A level examination passes are now essential if entry to any university is to be assured; however, until recently A level results were only part of the requirements for entry to the pinnacle of the system – the universities of Oxford and Cambridge. There, a complicated admissions system which required a separate stiff entrance examination and interview allowed boys from public schools a clear advantage in the competition for places.

We have seen that, historically, the links between public schools and the various Oxbridge colleges have been strong, many being forged centuries ago. When William of Wykeham, for example, founded Winchester College at the end of the fourteenth century, he also founded New College, Oxford, to act as the next stage in his education scheme for the training of new priests. The links continue, and there is still a group of boys who enter New College from Winchester each year. Until fairly recently places were actually 'reserved' for such boys in many of the older Oxbridge colleges, as were special closed entrance scholarships which were only open for competition by boys from specific public schools. Such gross and obvious inequalities have been gradually removed at both Oxford and Cambridge, but a far more important source of inequality in admissions has only been very recently dealt with. The special Oxbridge entrance examinations, which consist of specialist subject papers and usually at least one general paper, are taken in early December for entry the following October. The examination can thus be taken either before or after A level examinations. Public school entrants have traditionally taken the examination after A level and after an extra intensive seventh sixth-form term during which candidates are specially coached for these examinations. The general papers, in particular, often require rather different skills from those measured through A level specialist papers. The public school entrants were thus able to maintain a considerable advantage over candidates from state schools which were usually unable to provide this extra tuition either in the fourth or seventh terms.

Since the last war there has been slow but steady pressure on Oxbridge to move towards a more meritocratic selection system. The Robbins Report (1963) and the Franks Commission (1966) both found that male entrants from the maintained sector on average had better qualifications than those from independent schools. More damagingly, students from independent schools were more likely to get third class degrees and less likely to get first class degrees than were the students from state maintained schools. Ideas that the entrance examination and interview were able to select students with 'potential' as well as achievement were clearly incorrect. Pressures for change arose from within the universities, too, as an increasing number of dons who had not themselves been public school boys were appointed. The push towards a more single-minded academic excellence that occurred in the public schools was partly a reaction to the same changes that were occurring at Oxbridge. The Norrington table, which annually displays the academic character of each Oxford college in terms of the success of its members in their degree examinations, became a key indication of the 'worth' of each college. In an attempt to improve on poor performance, in the early 1970s Hertford College, Oxford, and some others started to admit some students who had not taken the entrance examination and jumped in its position on the Norrington table in the following years. Other colleges followed suit and by the end of the 1970s all of the colleges were prepared to admit some students on interview only, provided they obtained the minimum A level matriculation requirements, and some more students on condition they obtained good enough A level grades. However, even in 1983, some 88 per cent of places at Oxford were given to candidates who had taken the entrance examination. At Cambridge the figure was 66 per cent.

Oxford, however, has made the most recent moves towards a fairer entrance system when, in 1983, Sir Kenneth Dover was appointed to chair a committee on admissions which would consider the whole matter. The data collected by the committee showed that Oxford was still not attracting its fair share of high ability students from the state system and recommended major changes in the admissions system (Dover Report, 1983). Interestingly, once admitted, entrants from the two sectors are now scattered in exactly the same pattern between first, second and third class degrees. 'The differences found by the Franks commission in the 1960s seem to have disappeared by the 1980s' (Halsey, Heath and Ridge, 1984). Towards the end of 1983 both Oxford and Cambridge thus announced changes. At Oxford the entrance examination for post-A level candidates was abolished from 1986, but the option would still be available for pre-A level candidates. At both Oxford and Cambridge all entrance scholarships are to be abolished in a further attempt to try not to give advantages to independent school pupils. At the time of writing Cambridge intends to keep its post-A level entrance examination, but pressure from schools will probably force it to follow Oxford in the near future.

These changes in the Oxbridge admissions system will mean that the public schools will experience corresponding changes. About 4000 pupils stay on an extra term to prepare for the Oxbridge examinations, most of them in HMC schools. Stevens (1983) calculates that at Winchester, where about seventy stay on, the loss in income will be about £120,000 per year, while at Eton about £200,000 will be lost. Most of the schools have fewer candidates and thus would not be affected as greatly in this direct way. However, in the long term, the abolition of seventh term entry will mean that public schools may become less attractive at sixth form level. In 1983 9.2 per cent of acceptances were from sixth form colleges, which offer A level courses free but are less likely than HMC schools to be able to offer Oxbridge entrance examination tuition. The removal of these examinations might make sixth form colleges as attractive for some parents and pupils at A level as sixth form teaching in public schools. There are already many pupils who make this change after O level, and an increase in the numbers could cause far greater damage than the direct results of loss of fee income for the seventh term candidates.

9

A revolution in chains

He hadn't been prepared for separate studies, and was not a little astonished and delighted with the palace in question. It wasn't very large certainly, being about six feet long by four broad. . . . The space under the window at the further end was occupied by a square table covered with a reasonably clean and whole red and blue check tablecloth; a hard-seated sofa covered with red stuff occupied one side, running up to the end, and making a seat for one, or by sitting close, for two, at the table; and a good stout wooden chair afforded a seat to another boy. . . . Over the door were a row of hat-pegs, and on each side bookcases with cupboards at the bottom, shelves and cupboards being filled indiscriminately with school books, a cap or two, a mousetrap and candlesticks, leather straps, a fustian bag, and some curious looking articles.

(Hughes, 1857)

Tom's first sight of a Rugby boy's study or 'citadel' serves to remind us of the continuities of experience of boys in public schools as well as the changes. The studies may now be larger and the mousetrap and candlesticks replaced by stereo system and strobe lights, but the site for 'study room culture' remains much the same. While some aspects of life have changed considerably, there are others that have remained more or less constant.

The main theme in John Rae's *The Public School Revolution* (1981) is that between 1964 and 1979 the changes that occurred in Britain's public schools were so great as to constitute a revolution. Understandably, John Rae, as headmaster of Westminster School and one time chairman of the Headmasters' Conference, was keen to emphasize the discontinuities with past practice rather than the continuities. He was prepared to reveal a few of the minor warts, but wished to present an image of public schools which was radically different from the past – modern, relevant and enterprising. He was certainly correct that great changes did occur during his chosen fifteen-year timespan, but this chapter will argue that, rather than being revolutionary, these changes must be seen as part of a long process of adaption to new demands and circumstances. Further, the nature of public boarding schools is such as to present considerable constraints to rapid change. In short, if there was a revolution, it was a revolution in chains.

Changes beget changes

Salter and Tapper (1981) have argued, in a similar way to John Rae, that the rapidly growing emphasis on examination success has been one of the fundamental recent changes within public schools. They suggest that the major reasons for this development have been parental pressure and the increasingly bureaucratic and qualification orientated demands from the professions and industry. These arguments are in agreement with evidence already presented on the Rugby and Eton Group schools. For the major schools, this push towards becoming an 'examination mill' has only occurred recently. But this does not mean that the change has been revolutionary; rather, as a recent article by Christine Heward (1984) shows, the change must be seen as part of a wider pattern of adaption and adjustment to external pressures.

Heward's research is a historical case study of a single HMC school, which concentrates on the period before and after the Second World War. She shows that within her somewhat less prestigious Woodard school, the emphasis on examination success, encouraged by parental pressure and career requirements, has long historical roots. As industrial capitalism grew, there became greater need for trained professional officials selected through competitive examinations. By the time of the Taunton Commission in 1867, there was considerable concern that schools were not providing an adequate education for the middle classes, for – unlike the upper classes who could bestow wealth on their sons – the middle classes 'have only education to look to keep their sons on a high social level' (Taunton Commission, 1867). A group of new proprietary schools, in which middle-class parents sought to have their children educated at 'a price they could afford', arose primarily to fill this need. The Woodard schools, and many others, taught modern subjects such as English and mathematics alongside Latin, and structured the school in such a way that academic study and examination success were emphasized.

Heward uses a mixture of archival sources and oral evidence to document the ways in which middle-class parents at this school put pressure on the headmaster to ensure that they obtained value for money. Such parents, who were forced to rely on education as the most important means of ensuring that the family maintained or improved its social position from one generation to the next, made vigorous efforts to ensure that their sons entered a career giving security, a comfortable income and good long-term prospects. Entry into such careers required examination success which, it is made clear, is why these parents were prepared to invest in education at the school.

Thus, rather than being a revolution, the change at the Rugby and Eton Group schools has been a continuation of a long historic process. As entry to more and more occupations and the universities has become more bureaucratically organized and competitive, fewer and fewer families could be indifferent to their son's educational qualifications. The schools that had once been the preserve of an élite with substantial independent means, who required a classical education to distance their sons from the possible contamination of having to earn one's living, found that these parents, too, were demanding a more solid and encashable return on their investment. Indeed, it would seem that rather than the academic success of the independent sector being 'spearheaded by a handful of boys' public schools' as Rae suggests (1981: 161), it was the handful that were following the way the others had gone many years before. As Cross (1983) relates,

The transfer of competitiveness from the sports field to the examination hall has taken about fifty years. The '30s slump started it; the Second World War had its effect; more important, perhaps, was the expansion and opening up of the universities under the post-war Robbins plan. Now even the best-heeled people, apparently, are feeling the effect of the current recession and deindustrialization and are making plans for their children to be sheltered from them.

The old-boy network used to be seen as a way by which pupils could find out about, and were well placed to obtain, suitable jobs, but the increased bureaucratization of appointments procedures and the stiffening competition for available jobs has meant that this network has become less important at the early stages. Whether or not it will retain its importance in the later stages of career development, when promotions and transfers are being considered, is unknown, but what is clear is that the major public schools have responded to the new situation at the career entry stage. Careers guidance and information services have become a major part of school life.

Some schools run their own comprehensive careers advisory service, but most of the major schools are now members of ISCO (Independent Schools Careers Organization) which was formed as long ago as 1942 as the Public Schools Employment Bureau. Once again, the date of formation shows that the development of such services for pupils has been a gradual process of adaption to a changing situation rather than a sudden shift of emphasis. Some 300 schools are now in membership of ISCO which provides regular information, training for careers staff in schools and a series of tests and questionnaires for use by trained staff in the schools. ISCO also provides a continuing service for those who have left school until their twenty-third birthday.

At both of the research schools career guidance was taken very seriously. The tests of abilities and interests supplied by ISCO were used as a basis on which pupils and careers masters could explore possibilities for careers. The full programme included an occupational check list, the Rothwell-Miller interest blank, and the Connolly occupational interests questionnaire, all of which were used to 'get the boys thinking' and to widen their horizon of possibilities. Very few boys needed to be pushed into thinking about their future at all. As one of the careers masters explained:

16: I think the boys are far more aware than they used to be of the importance of working – far more aware of their futures. This is one of the reasons why the careers department has developed and expanded its operations – just to satisfy the consumer demand. There's a very serious and genuine worry about the future, whereas ten or fifteen years ago there wasn't. And they are absolutely right.

The careers department at this school was, indeed, a large operation with periodic interviews between boys and careers masters, a careers room with information on universities, colleges and the requirements of entry into various occupations, and a series of careers talks for the older boys. These career lectures were usually treated seriously by the boys. As the same careers master explained, with more than a hint of sadness in his voice,

16: It's quite interesting. We get careers speakers coming up to speak who start off by saying, 'You all probably think that industry and commerce and making money is a dirty word'. And I know they don't at all – it's ridiculous now. They don't think it's a dirty word at all. It's precisely what they are interested in, thank you very much, and they want to know how to get it – 'how do I get on to this rat race, and how do I make money, and how do I get a good job?'

Boys and parents have gradually become more calculating in their attitude towards the schools. There has been a move towards instrumentalism and individualism. Boys are still fiercely competitive, not for the traditional house or school cricket, but for their own individual and future successes.

This move towards greater individualism is also to be found in the sporting activities in the schools. Twenty years ago practically all sport played was in teams. Whether it be football, rugby, cricket or hockey the aim was to establish and develop feeling and attitudes of group solidarity and dependence on the collectivity. Such sports are still important within the schools – at the very least, team games are easier for masters to organize and oversee than the more individual games. The continuing popularity of rugby as against football probably owes something to its ability to keep thirty boys occupied rather than just twenty-two. But team games are now only a part of the sporting activities of these schools. A growing variety of more individually competitive sports is now part of the formal extra-curriculum, and boys may now play tennis, squash or golf, or learn fencing, judo or swimming whilst they are at the schools.

The change in sport has, again, not been a rapid revolution but has been a gradual accommodation of new demands. More importantly, although the actual form of sporting activity may have changed to a degree, sport still plays an important part in the lives of public school boys. It is often a political choice as to whether the continuities or the changes are emphasized. In the same way, chapel, although still compulsory in most schools, is now an infrequent activity, and Combined Cadet Force is now often voluntary and far less militaristic. Those wishing to present a dynamic image of the public schools will point to the changes; while those who wish to present them as anachronistic will emphasize that chapel, CCF and sport are still there, and that the changes are in degree rather than in substance.

For, in practice, any institution such as a public school has very great difficulty in making rapid and dramatic changes even where those with the power to initiate are agreed on a course of action. Public schools can only adapt and adjust to demands and perceived need for change slowly, for they are restricted in their possible actions by myriad constraints. Any revolution is a revolution which must take place within tight chains – chains which have the strength of tradition, geography, architecture and economics.

The nature and form of architecture and physical facilities of any school are, perhaps, the most enduring aspects of these institutions. When the old boys go back to the old school for a Gaudy, it is returning to the buildings themselves that is vital. The staff will have changed, the teaching will have changed, it may now accept girls, but the buildings will have remained more or less the same. The buildings will not only act as physical reminders of youth and vitality, but will reflect the educational ideologies of architects and educationalists of the time when they were built. The massive and central chapel now acts as a memorial to a time when Christianity, particularly the 'muscular' kind, was central to these institutions. The clustering of the main buildings of the school around the close, with its prominent cricket square, serves as a similar reminder of the importance of sport.

Although many of the schools are housed in splendidly impressive buildings, the influence of architecture on the nature of social relations may go almost unnoticed. Buildings provide the physical structure within which social relations are generated and maintained. They embody, in a physical form, the educational ideologies of past architects, educationalists and teachers, still granting room for manoeuvre for the present occupants, but acting as obstacles to dramatic shifts of emphasis. It is evident that most of the Rugby and Eton Group schools are housed in buildings which are now very different from those which any school would design for its present day purposes. The classrooms are either too small or too large, and spread over too large a geographical area. The houses were designed for a different era when all boys slept in spartan dormitories and heating costs were minimal. The chapel, which stands proudly at the centre, is used for at most one or two hours every week, while the dining hall is so small that the boys have to eat in shifts. The buildings themselves are not unloved by the occupants, and often act as a selling point to parents, but they are rarely ideally suited to modern requirements. Over the years the buildings can be added to and refurbished but this is expensive and can only occur slowly; meanwhile they act as solid reminders of past purposes and ideologies.

The houses are a very good example of the difficulties that schools face in adapting to change. Ideally many schools, under pressure from both boys and parents, would wish to house all of the older boys and many of the younger ones in single or shared bedsitting rooms which would give each boy a room where he can work and sleep undisturbed by others. Several of the boys and some of the masters pointed out to me that as term drew on boys got more and more tired, due, simply, to lack of sleep. As Graham Greene (1934) argued some fifty years ago, 'In a large dormitory hardly a quarter of an hour passes without someone snoring or talking in his sleep.' Most schools have now adapted their buildings or built additions so that some of the older boys can have bedsitting rooms. Charterhouse was able to sell land to raise sufficient money to totally rebuild seven of its eleven houses. These now offer study bedrooms for each boarder. At Eton this has long been the case, but most of the schools are unable to do anything more than gradually improve their present buildings. There are often more pressing needs on the boarding side than new buildings, too. Many of the houses give an immediate impression of squalor on entering them. Paintwork is plain and dull, sometimes peeling. The dormitories may have bare floorboards or perhaps hard wearing carpet, but they offer few luxuries. The ironframed, sagging beds offer little physical support or comfort. One of the research schools still had some hair rather than spring mattresses. It was not that it was thought that a spartan life was desirable for the boys, but that money spent on new mattresses could not be spent on anything else.

The question of priorities in the distribution of money available is an interesting one, for the agents of tradition and history often have a major influence. The ultimate financial responsibility for these schools lies not with the headmaster or bursar but with the governing body of the school, a group of about twenty eminent people, practically always male. Typically the governing body, council or trustees will consist of powerful and high ranking members of the Anglican church, the armed forces, universities, industry and the local community. There may also be some hereditary members who are distantly related to the original founders, and a few elected members. Many of the members will be old boys of the school. Uppingham's list of trustees is not untypical in having a colonel, a lord bishop, a cathedral dean, two university professors, a head of an Oxbridge college, a knight, an OBE, an MBE and a Lady. This group of people has to be convinced of the appropriateness of any major items of expenditure or any major changes within the school.

One would not expect such people to be amongst those most in favour of revolutionary changes. Not only has the established order of things ensured that they have achieved or maintained their positions of eminence, but, as many are old boys, to tamper with the school is to tamper with their own childhoods. Which old boy could countenance changing his old house to a girls' house, when so many memories, both good and painful, are reinforced by its remaining as it was when he was a boy? Which headmaster would be brave, or perhaps foolish, enough to suggest that the grossly underused and expensively heated chapel should be converted to a communal dining room, a move which would undoubtedly make excellent financial sense, but which would strike at the sanctity and centrality of both church and house?

In practice, the governing bodies of these schools seem to have been more forward looking than one might expect. They have responded to the direct pressures from headmasters and teachers and to the indirect ones from parents, boys and potential employers. Parents are simply not prepared to tolerate complete squalor in the houses, and schools have recognized that, with rising labour costs, hard wearing carpet may be easier to clean than floorboards, and thus represent a good investment. Money has also been found for new teaching equipment and many schools, fearing to be left out of the race, have rushed into lavish provision of now underused language laboratories and at present heavily used computer centres. Governing bodies are themselves, however, highly constrained in what they can do. Their primary consideration is that any improvement must be paid for either by direct additions to every school bill or through appeals or gifts. Governors now recognize that their responsibilities do not end with the distribution of money, but that they are also expected to act as fund raisers. Indeed, those governors or trustees who have high positions in industry and commerce are now amongst the most important to the school.

Fund raising and school appeals have become a major source of additional income for larger scale expenditure. It is the unusual school which now does not have a fairly regular programme of appeals which may be nominally a celebration of fifty or five hundred years, but without which new swimming pools, sports halls and teaching blocks would not have been built. The journal of the HMC, *Conference and Common Room*, regularly contains advertisements from fund raising consultants touting for business. One company advertises that it has been responsible for raising nearly ten million pounds in the last four years. Individual schools now launch appeals for at least a quarter of a million – some for much more. Such appeals have to be very carefully organized and are not primarily aimed at parents of boys at present at the school. Instead they aim to get a small number of large donations from major companies, institutions and possibly individuals, which can then be supplemented by a host of smaller contributions. Contacts with old boys who have risen in their careers to very senior posts are thus vital, for it is the directors of major companies who are able to ensure that their own public schools can receive a share of the company's regular charitable contributions. As the schools are registered charities, such donations can be claimed against tax and cost the company far less than would otherwise be the case. Such school fund-raising campaigns thus have to be carefully managed to ensure that those with the ability to make or direct contributions can see the wisdom of their doing so. The Appeal Prospectus must contain within it major items which can justify donations. Too dramatic changes in the character and nature of the school are thus to be avoided, for institutional giving is likely to support gradual innovation rather than revolutionary change.

Such constraints are likely to operate throughout the life of the school, for donations are not only given at times of special fund-raising appeals. Many of the schools have gradually built up good relationships with local industries and institutions of higher education. This is often particularly important within the sciences where it is not uncommon for schools to regularly receive 'cast-off' equipment and supplies which, while no longer suitable for high level research, are more than adequate for schools. The occasional supply of liquid nitrogen or solid carbon dioxide also often comes through local contacts. Such contacts are an important way whereby fees can be kept down and better facilities provided. Being mainly one-way relationships, they are essentially fragile, and masters need to cultivate them and ensure that nothing the school does is seen to be too unusual or against the interests of these other parties. The forces are thus again towards gradual adaption to external pressures rather than revolutionary change.

The continued existence of Combined Cadet Forces also owes much to questions of finance. CCF is much more voluntary than it used to be as pressure from boys and parents in this area coincided with the feelings of many of the younger masters who objected to all boys having to take part in what was seen as pre-military training. In some schools all boys do still take part. At Malvern, for example,

> Boys join the Combined Cadet Force in their second year in the school. At the end of his first half year a boy takes his basic Army or RAF Proficiency Test and after that he may choose from a variety of half-year courses. Amongst these are RAF, NCO Cadre, Royal Signals, Royal Engineers, REME (Motor Transport), REME (Radar), Royal Artillery, Advanced Infantry, Skill at Arms, Canoeing, First Aid, Casualty Simulation, Typing, Fire Fighting, Police and Band. All boys do a half-year course in Adventure Training culminating in a 48-hour ex-pedition in the Brecon Beacons in winter.
>
> (Malvern College Prospectus)

At Malvern CCF is thus a compulsory activity and some military activity must be undertaken, but a boy with distinct anti-military feelings can turn to first aid, band or typing if he is able to bear the taunts of his peers. More open alternatives are offered at Clifton where,

> boys are invited to join the voluntary school contingent of the Combined Cadet Force. After a trial term as a recruit, during which he will be introduced to the activities of the CCF, a boy may then choose to serve on a yearly basis, or may join one of the other activities offered at the same time on Mondays.
>
> (Clifton College Prospectus)

In spite of talk of revolutions occurring in public schools, CCF still retains a firm place, and it would appear that the Forces have recently risen again in importance in terms of providing careers for some of the less academically able boys. Yet objectively there is little reason why schools should provide training for this future career any more than many others. The others, however, do not give financial support as HM Forces do. The Ministry of Defence gives a grant to schools (state maintained as well as independent) according to the number of boys enrolled in the corps. This can be used to finance equipment and consumables which are related to CCF but not necessarily exclusively used by CCF. Thus a contribution can be obtained towards the cost of sports equipment, physical training apparatus, canoes, musical instruments, transport and so on, which can be used both for CCF and wider school activities. This financial support is part of the reason for the continued existence of CCF in so many schools and compulsion means that the number of boys in the corps is at a maximum to obtain the largest grant.

Teachers themselves can also often act to restrict dramatic changes. The long service at a single school that is so much a part of the housemaster system is such that the teachers with power and influence within the school often spend thirty or more years of their lives there. They are thus on the school staff for far longer than any headmaster, often serving under four or five in the time, weathering out the 'bad' headmasters and rejoicing with the 'good'. Their power to resist change is considerable. At the lowest level there is simply the problem that if a school, for example, has five classics masters who are largely unable to teach other subjects, classics must remain on the timetable until they retire or move. The problem is, unfortunately, at its worst with exactly those declining subjects that schools might most wish to change, for the lack of other opportunities in subjects such as Greek and Latin teaching means that staff movements are extremely rare. To be able to appoint a new computing specialist means that a vacancy must occur in an area in which the school is overstaffed.

At a deeper level, masters may resist change simply because they like the school the way it is. The man who chooses to teach at a public school in part because he is a keen cricketer will fight to ensure that cricket maintains a firm place on the sporting calendar, as will those who are keen on rowing or mountaineering. It must be remembered that for many of the staff one of the attractions of these schools is that they enable them to further their own sporting and other interests within their work environment, and, although they may complain of overwork, they also would not wish to see these formal extra-curricular activities removed. Many of the masters have also shown resistance to the greater stress on examination success. They willingly accept that the schools should try to teach as well as possible, try for examination successes and encourage university entry, but they reject the idea that the school should become an 'examination mill' in order to achieve these ends. Public schools, the majority of masters argue, are about educating the whole man and must be concerned with the cultural, aesthetic, moral and social aspects of education as much as the academic. Masters have actively tried to resist the calls from parents and boys for increased specialization and even greater emphasis on examinations. The area is very much a contested one, as it can be in state schools too (Cullingford, 1984). In one of the research schools, for example, I attended a sixth form parents' meeting where the headmaster was strongly criticized for his policy of forcing every student to take general studies. 'Why', asked one parent, 'can't they take an extra A level?' The headmaster initially argued in favour of a broader education than just that which was concerned with examination success, but was able to placate these parents finally only by using the argument that universities liked an element of wider study, and that the general studies in the school might help the pupils at interview. Pressure from parents and from boys was strong and constant. Almost without exception, masters resented this increased examination orientation. It severely restricted their autonomy by forcing them to neglect wider educational issues and confined their teaching to material on the examination syllabus. One very strong department at one of the schools was able to resist the pressure from its position of strength. The A level pupils did nothing whatever directly concerned with the A level syllabus in the first year of their A level studies. In the second year it was 'a headlong rush' to get it done, the pupils had no chance to get bored with it, and most achieved excellent results. Most teachers, not having the strength of such excellent results to back them, found that the increased examination pressure reduced their independent action, acted against their professional ideology and made the underlying worker/employer relationship more explicit (Walford, 1984).

For many masters it came down to the basic question of what is the purpose of education. Is it about offering opportunities for full personal development or is it simply a means by which parents can virtually ensure higher education for their children and thus give them a very good chance of obtaining a reasonable job? If the latter, then some of the masters would find the whole process of what they were doing objectionable, for they clung to the wider definition. In Lambert's (1975) terms, they were still concerned with the 'expressive goals' of the school, and laid stress on character training in moral, religious and/or cultural terms. Serving the community was a more desirable goal than the pursuit of individual success. The boys mainly saw it differently, as less than a quarter of those answering questionnaires at one of the research schools felt that the school promoted service to the community, and most were convinced that the school's main purpose should be to ensure that they got their required examination results.

This tension can be illustrated by one occasion in a masters' meeting where there was a long and heated discussion. It was one of the traditions of this particular school that various clubs and organizations for sixth form pupils went out of school, usually to a pub or hotel, and had a communal annual dinner. On the surface the problem was a simple one: the headmaster had refused to allow the debating club to have a club dinner whilst allowing some of the other clubs such a privilege. He justified his action in terms of ensuring that parents did not have to pay for too many extra celebratory meals, and reducing the possibility of bad publicity for the school if pupils behaved badly in public. In appropriate debating style, some of the masters argued strongly for the retention of dinners which they felt were a strong 'civilizing' influence on the boys. They felt that this, after all, was what the school should be about and that, if pupils did disgrace the school when in pubs, this was a sure sign that the dinners were even more necessary and that the school was failing in one of its major functions. The 'result' of the discussion was confused, but it seemed that the debating society would have its dinner the next year – a small victory for tradition, and a small reaction against the direction of change. Change, when it occurs, is a gradual process of accommodation to new circumstances; many constraints act to slow down the process.

Ten myths to be scotched

John Rae (1981) tells us that as far back as the early 1960s the Headmasters' Conference was concerned about its unfavourable popular image. It drew up a 'Programme for Action' which was based upon ten 'popular myths that need to be scotched'. These were that public schools:

(a) are a refuge for the brainless and the philistine
(b) are consecrated to Latin and teach no science
(c) are uninterested in sending boys to the new universities and redbricks
(d) have privileged access to Oxbridge places, for example through closed awards
(e) monopolize the City, Sandhurst, Whitehall and the Bar
(f) do not send boys into industry and are disdainful of modern technology
(g) foster bullying and sadism, particularly through corporal punishment and fagging
(h) have barbaric living conditions
(i) enjoy an unfairly high staff–pupil ratio
(j) promote homosexuality

(Rae, 1981: 31)

These ten points can act as convenient illustrations of the extent of change in public schools, whilst at the same showing the continued existence of constraints on change. The immediate reaction is that each of the ten is, indeed, a myth, but each point also needs further elaboration.

(a) *are a refuge for the brainless and the philistine*

Of the ten 'myths' this is perhaps the one that public schools must now feel they have effectively 'scotched'. We have seen already that present day public schools do certainly not now cater for the brainless offspring of the wealthy. The Common Entrance Examination, although retaining considerable flexibility, ensures that the lowest level of 'braininess' (if we can for a moment forget the problem of this rather floppy concept and equate it with performance in IQ tests) accepted by the Rugby and Eton Group schools is certainly above the national average. Parents now demand that their investment in the school is translated into examination success at O and A level, and this awesome responsibility to succeed academically is accepted by most of the boys as well. Less prestigious schools, of course, still accept children with lower ability and many of the independent non-HMC schools specifically aim for this end of the market, employing special teachers who are trained to help these less academically able pupils. For the HMC schools, however, not only must the child be able, but he or she must also be prepared to work hard while at the school. Consistent failure to do so results in expulsion.

While the first half of this 'myth' is thus firmly quashed, the second is more open to doubt. The schools themselves are certainly not philistine in the variety of cultural experiences that they encourage. Some of the larger schools may even act as cultural centres in music or art for the local community. But there is a considerable danger that a growing number of pupils within the schools are becoming philistine in the sense of having a material outlook and being indifferent to culture. The increasingly instrumental and individualistic attitude of both parents and pupils is seen by many masters as a threat to the wider educational purposes of the school. Philistines, so long as they are academically able ones, can indeed find a home in these schools.

(b) *are consecrated to Latin and teach no science*

We have seen that this second 'myth' also has very little truth in it. The days when boys spent all their time on classics have now long gone, and, far from teaching no science, it was shown in chapter eight that public schools were at the forefront of curriculum development in the sciences as in several other 'modern' subjects. Yet, while no one would now say that the schools are 'consecrated to Latin', they clearly give it far greater prominence than practically any other school in the country. Some schools still have Latin as a compulsory subject for all pupils, and Rugby, for example, still has more classics masters than English masters.

Most seem to still have more teachers of classics than of economics, politics or business studies.

In the same way, although science is now a major subject in these schools and 36 per cent of university entrants from HMC schools in 1983 were to study science and engineering, the national figure is 42 per cent for science and engineering. Thus, while the national figure for arts undergraduates in universities is about 49 per cent, some 55 per cent of students from HMC schools enter this area. Only in medicine do HMC schools enter about the same proportion of students as the national figure of 10 per cent. Thus, while the myth as plainly stated is untrue, the implication behind the statement, as with any good myth, still has some power.

(c) *are uninterested in sending boys to the new universities and redbricks*

When thinking about any institution there is always a danger that the various people within that institution will be taken to have homogeneous views and attitudes on policy concerned with the institution. Many masters, especially those most concerned with careers advisory work, are now often very keen to ensure that pupils find a higher education course that is the most suitable for him or her, no matter where it happens to be taught. The growing number of masters who themselves have been to new, redbrick and even technological universities also ensures that individual people within the schools are well aware of opportunities outside Oxbridge. But even so, most of the masters would still probably rather send boys to Oxbridge than the other universities or polytechnics. Indeed, as far as the polytechnics are concerned Greg Eglin (1984) has shown that state school sixth formers have far more knowledge of this sector than do those in independent school sixth forms. His study of sixth form pupils in four independent and seven state maintained schools in a single London borough showe l that, while aspirations for higher education were about the same for the two groups, those from the independent sector had far less knowledge of the polytechnics and much preferred to take a degree at a university if possible.

In general, public schools seem to be keen to send as many of their pupils as possible on to higher education, preferably to Oxbridge, but then to the other universities and lastly to the polytechnics and colleges of higher education. In practice, it would be difficult for any headmaster of a public school to move away from this emphasis even if he wished to, for it parallels the hierarchy of higher educational establishments held in the minds of most parents. The number of Oxbridge places achieved each year by individual schools is also one of the most easily available and public ways in which individual schools can now be ranked. Every year the major newspapers publish a list of Oxbridge places gained by individual schools as a proportion of the number of pupils in each sixth form. The list, which incidentally also includes state maintained schools and sixth form colleges, thus acts as a very public measure of the 'worth' of a school. The pressures are on each headmaster, and hence members of staff, to try to encourage pupils to enter Oxbridge if they have a chance of gaining a place. Schools are sending pupils to other universities, but usually only once it is clear that the pupil is unlikely to reach Oxford or Cambridge.

(d) *have privileged access to Oxbridge places, for example through closed awards*

It was shown in chapter eight that there are now no closed awards at either Oxford or Cambridge, and both universities have made considerable adjustments to their admissions system to make it easier for pupils from state schools to obtain places. In some colleges there is now felt to be a strong feeling against public school candidates, who are expected to be able to perform at a higher level than those from state schools because they have 'had the benefit of public school teaching'.

Even so, at Cambridge in 1983, 46 per cent of acceptances were from independent schools while only 36 per cent of the applications were, and at Oxford 47 per cent of acceptances came from 39 per cent of the applications. Independent schools are clearly much more successful in getting places than are the maintained schools and colleges. The figures show that one of the major problems is that proportionately fewer pupils from state schools apply, either because they feel they will not be accepted or because they simply do not see Oxbridge as desirable. But after application, candidates from independent schools still fare much better. Part of their greater success is undoubtedly due to their schools' greater knowledge of the system and of the individual Oxbridge colleges.

The application system for Oxford and Cambridge is still unique in the British university system, for candidates have to be accepted by an individual college for admission rather than the university as such. Once accepted by a college, the student has an automatic right to become a member of the university. Applicants have thus to make a very difficult choice between 24 colleges admitting ordinary undergraduates at Cambridge and 29 at Oxford. Without detailed knowledge of the individual college it is very much a matter of luck as to whether the choice gives a good chance of being accepted or a poor one. The chance depends on the particular subject and the individual college, for candidates are interviewed by fellows of the individual college and the chance of acceptance thus depends, to a degree, on the number of other applicants to that college in the particular subject and on how stiff the competition is. Many fellows take great care with the selection process and will try very hard to ensure that a good candidate who cannot be accepted by the first choice college gets accepted elsewhere, but, in practice, the number of acceptances by colleges other than the first choice college is small. In 1983 only 12 per cent of Cambridge applicants gained acceptance at a college other than their first preference and 11.5 per cent did so at Oxford. While the exceptional candidate will not be disadvantaged, those at the margin need to be very careful about their choice.

One of my research schools generously allowed me to attend a joint meeting of housemasters and heads of department at which Oxbridge strategy was discussed. In all there were about twenty masters who pooled their knowledge of the Oxbridge system to try to ensure that the candidates applied to the most 'appropriate' college. They drew upon their knowledge of individual college tutors who might be interviewing, the 'standing' of the college in each particular subject area, and their detailed records of what had happened to applicants in the previous years. The pupils' names were taken one by one and discussed by the group. X college had not accepted either of the applicants last year, Y college was looking for good geographers, Z college had few applicants in history. The recent move of a headmaster from a public school to the headship of an Oxbridge college was not looked on favourably – 'He'll be looking for state school boys.' There were difficult long- and short-term gains to be balanced in the process as, although the school wanted to get in as many pupils as possible, they also wanted to make sure that a 'poor' boy did not just scrape in and make the school's name 'mud' for next year's applicants. It was felt that they 'mustn't scupper a good college' with a boy who was marginal. 'Perhaps he should try [one of the former women's colleges]?'

Masters tried hard to make and retain contact with individual colleges. Links made while an undergraduate, or sometimes post-graduate, or during a one-term schoolmaster fellowship were exploited to try to gain a competitive edge through greater, or more up-to-date, information. The admissions tutors of some colleges were invited to dine with the headmaster. Masters would take small groups of boys on visits to colleges. The information was incomplete and far from perfect, but as a result of that meeting housemasters would advise applicants on which college to apply for, and if they heeded that advice it is likely that they had just that slightly better chance of being accepted.

It is thus no longer a case of public schools having privileged access to Oxbridge, merely that they are in a better position to be able to give appropriate advice. Nothing this school did could not be done by any state maintained school, but the greater number of applicants in the past and probably closer contacts now gave the school a greater depth of knowledge to draw upon and gave its pupils a head-start in the race.

(e) *monopolize the City, Sandhurst, Whitehall and the Bar*

While not a monopoly in the strict sense, there is little doubt that there are proportionately more people from public schools in the City, Sandhurst, Whitehall and the Bar, than from state main-tained schools. Given, however, that HMC schools, at least, have a highly academically able intake, this should be no surprise. The question is really one of whether, ability for ability, there are proportionately more public school boys than state school boys in these élite groups. However, even if the data were available to answer this question, it would only tell us the relationship between élites now and public schools as they were some forty or fifty years ago. It would tell us nothing about what we might expect the effect of a public school education to be on boys and girls who are at present attending public schools. The 'myth', if there is one, is thus concerned with the possible future rather than the present. It will be touched on again in the final chapter.

(f) *do not send boys into industry and are disdainful of modern technology*

This 'myth' is linked to the second concerning the teaching of Latin and science that has been already discussed. It is difficult to generalize about the whole range of public schools in this respect, but as an overall statement it is plainly no longer true that they are anti-industry and commerce. In the last few years there has been a dramatic growth in the number of school/industry link schemes and secondment schemes for teachers from both the state and independent sectors (see for example Watts, 1983; Thompson and Walford, 1983). Many of the major public boarding schools have played a part in these developments. Malvern, for example, appointed a master for a year who spent half of his time building links between the college and local industry, arranging visits and gathering information (Jenkins, 1982). Wellington has a similar scheme where about fifty sixth formers each year spend a few days on attachment to about twenty companies, which include such well known names as British Steel, Marks and Spencer and Racal (Hobson, 1983). There is now also a wide range of semi-autonomous groups working within both independent and state maintained schools to 'improve the image of industry' and to make the school curriculum more appropriate for the perceived needs of industry. These include the Schools Council Industry Project, Project Technology and Young Enterprise. In the latter, groups of pupils establish and own their own mini productive companies for a limited period. Although they have several adult advisers who may be drawn from the school and local industry and commerce, the pupils themselves make all the decisions as to production, finance, marketing and so on (Conference, 1979). By mid 1984, twenty-four of the HMC schools had been involved in Young Enterprise. In this area, too, the schools are responding to pressure from parents and boys as much as generating change internally. For most of the boys, it seems, industry is 'precisely what they are interested in, thank you very much, and they want to know how to get [money]' and enter the 'rat race'. The schools have thus been forced to oblige.

Modern technology, too, has a firm place in public schools, the first major injection, appropriately enough, being financed by industry. In the early 1950s there was considerable concern that the public schools might fall behind the state schools in science provision as they received no state grant. An Industrial Fund for the Advancement of Scientific Education was established which was sponsored by 141 industrial companies and raised £3.25 million. This was used to give grants to independent and the then direct grant schools for building, modernizing, expanding and equipping school chemistry and physics laboratories (Waring, 1979).

More recent modern technology has had to be financed on a more *ad hoc* basis, but computer centres have featured on several appeals and gifts of out-of-date computers by companies have helped elsewhere. At the beginning of 1982 the HMC established the Independent Schools' Microelectronics Centre, which is housed at Westminster College, Oxford. It was set up in parallel with the government's Microelectronics Programme and aims to act as an information centre and focus for independent schools. It is particularly concerned with in-service education and the development of materials for the whole curriculum, not just mathematics and the sciences (Conference, 1984). Some 81 per cent of HMC schools are in membership of the centre.

This still leaves, however, some forty HMC schools which are not in membership, and thus is indicative of the patchy response to industry and modern technology throughout the independent sector. While the major schools have been able to find the resources and a welcome response from industry, some of the less prestigious schools have been less successful or interested. Very well equipped computer laboratories are now to be seen at all of the major schools, but are sadly missing from many others. Again it must be remembered that, even though there has been considerable interest in technology and industry, this does not necessarily mean that pupils are entering industry in great numbers or doing so with scientific qualifications. Visits to factories and industry may well deter pupils as well as attract them, and the proportional numbers taking university science and engineering courses from public schools are still well below national figures.

(g) *foster bullying and sadism, particularly through corporal punishment and fagging*

The days of prefects 'roasting' young boys in front of an open fire or bellowing for a fag to do some menial duty have now gone, as have the cane-thrashing masters, long runs and cold showers. But it was shown in chapter three that the change has been one of degree rather than absolute nature. A good proportion of the younger boys in the main research school complained about being bullied and about some of the unofficial personal fagging that the older boys expected them to do. The fate of one boy who had become the 'butt of the year' was also described, showing that bullying and sadism still existed even amongst boys of the same age. However, the important question here is whether or not public schools still 'foster' bullying and sadism or whether the amount that is to be found within the schools now is more or less what, unfortunately, would be expected within any large group of boys. Within any school of 600 boys, or girls for that matter, there are bound to be some who delight in tormenting those younger or weaker than themselves. Adolescence is a time of personal insecurity and self-doubt, which can often be translated into particularly antisocial behaviour. A certain amount of bullying and sadism is thus to be expected; whether or not this is more or less than it would have been had those same boys attended state maintained schools is a matter for speculation.

It is clear that the various studies of boys in somewhat different circumstances reveal a depth of antisocial behaviour which is unmatched in the lives of most public school boys. The racist and sexist 'lads' in the West Midlands reported by Willis (1977), the street boys looking for excitement in Sunderland (Corrigan, 1979) or the gangs of Glasgow (Patrick, 1973) or Liverpool (Parker, 1972) appear to be in a different league of criminal activity from the boys in public school. But, of course, it is possible that they would still have been in a different league if these public school boys had attended their local schools. Fox (1984) has shown that parents are prepared to pay for their sons' education in public school not only because of their belief that the schools will enable their boys to gain better examination results, but because they feel that the school will 'develop character through discipline'. They believe that at public school they will have less chance of being badly influenced by others and thus less chance of becoming antisocial or criminal people. There is no way of testing whether they are correct, but it is likely that they are. Two factors, at least, point in favour. Firstly, as we have seen, the freedom allowed in studies, which act as sites for 'study room culture', allows 'weird ideas' to occur and work themselves through without any real danger or damage. The vast array of rules allows the younger boys at least to have a 'risky' and exciting time without getting into any real trouble. Secondly, the boys were aware that some of their parents were making considerable financial sacrifices on their behalf. Parents made this clear to boys, as they did their expectations as to their behaviour. The risk of expulsion that would be the inevitable result of involvement in gross bullying or sadism would be too great to take.

However, it is almost inevitable in an adolescent world that those older and more physically powerful will seek to make their lives more pleasant at the expense of younger boys. When there are mixed age dormitories, for example, the youngest boys will usually find themselves in the most uncomfortable bed and in the worst position. The older boys will move their more comfortable beds away from the banging door which would otherwise wake them every time any one goes to the toilet. This might be described as 'systematic bullying' or just a social norm of the group.

Indeed, one of the younger boys, perhaps wisely, argued that fagging was a good thing because the rules and regulations that accompanied it acted as a constraint on what otherwise would be much larger and more unreasonable demands made on him by older boys.

(h) *have barbaric living conditions*

The buildings in which pupils live vary widely in age, design and condition. At Charterhouse seven of the houses have been rebuilt and provide single study bedrooms for each boarder. The boys lucky enough to be members of these houses live in accommodation of a similar standard to that of many undergraduates in the newer universities. The floors are comfortably carpeted, the furniture and fittings are of a high standard and, perhaps most important, each boy has a door to close on the rest of the school should he wish to do so. But Charterhouse was lucky enough to be able to sell land to pay for new buildings; the vast majority of schools have either been unwilling or unable to do this and pupils are still accommodated in buildings dating from the last century or earlier which are far from ideally suited to present day demands.

There is little doubt that living conditions for pupils have gradually improved since the War. As schools have become more competitive, they have been forced by parents and pupils to update their accommodation in order to attract the most able. New buildings, however, are usually prohibitively expensive and schools have had to modify their existing ones as best they can. Brighter and cleaner paintwork is straightforward, as is hard-wearing carpet (which can have the additional advantage of actually reducing the labour of floorcleaning), but many of these older buildings simply cannot be refitted to provide the privacy of single study bedrooms. A common solution has been to provide a new wing of single rooms for the older boys, while the younger ones remain in dormitories which, as was shown in chapter three, can be somewhat spartan and cold in winter.

A source of some anger and envy in the schools is that, where girls have been admitted into the sixth form, they often have the best accommodation – which is usually the result of special new buildings for them rather than conscious sexism. For the boys, to describe living conditions as 'barbaric' may now be inaccurate, but life at school is certainly less comfortable than at their homes. With continual lack of privacy, uncomfortable beds, public washing facilities and sometimes even communal bathrooms, it is small wonder that many of the pupils looked forward to returning home at the end of term for rest and 'a bit of luxury'.

(i) *enjoy an unfairly high staff–pupil ratio*

The staff–pupil ratio for HMC schools in 1984 was 1 : 12.0 (ISIS, 1984) while for English state secondary schools the ratio for the same year was 1 : 16.2 (DES, 1985). On the surface, the question of whether this is 'unfairly higher' or just 'higher' is a political and ideological issue. However, the raw teacher–pupil ratios do not tell the whole story, because they do not compare like with like. It is generally accepted that the staff–pupil ratio should be better for older children than for younger ones. Thus in 1984 while the ratio for state secondary schools was 1 : 16.2, it was 1 : 22.1 for state primary schools. With the presence of middle schools the dividing age is not as clear as it was, but the majority of pupils reach the secondary stage at 11. Many HMC schools do not start until 13 and thus, by extrapolation, we might expect there to be a slightly better teacher–pupil ratio than in state secondary schools.

A greater difficulty is that while the majority of pupils in the state sector do not continue in the sixth form with A levels, the vast majority of public school pupils do. Again it is generally recognized that a better teacher–pupil ratio is required for sixth form work than for ordinary secondary school work. One way to deal with this, as is done in the state sector to calculate the nominal staff loading, is to weight sixth form pupils higher than other pupils in any calculation. Weighting factors are arbitrary constructs, but a common one used is simply to weight sixth form pupils twice as highly as other pupils.

In 1984 there were 225,000 teachers in state secondary schools with 3,646,000 pupils (t : p = 16.22). If we count those of 16 and above as all being sixth form pupils, there were 200,500 in sixth forms of these schools. If we count each of these as twice that of other pupils the new weighted ratio becomes 1 : 17.1. The same calculation for HMC schools, where there are far more sixth formers, gives a ratio of 1:15.2 for 1984.

While it would clearly be possible to argue over the weightings used, it is clear that there is actually very little difference in the overall ratios. In fact, if it is remembered that these same masters at public schools often have house, sporting and social activities also to look after, it might be more appropriate for parents to question why it is that the teacher–pupil ratio seems to be so bad at HMC schools compared with state maintained schools. There is, however, considerable variation within the HMC schools and those within the Rugby and Eton Group do fare better – though not dramatically so. This 'myth' seems to be untrue, although why the HMC should wish to scotch this particular myth is not clear.

(j) *promote homosexuality*

The Hite Report (1981), which questioned over 7000 American men on their sexuality, found that 43 per cent of men had sex with other boys when they were children or teenagers. This compares with Kinsey's *et al.* (1948) figure of 48 per cent.

> 43 per cent of those who answered had had some form of sex with another boy: most of these in mutual masturbation (not touching each other), or masturbation by one partner; but almost half (20 per cent) had masturbated each other; about one-third also did fellatio together; and a few had had anal intercourse, being the active and/or receptive partner.

She goes on to state

> There was no correlation between whether a boy had had sexual experience with other boys and whether he considers himself 'homosexual' or 'heterosexual' in later life. Many 'homosexual' men had never had relations with other boys in youth, and many 'heterosexual' men had had such relationships.
>
> (Hite, 1981: 45)

Hite makes it very clear that sexual activity of various kinds between boys does not necessarily lead to a homosexual lifestyle or to self-identification as homosexual. The numerous accounts that she gives show that many of these men had simply found such experiences 'a lot of fun'.

On the questionnaire given to the sample of 13- to 15-year-olds at one of the research schools there were three questions which gave some limited information on this aspect of life in public schools. Of slight interest was a question where respondents were asked to tick which out of thirteen attributes was likely to make a boy popular. Being 'reasonably good looking' was rated eleventh, well below practically anything else. A second question was more explicit, asking boys to tick what made a boy unpopular. Being 'too keen on own sex' was only ticked by about a quarter of the boys, less than for being 'unwilling to join in things', 'a hypocrite', 'interested mainly in himself', 'one who greases up to masters' or 'conceited'. Those who did tick this statement, however, often made their feelings clear by multiple ticks and comments on the side. The third question was even more explicit and asked pupils which of eighteen attributes they thought being at the school promoted. Homosexuality was ticked by about 18 per cent of the pupils, way below 'the habit of working thoroughly', 'concern for other people', 'self-reliance and independence' and so on. It scored about as well as 'Christian life and values', 'frustration' and 'snobbery'. Of more interest were the not unexpected comments which ranged from the emphatic 'public schools do not promote homosexuality' to 'not much', 'perhaps for some' and 'only done jokingly I think'. One argued that, 'Due to lack of girls, boys enter upon relationships which start from friendship and then build up and make them into a right load of benders.'

In summary, clearly sexual activity between boys in public schools does occur. Given that in most schools the boys are together in dormitories for most of the time it would seem unlikely that those having sexual experience of some kind would be less than the 43 per cent found by Hite (1981). It is also clear that the boys themselves were often able to distinguish between 'fun' and any self-identification as homosexual. In one of the questionnaire sessions, for example, with a group of reasonably able boys, one of them asked genuinely, 'But what do you mean by homosexuality? Do you mean when we're just mucking about or something serious?' showing that he was well able to separate the two, and not label himself as homosexual just because he had some 'fun' with his friends. Older boys confirmed this in conversations. One guessed that 'perhaps 60 per cent have been involved at one time' in sexual activity, but they, and he, had 'given it up' as they became older.

At least some of the boys at these schools would thus appear to have more balanced attitudes towards their sexuality than many adults. Not all of the boys are so lucky, for several masters told me that they had sometimes to 'counsel a boy who thought he might be homosexual'. Sexuality is not easily understandable in terms of the two usual separate categories – heterosexual and homosexual. In adolescence, however, the desire to 'clarify' sexuality and to identify with one or other of the labels (usually the first) is high. The danger in public schools is that the myth that they promote homosexuality may make acceptance of a range of youthful sexual activities more difficult. Boys may be more likely to believe that early sexual activity with other boys or sexual attraction towards other boys automatically puts them on the 'wrong' side of the divide, and that it is the 'fault' of their public school. Hite (1981) found differently. Of the 9 per cent of American men in her sample who classified themselves as homosexual, the majority had not had sexual experiences with other boys when they were young, and, conversely, of the 43 per cent who had had early sexual experiences with boys, the majority did not grow up to prefer to have sex with men rather than women.

Perhaps a more interesting question relates to that 9 per cent of boys at these schools who are likely to eventually prefer their own sex. A school of 600 boys might be expected to have 50 or so such boys. Is the atmosphere of the schools a suitable one for them to grow up in?

Conclusion

The essence of a myth is that it is a commonly held, but untrue, explanation or description of events. In the 1960s the HMC set out to 'scotch' ten of the myths associated with the public schools.

We have seen that, while some are completely unfounded, others still contain some underlying truth. These myths present us with illustrations of an alternative meaning of the term myth – one which emphasizes the aspect of a hidden meaning. Myths are not to be taken at face value, but are to be analysed for their deeper, underlying meanings.

That we are forced to look beyond the surface meanings of these myths to the veiled meanings is a measure of the extent of change in public schools. They have gradually adapted and developed to suit changing circumstances. The 'revolution' has not been a rapid one, nor has it been complete, for the constraints of geography, history, architecture, politics and tradition coupled with restricted finance, have meant that there are major areas of continuity as well as change. The historic buildings largely still remain in their ivy-encrusted splendour. There will be changes inside – the toilets will now have doors – but the multiple-bathed bathrooms and lines of open basins may still be retained. Thomas Hughes' description of a Rugby boys' citadel differs only in degree from the way a study might now be described, and the social interaction within these studies is no doubt fairly similar too. For the all essential distinction that separates the boys in public boarding schools from those elsewhere, that of living away from parents and spending the majority of one's time in the company of one's peers, still remains. While public schools are less closed and isolated from the community than they used to be, the social life that develops amongst peers, with its own joys and trials, norms, regulations and even language, is still heavily influenced by the constraints of history, architecture and tradition. While study room culture now differs considerably from that of Billy Bunter's peers as described by Orwell, boys still do spend time concerning themselves with the selection of the school soccer team and also still torment and laugh at the butt of their year.

The revolution is a revolution in chains.

10

Life in public schools?

In this final chapter, rather than discussing what life is like in public schools, the question is asked, 'Is there still life in public schools?' Will they survive and thrive in the future? It must, of necessity, be a speculative chapter, which attempts to draw on what evidence there is, but ultimately must make guesses as to what might occur in the future.

As Tapper and Salter (1984) argue, with certain reservations, 'the survival of independent schools in Britain is dependent upon the ability of the schools to attract a sufficient number of parents to pay the fees that enable them to meet their costs, and upon a willingness of governments to permit their continued existence'. Much thus depends on the image that is projected to parents and future pupils, politicians, decision shapers and decision makers. The image depends, indirectly at least, on the reality.

Attracting parents and future pupils

Irene Fox (1984, 1985; Bridgeman and Fox, 1978) has shown that parents who pay fees for their sons' education do so because they believe that independent schools are likely to 'produce better academic results and to develop the character by instilling discipline'. They believe that the ethos of these schools is such that boys will be encouraged to work hard at their examinations which will enable them to enter universities and, in turn, lead to secure and well paid careers. They also believe that the school will have a positive moral impact on the boy, and will encourage the development of maturity and culturally appropriate behaviour and interests.

To be able to attempt any predictions about the future it is necessary to look at the trend in information about the past. With regard to the first of those aspects that make independent schooling attractive to parents and pupils – examination success – a convenient summary is given by Halsey, Heath and Ridge (1984). They show that over the period 1961–81 the state sector, rather than the independent sector, obtained a greater share of both O and A level examination successes, but this was simply because the relevant age group grew during this period at a greater rate than the numbers of pupils in independent schools. In the vital area of success in three A levels, which is likely to lead to university entry, the independent schools held their own. 'The private schools produced 29 per cent of those obtaining three or more A levels in 1981 despite the fact that in the previous twenty years their share of pupils aged 17+ fell from 29 per cent to 19 per cent.' The schools were able to be more selective in their intake and have changed their emphasis and ethos such that, by 1981, 63 per cent left with at least one A level. Table 10.1 compares the output for maintained and independent schools.

Table 10.1 A level results for all school leavers for 1981 in percentages

	No A levels attempted	No A levels obtained	1 or 2 A levels	3 A levels	N
Independent schools	33.0	4.0	17.7	45.3	44,100
Maintained schools	84.6	1.9	6.4	7.1	689,900

Source: DES, 1983

The difference is startling, even when the raw data on all independent schools are considered. The figures for HMC schools would show an even greater difference.

Such information on trends, although interesting, does not give any idea of why it is that the independent schools have had their growing success at A level. One way of attempting to move beyond the descriptive to the explanatory is to postulate possible causes, such as social class, father's education, measured intelligence and so on, and then control for these statistically to see how much of the observed difference can be attributed to each of the possible causes. Needless to say, there are no data available which allows this sort of analysis to be conducted on the full range of desirable variables. While still having limitations (Walford and Miller, 1980), by far the most comprehensive data that we have is that collected by the Oxford Social Mobility Group in 1972 (Halsey, Heath and Ridge, 1980; Goldthorpe, 1980). They interviewed in depth a representative sample of about 10,000 men between the ages of 20 and 60, resident in England and Wales, and gathered data on familial, educational and occupational biographies. The data thus relate to men who were born between 1913 and 1952 and inevitably suffers from the main problem with any research of this kind – it can document and partially explain how the educational system worked in the past, but it can only give suggestions as to how the system might be working now or in the future. Gross average figures for all the sample would conceal the very real changes that occurred in education over this forty-year period, but division of the sample into four ten-year cohorts gives an idea of the underlying trends. The two last cohorts of those born between 1933–42 and 1943–52 are of the most interest here.

Halsey, Heath and Ridge (1984) construct a statistical model for the first of these two cohorts; the differences that were found in the proportion of pupils from the maintained and independent sectors who achieved at least one A level are reduced to insignificance once differences in social background and school leaving age are taken into account. Pupils in this 1933–42 birth cohort, with similar social backgrounds, simply stayed on longer in independent schools than did those in state maintained schools, and it is this difference in length of school career that accounts for the difference in examination performance. Halsey *et al.* go on to argue that 'there is no need to postulate school differences in the form of superior teaching or greater resources, except in so far as these may have encouraged pupils to stay on longer' (1984: 29). Once in the sixth form there were no significant advantages to be gained in the independent schools.

For the second, and younger cohort, however, this was not true. This group were in the sixth forms of their schools in the 1960s, and by this time pupils with similar family backgrounds and staying on at school the same length of time were more likely to get at least one A level pass in the independent sector than in the state maintained schools. The differences were small, but significant. A more detailed analysis, which looks at the various types of school in both the independent and maintained sectors, showed that in the 1960s the direct grant schools had a lead over the HMC schools (in terms of the advantage given to pupils from similar family backgrounds staying on the same length of time), with the grammar and non-HMC schools trailing badly. As Halsey *et al.* point out,

> This is an important result. It suggests that the rise in the relative success of the private sector predates comprehensive reorganization. In the period we are considering, the 1960s, it would still have been the grammar schools which catered for the growing numbers of sixth formers within the state sector, and it was against this competition from grammar schools that the private sector was already beginning to pull ahead.
>
> (1984: 31)

Patterns of numerical associations between variables do not, in themselves, provide answers to questions as to why it should be that the direct grant and HMC schools achieved their advantage. The researcher has to hypothesize reasonable explanations and see if they make sense in the light of the data and other information available. The three hypotheses suggested by Halsey *et al.* (1984) are that the differences may be due to increased academic selectivity, genuine 'school effects' in terms of better teaching and facilities, or an unintended consequence of larger sixth forms which generate, through increased competition, better pupil attitudes and motivation. They suggest that, while all three may be necessary for a full explanation, they would be inclined to put more weight on the unmeasured aspects of family background and least on actual school resources.

While this may have been the case in the 1960s, the ethnographic data presented earlier suggest that it is unlikely to be the case now. The gradually increasing emphasis on academic achievement has meant that teaching is now almost all orientated towards this objective, the work ethos of the large sixth form is not an unintended consequence within these schools, but is consciously generated and sought by the increasing numbers of academically highly qualified staff. It is not that unmeasured family background variables are not important too (the family prepared to invest in this way *is* qualitatively different from another of similar standing which chooses not to do so), but that the evidence points to schools 'making a difference' in terms of academic achievement. Part of this may be due to better teaching and facilities, while another part may be due to changing attitudes and motivation – they simply cannot be separated using present data. However, for many of the 14-year-old boys I spoke to, the fact of their parents' investment in them had a distinct effect on their motivation – indeed for some it had become an awesome responsibility. Once motivated they were able to take advantage of what the school offered.

From the evidence that is available, it is likely that parents *are* actually able to buy a competitive advantage for their sons at these schools in terms of academic success. In a world where stark social hierarchies have been partially replaced and legitimized by being converted into academic hierarchies, the public schools allow parents to use their cultural and financial capital to pass on their advantages to their sons, and increasingly also daughters, in a more socially acceptable way. In Bourdieu's (1977) terms, those parents with high cultural capital are able to legitimize that wealth through academic examinations and certification which, although ostensibly fair and open, in practice are structured so that those with most cultural capital gain the largest advantage. On the other hand, those parents with considerable financial capital, but less cultural capital, are able to use the public schools to convert between the two forms of capital, and again ensure a greater chance of passing on advantage to their children.

Tapper and Salter (1984) argue that a further important aspect for parents is that they feel they are able to purchase a distinctly different experience of schooling from that available in local comprehensives. They use data from the National Child Development Study to argue that there has been a convergence in the experiences of schooling between pupils in state maintained and public schools. They argue that the data on 16-year-old pupils from the two sectors show a considerable overlap in social-cultural pursuits. The patterns of reading, sports, watching TV, dancing, and being involved in voluntary work, for example, are shown to be statistically similar in terms of the frequency of involvement. They see 'powerful forces within contemporary society (such as segments of the media and those firms that produce goods and services for young people)' as having a vested interest in promoting a youth culture that cuts across class lines. Their assessment is that these forces have been largely successful, which has led to a decrease in the distinctiveness of educational and social experience in public schools. Further data from the same study on pupils' responses to their schooling are used to support this idea.

This argument is difficult to take seriously for schools in the Eton and Rugby Groups. At the first level, while it may be that similar proportions of pupils engage in sport, this says nothing about the nature of that cultural experience. Golf and cricket are associated with very different cultural forms from football. Again it is the nature of the books that are read that is important rather than the proportions who actually read them. At a deeper level, however, Tapper and Salter have not recognized the degree of independence that pupils have in selectively creating their own produced cultural forms. It was shown in chapter three that the boys creatively incorporate elements from various youth and popular cultures into their own cultural forms. Some of these elements (for example, tastes in popular music) may be indeed identical to those of many pupils in comprehensive schools but these are the superficial aspects of the cultural form which are built on a common core of very different attitudes, expectations and experience.

The simple fact of living away from home and family for long periods in an institution where most of the time is spent in the company of peers automatically makes it a very different school experience from that of day pupils in comprehensives. While some might argue that not all of these differences are desirable, it is hard to sustain the idea that the experiences are not distinctive. Just as importantly, the fact of paying for schooling puts parents and pupils in a very different relationship with the school and its teachers. Parents are investing in a service; pupils investing in their futures. Both groups appear to take long-term and largely instrumental views of the schooling process. From the interviews with schoolmasters and from the questionnaires and interviews with pupils, it was apparent that the relationship between these two groups was increasingly that of buyer–bought and, with teaching staff now coming from a wide range of social backgrounds, the relationship could be frequently interpreted in class terms. It was as if the dominant class was simply buying an efficient, complete private tutor system for their offspring in the same way as the dominant class of the fifteenth century might have done. The schools acted not only as sites for cultural reproduction, but also acted as minor sites for social reproduction, reproducing the relationships between classes.

The long-term survival of the schools, however, depends on the schools being able to play a part in class reproduction, too. If better qualifications lead nowhere there is little point in continuing to amass them. Here the trends are not so clear, and the future less easy to predict.

The fundamental problem is that while it is possible to gather information on the schooling of men at present in élite groups or in professional occupations and calculate the percentage who had a public school education, it is obviously not possible to find out what careers present pupils will eventually take up. We thus only know something about what the relationship is between occupations now and public schools some forty years ago – which may be very different from the similar relationships for boys now in public schools. Even from the data available, the trends are not particularly clear. In David Boyd's (1973) work, for example, which looked at élite groups at four different points from 1939 to 1970, it was found that the relationship between attendance at a public school and membership of an élite group had grown stronger over the period for the Royal Navy. Over the same period the relationship had shown no significant changes for ambassadors, judiciary, army, Royal Air Force and directors of clearing banks, and in only two of the groups Boyd looked at – Civil Service and the Church of England – had there been any significant decrease in the strength of the relationship. During this period, at least, public school boys appear to have retained their traditional stake in various élite groups. However, Boyd goes on to show that attendance at an ancient university (primarily Oxford and Cambridge) had actually increased in importance for three groups, remained unchanged for three groups and only decreased in the Church of England. Many would now question the importance of this last group, for their status has declined and their income is low, which suggests an overall tightening of the bond between higher education at Oxbridge and entry to élites over this period. The public schools may be correct in emphasizing their Oxbridge successes, for it would seem that this was a slightly more important attribute than public school attendance alone in entry to élite status. The recent changes at Oxbridge on admissions, where attempts are being made to widen the social class and educational backgrounds of students, thus must be seen as potentially harmful to the public schools. Parents would be far less willing to pay for their sons' education if the links between school and university and prestigious occupations were weaker.

Entry into professional occupations may be mainly dependent on academic success, especially at Oxbridge, but a successful career demands more than this. To rise to the top of a chosen professional career demands particular social and interpersonal skills and abilities, contacts, hard work and single-minded determination. This, of course, is closely related to parents' second main reason for being prepared to pay for their sons' schooling – 'to develop the character by instilling discipline'. Do the trends indicate an increase or decrease in the public schools' abilities to develop these attributes?

The evidence on social and interpersonal skills and abilities is mixed. On the one hand, some aspects of life in public schools have changed in a direction which encourages appropriate skills. In sport, for example, there has been a move away from the dominance of team games towards more individual and socially exploitable sports. Ability and interest in golf, tennis or squash are far more of an advantage in terms of advancement in business or the professions than are football or rugby, for the squash or golf clubs are sites at which informal business discussions can be held. The chance to be able to strike the apocryphal million pound deal at the nineteenth hole depends on a certain amount of skill in the preceding eighteen. Public schools increasingly are providing these skills as a necessary component of their finished product.

On the other hand, there appears to be a change in the opposite direction with regard to qualities of 'leadership' so widely regarded as the justification for the prefect system. The increased academic emphasis has resulted in greater direct control and organizational responsibility by masters. Pupils appear to be more reluctant to take on prefectural duties, which may interfere with their examination work, and thus are less able to develop leadership skills in the house or school. Whether or not such schoolboy responsibilities did, in fact, have an advantageous effect in later occupational success is open to doubt, but, if so, the effect is likely to be declining.

On the other hand, individualistic, goal-orientated striving is very strong. The boys know that a considerable financial investment has been made in them by their parents and recognize that they are expected to 'do well' as a result. Naturally, not all of the boys respond positively to this moral obligation but, for the most part, boys recognize that if they want to share in the affluence of their parents they will have to work for it. Most boys in public schools appear to be highly ambitious and determined. Eglin (1984) has given some information on the higher educational aspirations of pupils from independent schools, where he shows that, for the sixth formers in his sample, the same percentage of pupils from state and independent schools aspire to higher education, but many more in the independent sector expect this to be in universities rather than polytechnics or colleges of higher education. High aspirations for eventual occupation were also found in answers to questionnaire items from the boys at one of the research schools of the present research. Although a few expressed doubts as to whether they would be able to get a job at all due to rising unemployment, the vast majority of boys at age 13 to 15 already had firm ideas of possible careers in mind. Almost without exception these were Social Class I occupations. With a large sixth form of pupils aiming for influential jobs, the success of some may provide just the necessary contacts to ensure the success of others as well.

The times when public schools merely had to be attractive to parents while pupils had little say in their own schooling have now long gone, if they ever existed. Boys and girls now appear to negotiate with their parents about their education (as, indeed, did Tom Brown) and schools have to be attractive to pupils as well as parents. Before a boy is accepted into a house, conditional on Common Entrance Examination success, he is interviewed with his parents by the housemaster. The occasion is recognized as a two-way process, for the school is just as interested in impressing the boy and parents as they are in impressing the housemaster. They, in fact, may have far more choice than he. At the sixth form, in particular with girls, the major schools have greater choice, but it is still the pupils who make the decisions rather than their parents, and it is they who now quite often decide to attend a sixth form college rather than endure the restrictions of school any longer. This need to be attractive to pupils has been a major cause of changes within the schools. Reductions in compulsory chapel, greater free time, more freedom to wear or do most things people of their age take for granted, and generally fewer restrictions, have resulted from pressure from pupils. Ultimately, pupils have the ability to ensure their own removal from a school they dislike. From the data gathered from the two research schools, it would appear that the public schools have had considerable success in becoming attractive to pupils. The vast majority of pupils were more than satisfied with both the teaching, which they value highly, and the sort of life they led at the schools. Part of this may be due to lack of other experience with which to compare their lives at boarding school, but when three-quarters of the pupils claim to either thoroughly enjoy or have a reasonably pleasant time at the school and only 6 per cent claim to be really unhappy, most of the boys clearly find that the advantages of their boarding lives outweigh the problems.

However, as the pupils at the research schools were largely a self-selected group, this tells little about overall trends in attractiveness of the schools to either pupils or parents. While the pupils there generally find the life attractive, they may be drawn from a declining population of similar children who would do so. National figures from the Independent Schools Information Service (1984) can give some information on this aspect.

In the years from 1981 to 1983 there was a gradual decline in the number of pupils in independent schools as a whole. 1984 saw an increase over the previous year of about $\frac{1}{4}$ per cent. In terms of the proportion of the age range, however, independent schools have increased their share over the same period, and for the last decade or more. For, at present, the total school-age population in Britain is falling by about 3 per cent per year, and the independent schools are actually gaining a larger proportion of the declining population. As was shown in chapter six, these figures conceal internal changes, for while the overall numbers are healthy, there have been losses in the number of boarders and gains in the number of day pupils. This is as true in the HMC schools as it is in the overall figures for the independent schools. The decrease in absolute numbers of boy boarders has been partially compensated by a gain in girl boarders, but the trend is downwards – whether it be for financial or social reasons, boarding does not appear to be as attractive as it was to parents and/or pupils. In the year 1983–4, for example, there was a loss of 1542 boarding pupils (1.4 per cent) and a gain of 2550 day pupils (0.9 per cent) in independent schools. The available figures for HMC schools indicate the same trend, but it should be noted that the proportional decrease in boarding places is still less than the proportional decrease in school population in Britain. There is a sense in which even boarding places have become more popular, but it is the day places that have risen most rapidly. Boarders now form 27 per cent of the total number of school pupils for those independent schools in membership of ISIS.

Public boarding schools like the two research schools may thus have to adapt faster than the day schools. Indeed both of my research schools had gradually increased the proportion of day boys over the last decade. The HMC has shown some concern for the problems of boarding schools, and has proposed that the Assisted Places Scheme might be extended to cover some boarding element as well as tuition. However, even though the waiting lists for places at most Rugby and Eton Group schools may not be over-long, it is unlikely that these particular schools will suffer. Some of the boarding schools at the lower end of the hierarchy, especially those that are geographically isolated, may be under pressure from the drop in boarders, but it is likely that the major schools will be able to retain their boarding character, with just a somewhat higher proportion of day pupils.

Statistical material from ISIS (1984) shows that there have been other changes in the pupil population too. Over the last decade there has been a gradual increase in the proportion of girls being educated independently. They now form 42 per cent of pupils – 33 per cent of boarders and 45 per cent of day pupils. This change has meant that the girls' schools have not suffered as greatly as might have been thought as a result of the moves to co-education of so many former boys-only schools. The number of foreign pupils has also decreased recently, probably due to increased university fees, showing that the increase in numbers of British pupils is even greater than the overall percentage.

To return to Tapper and Salter's (1984) argument, it would seem that the Rugby and Eton Group schools at present are able to attract a sufficient number of parents and pupils to enable them to meet their costs. These costs have risen far more rapidly than inflation for several years, yet parents are still willing to pay for the advantages they feel the schools promote. The various pressures on the schools have ensured that they have adapted in such a way that, while retaining links with the past, they have been able to present themselves as offering value for money. In the restricted terms of offering a better chance of examination success this appears to be an accurate perception, but the very pressures that have ensured the increased academic emphasis also seem to have caused changes in the ethos of the school, some of which may, in the long term, be detrimental. In the short term, however, a decline in popularity is not to be expected.

The immediate threats to the future of these public schools, if
there are any, come from Tapper and Salter's second criterion –
'willingness of governments to permit their continued existence'
– rather than from any internal problems within the schools.
Behind the banners of 'equality of opportunity' and 'reducing the
burden of taxation' the Conservative Party firmly supports
independent schools (CISC, 1983). Its support has even gone so
far as to finance the Assisted Places Scheme where a limited
number of pupils selected on merit have part or all of their fees
paid by the state according to parental income (DES, 1980b). It is
too early to know whether the scheme actually lives up to its
claim to be increasing equality of opportunity. An evaluation of
the project is underway (see Whitty and Edwards, 1984). The
Labour Party, on the other hand, is now firmly committed to the
concept of equality and to the abolition of independent education. How significant a threat to the public schools does the
Labour Party represent?

If the Labour Party were returned to power it is likely that its
policy on independent schools would be similar to that on which
it fought the 1983 general election (Labour Party, 1980, 1983). If
so, the attack would have several graded levels. The Assisted
Places Scheme and the buying of places by local education authorities would almost certainly quickly be axed. Withdrawal of
charitable status and imposition of VAT on fees might take a little
longer, but are well within possibilities. These changes would
have serious effects on some independent schools, but are
unlikely to bring about the closure of more than a few of the less
prestigious schools. The remainder would simply charge higher
fees to compensate for their loss of income and new expenditure,
and some categories of parents would be financially squeezed
out. The result would be a more socially homogeneous and élite
private educational system than now. The Labour Party's other
plans would take rather longer and would be far more difficult to
implement. It might appear at first that making the charging of
school fees illegal is a relatively easy legislative move. The
problem, however, is that this would mean that state schools
would have to accommodate an increase of some 6 per cent of
pupils at enormous cost. It is unlikely that the match between the

geographical spread of population decline and that of new requirements would be great, so school building in substantial amounts would probably be necessary. The phasing out of boarding allowances paid to government personnel for their children to attend independent schools might also prove to be prohibitively expensive, for some, at least, of these pupils would require alternative boarding accommodation to be available. This could only be provided by further new building or purchase of ex-independent school buildings. In practice, new expenditure of this sort is unlikely to be given a high priority by any returning Labour government, for renovation of the presently dramatically underfinanced state sector would probably already necessitate a far larger slice of the budget than any government could justify. The immediate outcome of Labour policy would be thus likely to be a decrease in equality rather than an increase. A few schools would be forced to close, but the major schools would remain intact, merely serving a more restricted clientele.

In summary, it would appear that public schools will remain a significant part of the educational landscape for many years to come. They have become an attractive alternative to the state comprehensive system for many parents and pupils, and there are still sufficient parents who can afford the rapidly rising fees. Additionally, while any future Labour government would probably make life harder for the schools, it would be difficult to abolish public schools completely without incurring an unmanageable financial burden. Some of the less well known schools may be faced with closure due to high costs and the trend against boarding. The changes in Oxbridge admissions policies, with the ending of the seventh term for sixth formers, and the increased attractiveness of sixth form colleges, may well close a few more, but it is highly unlikely that any of the major public schools will suffer. They will certainly continue to adapt to changing circumstances – more Rugby and Eton Group schools are likely to become co-educational, there will be more day pupils rather than boarders and there could be an extension downwards to take more pupils in the 11 to 13 age range – but the schools will survive for the foreseeable future.

The gradual changes that have occurred within public schools, coupled with the Conservative government's declining commitment to the state system both ideologically and financially, have made it increasingly certain that privilege can indeed be bought by those parents rich enough to pay for their children's schooling. These changes have also made clear the nature of this relationship between parents and the schools – schools must be seen as providing a service for customers and will stand or fall according to the quality of that service and whether or not they can retain their ability to offer advantaged entry into universities, professions and the various élite groups in society. The changes have made the political and ideological questions of whether or not a democratic society should retain purchasable privilege for the children of the wealthy more stark. Put simply, the market position of public schools is such that they can only survive if they act, and are seen to act, in such a way that inequality in society is reinforced and widened. In this it is likely that they will be successful.

If the public schools are to survive, the brute facts of inequality must remain an essential accompaniment to the experience. While Hughes may claim that, in the time of Tom Brown, ideas of inequality were only implanted into the minds of young boys by 'Jack Nastys and fine ladies' maids', present day parents have taken over these two roles, and have acted to ensure that their children are well aware that they will have a good chance of benefiting from inequality if they are individually competitive enough to exploit their advantage. Once again there are elements of both continuity and change.

> . . . and Tom and his younger brothers, as they grew up, went on playing with the village boys, without the idea of equality or inequality (except in wrestling, running and climbing) ever entering their heads, as it doesn't till it's put there by Jack Nastys or fine ladies' maids.
>
> (Hughes, 1857)

Bibliography

Acker, Sandra (1980) 'Women: the other academics', *British Journal of Sociology of Education*, 1(1), 81–91.

Althusser, Louis (1971) *Lenin and Philosophy and Other Essays*, London, New Left Books.

Annan, Noel (1965) *Roxburgh of Stowe*, London, Longmans.

Apple, Michael W. (1979) *Ideology and Curriculum*, London, Routledge & Kegan Paul.

Association for Science Education (1981) 'ASE Committees 1981', *Education in Science*, 91, 17.

Baldwin, Stanley (1926) *On England and Other Addresses*, London, Philip Allan.

Ball, Steven J. (1981) *Beachside Comprehensive*, Cambridge, Cambridge University Press.

Ball, Stephen J. (1983) 'A subject of privilege: English and the school curriculum 1906–35', in Hammersley, M. and Hargreaves, A. (eds) *Curriculum Practice*, Lewes, Falmer Press.

Bamford, T. W. (1967) *The Rise of the Public Schools: A study of boys' public boarding schools in England and Wales from 1837 to the present day*, London, Nelson.

Barker, D. L. and Allen, S. (eds) (1976) *Sexual Divisions and Society*, London, Tavistock.

Baron, S., Finn, D., Grant, N., Green, M. and Johnson, R. (1981) *Unpopular Education: Schooling and Social Democracy in England since 1944*, London, Hutchinson.

Barron, R. D. and Norris, G. M. (1976) 'Sexual divisions and the dual 'labour market', in Barker, D. L. and Allen, S. (eds) *Dependence and Exploitation in Work and Marriage*, London, Longmans.

Beechey, V. (1978) 'Women and production: a critical analysis of some sociological theories of women's work', in Kuhn, A. and Wolpe, A. M. (eds) *Feminism and Materialism*, London, Routledge & Kegan Paul.

Benn, S. I. and Peters, R. S. (1959) *Social Principles and the Democratic State*, London, Macmillan.

Bernstein, Basil (1971) 'On the classification and framing of educational knowledge', in Young, M. F. D. (ed) *Knowledge and Control*, London, Collier-Macmillan.

Bernstein, Basil (1973) 'Class and pedagogies: visible and invisible', reprinted as chapter 6 of *Class, Codes and Control*, Vol. 3, 1st edn, London, Routledge & Kegan Paul.

Bernstein, Basil (1975) Introduction to *Class, Codes and Control*, Vol. 3, London, Routledge & Kegan Paul.

Bernstein, Basil (1977) 'Aspects of the relation between education and production', chapter 8 of *Class, Codes and Control*, Vol. 3, 2nd edn, London, Routledge & Kegan Paul.

Bernstein, Basil (1982) 'Codes, modalities and the process of cultural reproduction: a model', in Apple, M. W. (ed) *Cultural and Economic Reproduction in Education*, London, Routledge & Kegan Paul.

Binns, David and Mars, Gerald (1984) 'Family, community and unemployment: a study in change', *Sociological Review*, 32(4), 662–95.

Bishop, T. J. H. and Wilkinson, Rupert (1967) *Winchester and the Public School Elite*, London, Faber & Faber.

Blandford, Linda (1977) 'The making of a lady', in Macdonald Fraser, George (ed) *The World of the Public School*, London, Weidenfeld & Nicolson.

Blumenau, Ralph (1965) *A History of Malvern College 1865–1965*, London, Macmillan.

Bosanquet, N. and Doeringer, P. D. (1973) 'Is there a dual labour market in Great Britain?', *Economic Journal*, 83, 421–35.

Bourdieu, Pierre (1977) 'Cultural reproduction and social reproduction', reprinted in Karabel, J. and Halsey, A. H. (eds) *Power and Ideology in Education*, Oxford, Oxford University Press.

Bourdieu, Pierre and Passeron, Jean-Claude (1977) *Reproduction in Education, Society and Culture*, London, Sage.

Bowen, Margaret (1983) 'Teachers in a sixth-form college', paper given at Teachers' Careers and Life Histories Conference, St Hilda's College, Oxford, September.

Bowles, S. and Gintis, H. (1976) *Schooling in Capitalist America*, London, Routledge & Kegan Paul.

Boyd, David (1973) *Elites and their education*, Slough, NFER.

Braverman, H. (1974) *Labour and Monopoly Capital*, London, Monthly Review Press.

Bridgeman, Tessa and Fox, Irene (1978) 'Why people choose private schools', *New Society*, 44, 702–5.

Bruegel, I. (1979) 'Women as a reserve army of labour: a note on recent British experience', *Feminist Review*, 1(3), 14.

Bucher, Rue and Strauss, Anselm (1961) 'Professions in process', *American Journal of Sociology*, 66, 325–34.

Burgess, Robert G. (1983) *Experiencing Comprehensive Education*, London, Methuen.

Burke, John (1983) 'The routinized experience of the sixth form college teacher and the process of status differentiation', paper given at Teachers' Careers and Life Histories Conference, St Hilda's College, Oxford, September.

Burnet, J. F. (ed) (1978) *The Public and Preparatory Schools Year Book 1978*, London, Adam & Charles Black.

Burnet, J. F. (ed) (1982) *The Public and Preparatory Schools Year Book 1981*, London, Adam & Charles Black.

Campbell, F. (1970) 'Latin and the elite tradition in education', in Musgrave, P. W. (ed) *Sociology, History and Education*, London, Macmillan.

Campbell-Jones, Suzanne (1979) *In Habit*, London, Faber & Faber.

Chetwynd, Jane and Hartnett, Oonagh (eds) (1978) *The Sex Role System*, London, Routledge & Kegan Paul.

Coleman, J. S. *et al.* (1966) *Equality of Educational Opportunity*, Washington D.C., Government Printing Office.

Conference (1979) 'Young enterprise. Oundle and Clifton', *Conference*, 16(1), 13–16.

Conference (1981) 'Editorial; No special arrangements . . .', *Conference*, 18(1), 1–3.

Conference (1984) 'Microelectronics. A feature on microelectronics and computers in education', *Conference* 21(1), 9–21.

Connell, R. W., Ashenden, D. J., Kessler, S. and Dowsett, G. W. (1982) *Making the Difference*, Sydney, George Allen & Unwin.

Conservative Independent Schools Committee (1983) *Independent Schools. Speakers' Notes*, London, CISC.

Cooper, Barry (1983) 'On explaining change in school subjects', *British Journal of Sociology of Education*, 4(3), 207–22.

Corrigan, Paul (1979) *Schooling the Smash Street Kids*, London, Macmillan.

Coser, Lewis A. (1974) *Greedy Institutions. Patterns of Undivided Commitment*, New York, Free Press.

Cross, Jack (1983) 'Prospects', *The Guardian*, 22 November, 17.

Cullingford, Cedric (1984) 'The battle for the schools: attitudes of parents and teachers towards education', *Educational Studies*, 10(2), 113–19.

Curtis, S. J. and Boultwood, M. E. A. (1966) *An Introductory History of English Education Since 1800*, 4th edn, London, University Tutorial Press.

Custance, Roger (ed) (1982) *Winchester College: 6th Centenary Essays*, Oxford, University Press.

Dale, R. R. (1975) 'Education and sex roles', *Educational Review*, 27(3), 240–8.

Dancy, John C. (1963) *The Public Schools and the Future*, London, Faber & Faber.

Davis, Kingsley and Moore, Wilbert E. (1945) 'Some principles of stratification', *American Sociological Review*, 10, 242–7.

Deem, Rosemary (ed) (1980) *Schooling for Women's Work*, London, Routledge & Kegan Paul.

Deem, Rosemary (1981) 'State policy and ideology in the education of women', *British Journal of Sociology of Education*, 2(2), 131–44.

Delamont, Sara (1976a) 'The girls most likely to: cultural reproduction and Scottish elites', *Scottish Journal of Sociology*, 1, 29–43.
Delamont, Sara (1976b) *Interaction in the Classroom*, London, Methuen.
Delamont, Sara (1980) *Sex Roles and the School*, London, Methuen.
Delamont, Sara (1984) 'Debs, dollies, swots and weeds: classroom styles at St Luke's', in Walford, Geoffrey (ed) *British Public Schools: Policy and Practice*, Lewes, Falmer Press.
Delderfield, R. F. (1972) *To Serve Them All My Days*, London, Hodder & Stoughton.
Department of Education and Science (1980a) *Statistics of Education 1978. Vol. 2 School Leavers*, London, HMSO.
Department of Education and Science (1980b) *Assisted Places at Independent Schools. A brief guide for parents*, London, DES.
Department of Education and Science (1983) *Education Statistics for the United Kingdom*, London, HMSO.
Devlin, Tim (1984) *Choosing Your Independent School*, London, ISIS and Arrow Books.
Dingwall, R. (1976) 'Accomplishing profession', *Sociological Review*, 24, 331–49.
Dod (1982) *Dod's Parliamentary Companion 1982*, London, Dod's Parliamentary Companion Ltd.
Doeringer, P. B. and Piore, M. J. (1972) *Internal Labor Markets and Manpower Analysis*, Lexington, Mass., D. C. Heath & Co.
Dover Report (1983) *Report of the Committee on Undergraduate Admissions*, Oxford, Oxford Colleges Admissions Office.
Edwards, Tony, Fulbrook, Mary and Whitty, Geoff (1984) 'The state and the independent sector: policies, ideologies and theories', in Barton, Len and Walker, Stephen (eds) *Social Crisis and Educational Research*, Beckenham, Croom Helm.
Eggleston, J. F., Galton, M. J. and Jones, M. E. (1976) *Processes and Products of Science Teaching*, London, Macmillan.
Eglin, Greg (1984) 'Public schools and the choice at 18+', in Walford, Geoffrey (ed) *British Public Schools: Policy and Practice*, Lewes, Falmer Press.
Ellis, Joseph and Moore, Robert (1974) *School for Soldiers*, New York, Oxford University Press.
Everhart, Robert B. (1983) *Reading, Writing and Resistance. Adolescence and labor in a junior high school*, Boston, Mass., Routledge & Kegan Paul.
Fairhall, J. (1982) 'Boys only school rule', *The Guardian*, 17 March, 3.
Farrar, Frederick W. (1858) *Eric, or Little by Little*, Edinburgh, Adam & Charles Black.
Finch, Janet (1983) *Married to the Job*, London, George Allen & Unwin.
Flanders, Ned A. (1970) *Analysing Teaching Behaviour*, New York, Addison-Wesley.
Fleming Report (1944) *The Public Schools and the General Education System*, Report of the Board of Education, Committee on Public Schools, London, HMSO.

Fletcher, Ronald (1984) *Education in Society: The Promethean Fire. A new essay in the sociology of education*, Harmondsworth, Penguin.

Floud, J., Halsey, A. H. and Martin, F. M. (1956) *Social Class and Educational Opportunity*, London, Heinemann.

Fogarty, M., Rapoport, R. and Rapoport, R. (1971) *Sex, Career and Family*, London, Allen & Unwin.

Fox, Irene (1984) 'The demand for a public school education: A crisis of confidence in comprehensive schooling', in Walford, Geoffrey (ed) *British Public Schools: Policy and Practice*, Lewes, Falmer Press.

Fox, Irene (1985) *Public Schools and Private Issues*, London, Macmillan.

Franks Commission (1966) *Report of Commission of Enquiry*, Oxford, Clarendon Press.

Furlong, Viv J. (1976) 'Interaction sets in the classroom: Towards a study of pupil knowledge', in Stubbs, Michael and Delamont, Sara (eds) *Explorations in Classroom Observation*, Chichester, Wiley.

Galton, M. J., Simon, B. and Croll, P. (1980) *Inside the Primary Classroom*, London, Routledge & Kegan Paul.

Gannaway, H. (1976) 'Making sense of school', in Stubbs, Michael and Delamont, Sara (eds) *Explorations in Classroom Observation*, Chichester, Wiley.

Gathorne-Hardy, Jonathan (1977) *The Public School Phenomenon*, London, Hodder & Stoughton.

Gibson, Rex (1977) 'Bernstein's classification and framing: a critique', *Higher Education Review*, 9, 23–45.

Ginsburg, M. B., Meyenn, R. J. and Miller, H. D. R. (1980) 'Teachers' conceptions of professionalism and trades unionism: An ideological analysis', in Woods, Peter (ed) *Teacher Strategies*, London, Croom Helm.

Glaser, B. and Strauss, A. (1967) *The Discovery of Grounded Theory*, Chicago, Aldine.

Glass, G. V., Cohen, L. S., Smith, M. L. and Filby, N. N. (1982) *School Class Size. Research and Policy*, Beverly Hills, Sage.

Goffman, Ervin (1961) *Asylums*, New York, Doubleday.

Goffman, Ervin (1963) *Stigma: Notes on the Management of a Spoiled Identity*, Englewood Cliffs, New Jersey, Prentice Hall.

Goldthorpe, J. H. (1980) *Social Mobility and Class Structure in Modern Britain*, Oxford, Clarendon Press.

Goodson, Ivor (1983a) *School Subjects and Curriculum Change*, Beckenham, Croom Helm.

Goodson, Ivor (1983b) 'Defining and defending the subject: geography versus environmental studies', in Hammersley, Martin and Hargreaves, Andy (eds) *Curriculum Practice*, Lewes, Falmer Press.

Graves, Robert (1929) *Goodbye to All That*, London, Jonathan Cape (Penguin Books, 1960).

Greene, Graham (1984) *The Old School*, Oxford, University Press (first published by Jonathan Cape, 1934).

Guardian (1984) 'Public schoolboys' bomb hoax on Neave's widow', 2 August, 3.

Halls, W. D. (1971) 'Cultural ideals and elitist education in England', *Comparative Education Review*, 15(3), 317–29.

Halsall, Martyn (1981) 'Balancing the fees and the faith', *The Guardian*, 22 December, 13.

Halsey, A. H. (1981) 'Democracy in education', *New Society*, 28 May.

Halsey, A. H., Heath, A. F. and Ridge, J. M. (1980) *Origins and Destinations: family, class and education in modern Britain*, Oxford, Clarendon Press.

Halsey, A. H., Heath, A. F. and Ridge, J. M. (1984) 'The political arithmetic of public schools', in Walford, Geoffrey (ed) *British Public Schools: Policy and Practice*, Lewes, Falmer Press.

Hamblin, D. (1978) *The Teacher and Pastoral Care*, Oxford, Blackwell.

Hammersley, Martyn and Atkinson, Paul (1983) *Ethnography. Principles in practice*, London, Tavistock.

Hammersley, Martyn and Hargreaves, Andy (eds) (1983) *Curriculum Practice*, Lewes, Falmer Press.

Hargreaves, David H. (1967) *Social Relations in a Secondary School*, London, Routledge & Kegan Paul.

Harker, Richard K. (1984) 'On reproduction, habitus and education', *British Journal of Sociology of Education*, 5(2) 117–27.

Hebdige, D. (1979) *Subculture: The Meaning of Style*, London, Methuen.

Heward, Christine M. (1984) 'Parents, sons and their careers: A case study of a public school, 1930–50', in Walford, Geoffrey (ed) *British Public Schools: Policy and Practice*, Lewes, Falmer Press.

Hilton, James (1934) *Goodbye Mr Chips*, London, Collins.

Hine, B. J. (1975) 'Political bias in school physics', *Hard Cheese*, 4/5, 93–6.

Hirst, P. M. and Peters, R. S. (1970) *The Logic of Education*, London, Routledge & Kegan Paul.

Hite, Shere (1981) *The Hite Report on Male Sexuality*, London, Macdonald.

Hobson, Peter (1983) *The Wellington College School-Industry Link Scheme. A Report on its first five years 1977–82*, Berkshire, Wellington College.

Honey, J. R. de S. (1977) *Tom Brown's Universe: The development of the public school in the 19th century*, London, Millington Books.

Hughes, Thomas (1857) *Tom Brown's Schooldays*, London, Macmillan.

ISIS (1982) *Annual Census 1982. Statistical Survey of Independent Schools*, London, Independent Schools Information Service.

ISIS (1984) *Annual Census 1984*, London, Independent Schools Information Service.

Jenkins, E. W. (1979) *From Armstrong to Nuffield. Studies in twentieth-century science in England and Wales*, London, John Murray.

Jenkins, Jack (1982) 'Industry across the curriculum at Malvern', *Education*, 19 November, 396–7.

Jenkins, Richard (1983) *Lads, Citizens and Ordinary Kids*, London, Routledge & Kegan Paul.

John, D. (1980) *Leadership in Schools*, London, Heinemann.

Kalton, G. (1966) *The Public Schools*, London, Longmans.

Kelly, Alison (1979) 'Where have all the women gone?', *Physics Bulletin*, 30, 108–11.

Kelly, Alison (ed) (1981) *The Missing Half. Girls and Science Education*, Manchester, University Press.

King, Ronald (1978) *All Things Bright and Beautiful?*, Chichester, Wiley.

King, Ronald (1983) *The Sociology of School Organisation*, London, Methuen.

Kinnock, Neil (1981) 'Private schools', news release, Labour Party, 13 July 1981.

Kinsey, A. *et al.* (1948) *Sexual Behaviour in the Human Male*, Philadelphia, W. B. Saunders.

Kipling, Rudyard (1899) *Stalky and Co*, London, Macmillan.

Kogan, Maurice (1971) *The Politics of Education*, Harmondsworth, Penguin.

Labour Party (1980) *Private Schools – A Labour Party Discussion Document*, London, Labour Party.

Labour Party (1983) *The New Hope for Britain. Labour's Manifesto 1983*, London, Labour Party.

Lacey, Colin (1966) 'Some sociological concomitants of academic streaming in a grammar school', *British Journal of Sociology*, 17(3).

Lacey, Colin (1970) *Hightown Grammar*, Manchester, University Press.

Lacey, Colin (1976) 'Problems of sociological fieldwork: A review of the methodology of Hightown Grammar', in Shipman, Marten (ed) *The Organisation and Impact of Social Research*, London, Routledge & Kegan Paul.

Lacey, Colin (1982) 'Freedom and constraints in British education', in Frankenberg, Ronald (ed) *Custom and Conflict in British Society*, Manchester, Manchester University Press.

Lamb, F. and Pickthorne, H. (1968) *Locked-up Daughters: a parents' look at girls' education and schools*, London, Hodder & Stoughton.

Lambart, Audrey M. (1976) 'The sisterhood', in Hammersley, Martyn and Woods, Peter (eds) *The Process of Schooling*, London, Routledge & Kegan Paul.

Lambart, Audrey (1982) 'Expulsion in context: A school as a system in action', in Frankenberg, Ronald (ed) *Custom and Conflict in British Society*, Manchester, Manchester University Press.

Lambert, Royston (1968) 'Religious education in the boarding school', in Jebb, Dom Phillip (ed) *Religious Education*, London, Darton, Longman & Todd.

Lambert, Royston (1975) *The Chance of a Lifetime? A study of boarding education*, London, Weidenfeld & Nicolson.

Lambert, Royston and Millham, Spencer (1968) *The Hothouse Society*, London, Weidenfeld & Nicolson.

Lambert, Royston, Bullock, Roger and Millham, Spencer (1970) *A*

Manual to the Sociology of the School, London, Weidenfeld & Nicolson.

Lambert, Royston, Hipkin, John and Stagg, Susan (1968) *New Wine in Old Bottles?*, Occasional Papers in Social Administration, Number 28, London, Bell.

Leach, Arthur F. (1899) *A History of Winchester College*, London, Duckworth.

McConnell, J. D. R. (1967) *Eton: How It Works*, London, Faber.

Macdonald, K. M. (1980) 'The persistence of an elite: The case of British army officer cadets', *The Sociological Review*, 28(3), 635–40.

MacDonald, Madeleine (1977) *The Education of Elites*, Unit 29, E202, Schooling and Society, Milton Keynes, Open University.

MacDonald, Madeleine (1980) 'Socio-cultural reproduction and women's education', in Deem, Rosemary (ed) *Schooling for Women's Work*, London, Routledge & Kegan Paul.

MacDonald, Madeleine (1981) *Class, Gender and Education*, Block 4, Units 10–11, E353, Milton Keynes, Open University Press.

MacDonald Fraser, George (ed) (1977) *The World of the Public School*, London, Weidenfeld & Nicolson.

Marland, M. (1974) *Pastoral Care*, London, Heinemann.

Metz, Mary Haywood (1978) *Classrooms and Corridors*, Berkeley,University of California Press.

Meyenn, Robert J. (1980) 'School girls' peer groups', in Woods, Peter (ed) *Pupil Strategies*, Beckenham, Croom Helm.

Miller, Henry and Walford, Geoffrey (1985) 'University cut and thrust', in Walford, Geoffrey (ed) *Schooling in Turmoil*, Beckenham, Croom Helm.

Musgrove, Frank (1968) 'The contribution of sociology to the study of the curriculum', in Kerr, J. F. (ed) *Changing the Curriculum*, London, University of London Press.

Neill, A. S. (1962) *Summerhill*, London, Victor Gollancz.

Okely, Judith (1978) 'Privileged, schooled and finished: Boarding education for girls', in Ardener, Shirley (ed) *Defining Females*, London, Croom Helm.

Orwell, George (1940) 'Boys' weeklies', *Horizon*, 3, reprinted in *Inside the Whale* (1940) and *Selected Essays* (1957), Harmondsworth, Penguin.

Otley, C. B. (1978) 'Militarism and militarization in the public schools, 1900–1972', *British Journal of Sociology*, 29(3), 321–39.

Ozga, J. T. and Lawn, M. A. (1981) *Teachers, Professionalism and Class*, London, Falmer Press.

Parker, Howard (1972) *View From the Boys*, London, David & Charles.

Patrick, James (1973) *A Glasgow Gang Observed*, London, Eyre Methuen.

Plowden Report (1967) *Children and their Primary Schools*, London, HMSO.

Prescott, Peter S. (1970) *A World of Our Own*, New York, Dell Publishing.

Pring, Richard (1975) 'Bernstein's classification and framing of knowledge', *Scottish Educational Studies*, 7, 67–74.

Public Eye (1981) 'Free sixth forms lure hard-hit parents', *The Observer*, 13 September, 2.

Punch, Maurice (1974) 'The sociology of the anti-institution', *British Journal of Sociology*, 25(3).

Punch, Maurice (1977) *Progressive Retreat*, Cambridge, University Press.

Punch, M. and Swirsky, R. (1974) 'Freedom for what? The Scotland Road Free School', *The Teacher*, 8 February 1974.

Quigly, Isabel (1982) *The Heirs of Tom Brown*, Oxford, University Press.

Raby, Leo and Walford, Geoffrey (1981a) 'Career related attitudes and their determinants for middle- and low-stream pupils in an urban, multi-racial comprehensive school', *Research in Education*, 25, 19–35.

Raby, Leo and Walford, Geoffrey (1981b) 'Job status aspirations and their determinants for middle and lower stream pupils in an urban, multi-racial comprehensive school', *British Educational Research Journal*, 7(2) 173–81.

Rae, Daphne (1983) *A World Apart*, Guildford, Lutterworth.

Rae, John (1981) *The Public School Revolution*, London, Faber & Faber.

Redican, Bede (1985) 'Subject teachers under stress', in Walford, Geoffrey (ed) *Schooling in Turmoil*, Beckenham, Croom Helm.

Richardson, E. (1973) *The Teacher, the School and the Task of Management*, London, Heinemann.

Richardson, R. and Chapman, J. (1973) *Images of Life*, London, SCM.

Robbins Report (1963) *Higher Education*, Cmnd 2154, Committee on Higher Education, London, HMSO.

Rubery, J. (1978) 'Structured labour markets, worker organisation and low pay', *Cambridge Journal of Economics*, 4, 17–36.

Salter, Brian and Tapper, Ted (1981) *Education Politics and the State. The theory and practice of educational change*, London, Grant McIntyre.

Scott, John (1982) *The Upper Classes*, London, Macmillan.

Shaw, Jennifer (1976) 'Finishing school – some implications of sex-segregated education', in Barker, D. L. and Allen, S. (eds) *Sexual Divisions and Society*, London, Tavistock.

Shaw, Jennifer (1980) 'Education and the individual: schooling for girls or mixed schooling – a mixed blessing?', in Deem, Rosemary (ed) *Schooling for Women's Work*, London, Routledge & Kegan Paul.

Shaw, Jennifer (1984) 'The politics of single sex schools', in Deem, Rosemary (ed) *Co-education Reconsidered*, Milton Keynes, Open University Press.

Simon, Brian and Bradley, Ian (eds) (1975) *The Victorian Public School*, Dublin, Gill & Macmillan.

Spender, Dale (1979) *Man Made Language*, London, Routledge & Kegan Paul.

Stanworth, Philip (1984) 'Elites and privilege' in Abrams, Philip and Brown, Richard (eds) *UK Society*, London, Weidenfeld & Nicolson.

Stanworth, Philip and Giddens, Anthony (eds) (1974) *Elites and Power in British Society*, Cambridge, Cambridge University Press.

Stevens, Auriol (1983) 'Exam blow to public school fees', *Observer*, 5 June 1983, 5.

Tapper, Ted and Salter, Brian (1984) 'Images of independent schooling: Exploring the perceptions of parents and politicians', in Walford, Geoffrey (ed) *British Public Schools: Policy and Practice*, Lewes, Falmer Press.

Taunton Commission (1867) *Schools Inquiry Commission*, Cmnd 3966, Report of the Commissioners appointed by Her Majesty to inquire into the education given in schools in England not comprised within Her Majesty's two recent commissions on popular education and on public schools, London, HMSO.

Thomas, Bernard (ed) (1957) *Repton 1557 to 1957*, London, Batsford.

Thompson, Richard and Walford, Geoffrey (1983) *Teachers into Industry. An evaluation of an Understanding British Industry teacher scheme*, Birmingham, University of Aston. Also published in *Collected Original Resources in Education* (1984), 8(1), 1–178.

Tumin, Melvin M. (1953) 'Some principles of stratification: A critical analysis', *American Sociological Review*, 18, 387–94.

Turner, Glenn (1983) *The Social World of the Comprehensive School*, Beckenham, Croom Helm.

Wakeford, John (1969) *The Cloistered Elite. A sociological analysis of the English boarding school*, London, Macmillan.

Walford, Geoffrey (1981) 'Tracking down sexism in physics textbooks', *Physics Education*, 16, 261–5.

Walford, Geoffrey (1983a) 'Girls in boys' public schools: a prelude to further research', *British Journal of Sociology of Education*, 4(1), 39–54.

Walford, Geoffrey (1983b) 'Science textbook images and the reproduction of sexual divisions in society', *Research in Science and Technological Education*, 1(1), 65–72.

Walford, Geoffrey (1984) 'The changing professionalism of public school teachers', in Walford, Geoffrey (ed) *British Public Schools: Policy and Practice*, Lewes, Falmer Press.

Walford, Geoffrey (1985) 'The construction of a curriculum area: science in society', *British Journal of Sociology of Education*, 6, 155–72.

Walford, Geoffrey and Miller, Henry (1980) Review Essay, *Origins and Destinations* by Halsey, A. H., Heath, A. F. and Ridge, J. M., and *Social Mobility and Class Structure in Modern Britain* by Goldthorpe, J. H. with Llewellyn, C. and Payne, C., *Research in Education*, 24, 63–75.

Walker, William George (1956) *A History of the Oundle School*, London, The Grocer's Company.

Waring, Mary (1979) *Social Pressures and Curriculum Innovation. A study of the Nuffield Foundation Science Teaching Project*, London, Methuen.

Watts, A. G. (ed) (1983) *Work Experience and Schools*, London, Heinemann.

Waugh, Alec (1917) *The Loom of Youth*, London, Grant Richards.

Weinberg, Ian (1967) *The English Public Schools*, New York, Atherton.

Weis, Lois (1983) 'Schooling and cultural production: A comparison of black and white lived culture', in Apple, M. W. and Weis, L. (eds) *Ideology and Practice in Schooling*, Philadelphia, Temple University.

Weppner, Robert S. (ed) (1977) *Street Ethnography*, Beverly Hills, Sage.

Whitty, Geoff and Edwards, Tony (1984) 'Evaluating policy change: The Assisted Places Scheme', in Walford, Geoffrey (ed) *British Public Schools: Policy and Practice*, Lewes, Falmer Press.

Whyte, W. H. (1943) *Street Corner Society*, Chicago, University Press.

Wiener, M. J. (1982) *English Culture and the Decline of the Industrial Spirit*, Cambridge, Cambridge University Press.

Wilby, Peter (1981) 'A parents' guide to private education', *Sunday Times Magazine*, 22 November, 31–55.

Wilkes, John (1980) 'Sources of authenticity in state and public schools: an historical approach', *Westminster Studies in Education*, 3, 91–103.

Wilkinson, R. (1964) *The Prefects. British Leadership and the Public School Tradition*, Oxford, Oxford University Press.

Willis, Paul (1977) *Learning to Labour*, Farnborough, Saxon House.

Willis, Paul (1981) 'Cultural production is different from cultural reproduction is different from social reproduction is different from reproduction', *Interchange*, 12(2–3) 48–67.

Willis, Paul (1983) 'Cultural production and theories of reproduction', in Barton, L. and Walker, S. (eds) *Race, Class and Education*, Beckenham, Croom Helm.

Willis, Paul (1984) 'Conclusion: Theory and practice', in Bates, I., Clarke, J., Cohen, P., Finn, D., Moore, R. and Willis, P., *Schooling for the Dole?*, London, Macmillan.

Wilson, John (1962) *Public Schools and Private Practice*, London, Allen & Unwin.

Wober, Mallory (1971) *English Girls' Boarding Schools*, London, Allen Lane.

Wodehouse, P. G. (1909) *Mike, a Public School Story*, London, Herbert Jenkins.

Wolfe, A. M. (1974) 'The official ideology of education for girls', in Flude, M. and Ahier, J., *Educability, Schools and Ideology*, Beckenham, Croom Helm.

Wolfe, A. M. (1978) 'Education and the sexual division of labour', in Kuhn, A. and Wolpe, A. M. (eds) *Feminism and Materialism*, London, Routledge & Kegan Paul.

Wood, Stephen (1981) 'Redundancy and female employment', *Sociological Review*, 29(4), 649–83.

Woods, Peter (1979) *The Divided School*, London, Routledge & Kegan Paul.

Wragg, Ted and Dooley, Pauline (1984) 'Class management during teaching practice', in Wragg, E. C. (ed) *Classroom Teaching Skills*, Beckenham, Croom Helm.

Young, Michael (1983) *The Elmhursts of Dartington*, London, Routledge & Kegan Paul.

Young, Michael F. D. (1971a) 'An approach to the study of curricula as socially organized knowledge', in Young, M. F. D. (ed) *Knowledge and Control*, London, Collier-Macmillan.

Young, Michael F. D. (ed) (1971b) *Knowledge and Control*, London, Collier-Macmillan.

Young, Michael F. D. (1976) 'The schooling of science', in Whitty, Geoff and Young, Michael (eds) *Explorations in the Politics of School Knowledge*, Driffield, Nafferton Books.

Name index

Subject index